GENDER, DISCOURSE, AND DESIRE IN TWENTIETH-CENTURY BRAZILIAN WOMEN'S LITERATURE

Purdue Studies in Romance Literatures

Editorial Board

Floyd Merrell, Series Editor
Jeanette Beer
Paul B. Dixon

Benjamin Lawton
Howard Mancing
Allen G. Wood

Associate Editors

French
Paul Benhamou
Willard Bohn
Gerard J. Brault
Mary Ann Caws
Gérard Defaux
Milorad R. Margitić
Glyn P. Norton
Allan H. Pasco
Gerald Prince
David Lee Rubin
Roseann Runte
Ursula Tidd

Italian
Fiora A. Bassanese
Peter Carravetta
Franco Masciandaro
Anthony Julian Tamburri

Luso-Brazilian
Fred M. Clark
Marta Peixoto
Ricardo da Silveira Lobo Sternberg

Spanish and Spanish American
Maryellen Bieder
Catherine Connor
Ivy A. Corfis
Frederick A. de Armas
Edward Friedman
Charles Ganelin
David T. Gies
Roberto González Echevarría
Patricia Hart
David K. Herzberger
Emily Hicks
Djelal Kadir
Amy Kaminsky
Lucille Kerr
Alberto Moreiras
Randolph D. Pope
Francisco Ruiz Ramón
Elżbieta Skłodowska
Mario Valdés
Howard Young

 volume 29

GENDER, DISCOURSE, AND DESIRE IN TWENTIETH-CENTURY BRAZILIAN WOMEN'S LITERATURE

Cristina Ferreira-Pinto

Purdue University Press
West Lafayette, Indiana

Copyright ©2004 by Purdue University. All rights reserved.

08   07   06   05   04   5   4   3   2   1

∞The paper used in this book meets the minimum requirements of American National Standard for Information Sciences—Permanence of Paper for Printed Library Materials, ANSI Z39.48-1992.

Printed in the United States of America
Design by Anita Noble

Library of Congress Cataloging-in-Publication Data
  Pinto, Cristina Ferreira, 1960–
    Gender, discourse, and desire in twentieth-century Brazilian women's literature / Cristina Ferreira-Pinto.
      p.   cm. — (Purdue studies in Romance literatures ; v. 29)
    Includes bibliographical references and index.
    ISBN 1-55753-352-0 (pbk.)
    1. Brazilian literature—Women authors—History and criticism. 2. Brazilian literature—20th century—History and criticism. 3. Women in literature. 4. Sex role in literature. 5. Desire in literature. I. Title II. Series.

  PQ9533.P56 2004
  869.09'3538'0820981—dc22   2003025959

To my daughters, Nina Clara and Ana Camila,
and the women of the New Millennium

Contents

ix **Acknowledgments**
x **Brazilian Women in Society and Literature**
A Chronology
1 **Introduction**
Brazilian Women's Literature as a Counterideological Discourse
8 **Chapter One**
Female Body, Male Desire
38 **Chapter Two**
Brazilian Women Writers: The Search for an Erotic Discourse
75 **Chapter Three**
Representation of the Female Body and Desire: The Gothic, the Fantastic, and the Grotesque
93 **Chapter Four**
Sonia Coutinho's Short Fiction: Aging and the Female Body
113 **Chapter Five**
Contemporary Brazilian Women's Short Stories: Lesbian Desire
143 **Chapter Six**
The Works of Márcia Denser and Marina Colasanti: Female Agency and Heterosexuality
159 **Conclusion**
Brazilian Women Writers in the New Millennium
165 **Appendix**
English Translations
179 **Notes**
185 **Bibliography**
199 **Index**

Acknowledgments

This book has been some years in the making. In a sense, it started many years ago, as I began reading, teaching, and writing about Brazilian women writers and their works.

I wish to thank Fred Ellison, Maria José Somerlate Barbosa, and Matthew Bailey, who read earlier versions of this book at different times and offered valuable comments and encouragement; and the Purdue Studies in Romance Literatures readers, whose useful suggestions for revisions helped improve the manuscript. Thank you also to the participants in the graduate seminar on Feminist Criticism I taught at the Pontifícia Universidade Católica do Rio Grande do Sul, in the summer of 2001. The vibrant discussions we held there and their keen contributions helped me think through and revisit some of the issues I address in this book. In this regard, I am grateful to Dr. Regina Zilberman, who made that experience possible.

An NEH Summer Stipend in 1999 allowed me time to carry out some initial research, and for that I am thankful.

* * *

A small portion of Chapter 2, on Helena Parente Cunha, was published in "Escrita, auto-representação e realidade social no romance feminino latino-americano," in *Revista de Crítica Literaria Latinoamericana* 45 (1997): 81–95.

An earlier version of Chapter 3 appeared as "The Fantastic, the Gothic and the Grotesque in Contemporary Brazilian Women's Novels," in *Chasqui: Revista de Literatura Latinoamericana* 25.2 (Nov. 1996): 71–80.

Parts of Chapters 4 and 5 appeared, respectively, as "Sonia Coutinho: Desconstruindo mitos de feminilidade, beleza e juventude," in *Hispania* 82.4 (Dec. 1999): 713–24, and as "O desejo lesbiano no conto de escritoras brasileiras contemporâneas" in *Revista Iberoamericana* 187 (Apr.–June 1999): 405–21.

These earlier works have been here substantially revised and expanded. They are used here with permission.

Brazilian Women in Society and Literature:
A Chronology

1752: Margarida Teresa da Silva e Orta's (1711?–93) *Aventuras de Diófanes* [Diófanes's adventures], considered by many the first Brazilian novel and the first literary work by a Brazilian woman, is published in Portugal.

1822: Brazil's political independence from Portugal.

1827: First legislation concerning women's education approved in Brazil. The new law gave female students access to elementary schools.

1832: Nísia Floresta Brasileira Augusta (1810–85), a poet, educator, feminist, and antislavery activist, translates and publishes Mary Wollstonecraft's *Vindication of the Rights of Woman*.

1852: Premiere issue of *O jornal das senhoras* [The ladies' journal], edited by Joana Manso, is published in Rio de Janeiro; this and other women's journals that followed served as channels for Brazilian women to express their ideas and to publish their poems, essays, and short fiction.

1859: Maria Firmina dos Reis (1825–1917), a mulatto woman, publishes *Úrsula,* in which she attacks slavery and defends its abolition; for many critics, who do not consider Margarida Teresa da Silva e Orta as part of the Brazilian literary canon, since she grew up in Portugal, Reis is the first true Brazilian woman novelist.

1876: Female students are allowed to attend teachers' schools, previously restricted to men.

1879: Coeducation allowed in elementary schools; institutions of higher education open to women.

1881: First female student begins medical school in Rio de Janeiro; the newspaper *A mulher* [Woman] is published in New York by Brazilian female students.

1888: Slavery abolished in Brazil.

1889: End of the Monarchy and establishment of the Republic.

1897: Premiere issue of *A mensageira* [The female messenger], edited by Presciliana Duarte de Almeida, is published in São Paulo; the editorial celebrates the "intellectual development of Brazilian women" and their participation in the national arts and sciences, and seeks to give voice to the ever-growing number of women who write.

1919: Bertha Lutz (1894–1976), feminist leader and politician, represents Brazil in the International Women's Council of the International Workers' Organization; in 1922 Lutz founds the Brazilian Federation for Women's Progress, and two years later represents Brazil in the first Pan-American Women's Conference, held in the United States.

1919: Júlia Lopes de Almeida (1862–1934), journalist, novelist, and playwright, organizes the Feminine Literary and Artistic University. Lopes de Almeida, a member of Lutz's Brazilian Women's Legion, also helped organize the Brazilian Academy of Letters, even though she could not join it because she was a woman.

1921: First women's soccer game played in São Paulo.

1924: Maria Lacerda de Moura (1887–1945), feminist activist, educator, and writer, publishes *A mulher é uma degenerada?* [Are women depraved?]; in this and in other works the author defends free love, polygamy for women, and sexual education, and speaks against women's ignorance of their own bodies and against dominant gender relations. In 1932 she publishes *Amai e . . . não vos multipliqueis* [Love but . . . do not multiply], in which she addresses love, marriage, and responsible maternity.

1928: Women granted the right to vote in the state of Rio Grande do Norte.

1930: Rachel de Queiroz (1910–2003) publishes *O quinze* [The year fifteen]; critics praised the novel's depiction of the drought and human suffering in Northeastern Brazil, but mostly ignored the plot involving the female protagonist, a teacher who forgoes marriage so as to preserve her freedom and independence.

1932: Women granted the right to vote by a new national electoral code.

A Chronology

1933: First female representative elected.

1937: The government names a committee to prepare the Statutes of Women to be added to the Constitution.

1944: Clarice Lispector (1920–77) publishes *Perto do coração selvagem* (*Near to the Wild Heart,* 1991), a novel extremely well received by the critics for its innovative prose, psychological introspection and philosophical dimension. Lispector was to become one of the most renowned and influential Brazilian writers of the twentieth century.

1962: Married women are granted a new civil status, whereby a woman is no longer considered a minor and dependent on her husband before the law.

1964: On March 31, a coup d'état inaugurates a right-wing military dictatorship that lasts through 1985.

1968: Thousands of mothers and housewives march in the streets to denounce the torture by the military government of students involved in previous demonstrations and protests.

1969: The award-winning play *Fala baixo senão eu grito* [Speak softly or I'll scream] by Leilah Assunção (1943) is one of several woman-authored plays to open in Brazil this year. In their plays, Assunção and other female playwrights focus on women's issues within the political context of the military dictatorship.

1975: The United Nations declares 1975 the International Women's Year, opening the Decade for Women (1975–85); the United Nations sponsors a weeklong seminar on the role of women in Brazilian society, held at the Associação Brasileira de Imprensa [Brazilian Press Association]. This same year the Movimento Feminino pela Anistia [Women's Movement for Amnesty] is created in Brazil.

1977: Rachel de Queiroz is the first woman to join the Brazilian Academy of Letters; subsequently, other women are elected to the Academy: Dinah Silveira de Queiroz (1917–82) in 1980, Lygia Fagundes Telles (1923) in 1985, and Nélida Piñon (1937) in 1989.

A Chronology

1979: Women begin to achieve new and higher positions in politics and the government; this year the first female senator takes her seat, when it becomes open due to the death of the male senior senator, but only in 1990 is the first woman elected to the Senate. Meanwhile, the first female Minister is appointed to the Ministry of Education in 1982.

1980: United Nations World Conference on Women; the Grupo Lésbico Feminista [Feminist Lesbian Group] is created, followed by the creation of other political and cultural groups who address issues concerning female homosexuality. This same year, journalist and short-story writer Márcia Denser (1949) edits the anthology of female erotic short stories *Muito prazer* [Pleased to meet you / Much pleasure], followed by *O prazer é todo meu* [The pleasure is all mine] in 1984.

1985: The National Council on Women's Rights is established; state and local councils are also created. This same year the first *delegacia da mulher* [women's police station], staffed by women police officers, is open to help female victims of sexual assault and harassment, and of domestic abuse.

1987: I Conferência Nacional sobre a Saúde da Mulher [First National Conference on Women's Health] addresses, among other issues, sexual reproduction and abortion.

1988: Women are recognized as equal to men by the newly revised Federal Constitution. The law no longer considers men the head of the household; rather, men and women are to share all rights and responsibilities within the marriage.

1993: The prestigious Editora Brasiliense publishes *Erotica*, a selection of short stories submitted to a national competition of erotic fiction by women; about a thousand women—most of them unpublished writers—participated in the competition, with texts that ranged from platonic to very explicit, and that included numerous depictions of lesbian eroticism.

1995: Fourth World Conference on Women; Rosiska Darcy de Oliveira (194?), a writer, university professor, and

A Chronology

political exile during the military dictatorship, is named president of the National Council on Women's Rights by the newly inaugurated President Fernando Henrique Cardoso.

1996: Nélida Piñon elected president of the Brazilian Academy of Letters, the first woman to be awarded such distinction.

2000: Celebration of the 25th anniversary of the Associação Brasileira de Imprensa seminar on the role of women in Brazil.

Introduction
Brazilian Women's Literature as a Counterideological Discourse

Before the mid-1900s, the number of female names that were part of the Brazilian literary canon was rather small, although women had certainly engaged in writing, first as a hobby or as a private way of self-expression and, around the beginning of the twentieth century, as a profession. Those few women whose names were part of the national canon seemed to represent isolated and sporadic exceptions, and are viewed today as pioneers who first opened the doors to the wide acceptance of women writers in Brazil. Even though most of Brazil's female literary production before the late 1800s was all but forgotten along with the authors' names, a tradition of women's literature has indeed existed in the country.

This tradition may have begun with the letters a sixteenth-century woman, Felipa de Souza, wrote to her female lover, causing her arrest by the Inquisition; it continued with the poems and chronicles published under pseudonyms in nineteenth-century periodicals, and with the novels and short stories of a pioneering group of female authors such as Rachel de Queiroz, Lygia Fagundes Telles, and Clarice Lispector.[1] These modern Brazilian writers constituted in the 1930s and 1940s the first group of women openly acclaimed by the male-dominated literary canon. In this way, over the years and through various generations, Brazilian women writers have slowly made their way into the public space, forming a female literary lineage that only in the last quarter of the twentieth century has started to be recovered. Brazilian critic Zahidé Lupinacci Muzart's *Escritoras brasileiras do século XIX* [Nineteenth-century Brazilian women writers] (1999) is an example of the efforts by Brazilian scholars in the critical recovery of previously forgotten or ignored women writers.

Introduction

Brazil's female literary production has emerged against the canonical, male-produced literary and cultural discourse, and has often served as a counterpoint to a patriarchal, masculinist ideology that remained pervasive throughout the twentieth century.[2] However sporadic and isolated before 1900, in the twentieth century, and particularly from the 1960s on, Brazilian women have deconstructed in their literature cultural myths of femininity, beauty, and youth, and myths about women's social roles, identity, bodies, sexuality, and desire. As a consequence, their works often render problematic gender relations in Brazilian society. These myths of femininity begin to be more radically undermined in the second half of the twentieth century, when Western cultures witness the crisis of modernity and the failing of logocentrism. In Brazil, this crisis is announced by the counterideological discourses of cultural and political groups such as women's associations, workers' unions, the Black Movement, and Gay Pride alliances that up until then had been more or less marginalized or ignored by the dominant discourse.

Even though this cultural crisis must be understood in the aftermath of the military dictatorship in Brazil, it did not happen "unexpectedly." In the decades leading to the 1960s and during the 1970s, women had become the strongest voices among those in Brazilian literature that sought to deconstruct the dominant discourse, and their presence in the national cultural scene helped open a space for the literature of other minority groups. This phenomenon takes place within the context of a wider women's movement in the country, in the 1970s and 1980s, "arguably the largest, most diverse, most radical, and most successful women's movement in Latin America" (Alvarez 3). Since the 1960s, Brazilian female authors had lived through the impact of the Cultural Revolution that brought new lifestyles, drug experimentation, the pill, and the sexual revolution to Brazil. In 1975, the International Women's Year, introduced by the United Nations and celebrated around the world, also had significant repercussions in Brazil. From that year on, a considerable number of important works about and by women came out in various fields, particularly in sociology, psychology, and public policies. With the political amnesty in 1979, Brazilian exiles began to return to the country. Among them were women who had witnessed and sometimes

Introduction

participated in women's movements abroad, such as Rosiska Darcy de Oliveira. All these factors have placed women in the cultural avant-garde against the dominant discourse in Brazil.

In the last decades of the twentieth century, female poets, fiction writers, and playwrights have produced the most important counterideological discourse in Brazilian literature, as they have strived to create an authentic language and fresh images suitable for the expression of new voices and a changing reality. Many, as well as diverse, names have given shape to such discourse. In addition to Lispector, Telles, Leilah Assunção, Nélida Piñon, and Márcia Denser, are Hilda Hilst (1930), Marina Colasanti (1937), Sonia Coutinho (1939), and Consuelo de Castro (1946), among others. Some of these women writers (for example, Lispector) have denied that sexual difference is relevant in the critical assessment of their works; others (Colasanti, for instance), on the contrary, have not been concerned about hiding their feminist stance. However, what should be taken into account is that Brazilian women writers, either seen as a group or individually, have developed a feminist critique of the Brazilian "master narrative," particularly as it concerns the representation of the female body, sexuality, and desire.

* * *

In the chapters ahead I discuss a significant number of poems, short stories, and novels by Brazilian female authors in order to identify and analyze the poetic and discursive strategies employed to deconstruct cultural myths and stereotypes, and to defy traditionally accepted patterns of female behavior. The work of Brazilian women playwrights, while not the object of my study here, has also been a part in this process of deconstruction of cultural myths. However, as David S. George has stated, "as writers, women came late to the Brazilian stage. Their way was paved by poets and especially by fiction writers" (57). Plays by Hilst, Assunção, de Castro, as well as Edla Van Steen (1936), Maria Adelaide do Amaral (1942), and a few others, share with Brazilian women's poetry and fiction certain thematic aspects, specifically the discussion of women's roles in society, gender relations, and women's search for emotional, sexual, and intellectual self-realization. For this reason, George

Introduction

places Brazilian women's plays within a tradition of "quest for identity" literature previously initiated in Brazil by women fiction writers (cf. George 57–66), and also developed by Brazilian women poets.³

I focus on the strategies Brazilian female poets and fiction writers utilize to achieve new forms of representation of the female body, sexuality, and desire. Sexuality and desire are intrinsically linked to an individual's sense of identity, and are of particular importance for women, given the historical repression of their bodies and sexualities; the double standard of morality still often applied to men and women in many Western cultures, and specifically in Latin America; institutional heterosexuality as the accepted norm; and the assignment of rigid social roles for women. Therefore, I will examine the narrative and poetic strategies Brazilian female writers have employed in portraying the female body, in the representation of female sexuality and eroticism, and in the discussion of social and cultural issues that, in one way or another, relate to a woman's sense of her own body and sexuality. Among these issues are: the characterization of women based on racial features and class hierarchy, marriage, motherhood, and aging.

In Chapter 1, I establish what had been the cultural "norm" of femininity or, in other words, the ideas about women's bodies, sexuality, and social roles predominant in Brazil throughout the twentieth century. In order to do so, I discuss the representation of women and female sexuality in Brazilian literature by male authors as seen in four nineteenth-century novels. These novels are *Memórias de um sargento de milícias* (1853; *Memoirs of a Militia Sergeant,* 1959; 1999), by Manuel Antônio de Almeida; *Iracema* (1865; English translations 1886; 2000), by José Martiniano de Alencar; Aluísio Azevedo's *O cortiço* (1890; *A Brazilian Tenement,* 1926; 1976; *The Slum,* 2000); and Joaquim Maria Machado de Assis's *Dom Casmurro* (1899; English translations 1953; 1997). These four canonical works have helped define and establish some stereotypes about female sexuality well rooted in Brazilian culture, such as the sensual mulatto woman; the seductive, unfaithful woman; the pure, white, married woman; and lesbians as perverted and/or frustrated women.

In Chapter 2, I take as a point of departure the poetry of Gilka Machado (1893–1980), who, at the beginning of the twentieth century, sent shock waves through the literary public and critics with the publication in 1915 of her first book, *Cristais partidos* [Shattered crystal]. Machado's subversion lay mainly in her claims of women's subordination in society and in her erotic poems. These claims were cause for scandal, fueled in part by the sensationalist treatment the author received in the media at the time. Machado has been recognized as an important precursor of contemporary literature by Brazilian female authors who recurrently focus on problems affecting women's social situation, their sense of identity, and their sexuality.

One of Gilka Machado's most significant achievements, which underlies the "offensive" quality her early critics and readers found in her poetry, is the very fact that men are often absent from her erotic poems, either as the subject of desire or even as its object. In all her poetry, the poetic voice is female and takes the role of the desiring subject. At the same time, a woman may be also the source of pleasure, and even the explicit object of desire. The exclusion of a masculine figure from the erotic exchange becomes problematic in a male-centered society such as Brazil. In a country famous for being sexually "free," female autoeroticism and lesbian desire, which Machado's poetry hints at, are tolerated only as far as they may be erotic stimuli for the male voyeur.

For many decades, Gilka Machado was an isolated and often marginalized figure within the Brazilian literary canon. She was certainly not the only writer of that period to have raised issues relating to female sexuality. We only have to think of Rachel de Queiroz, one of the most important authors of the 1930s Novel of the Northeast, or of Patrícia Galvão (pseud. Pagu; 1910–62), whose novel *Parque industrial* (1933; *Industrial Park,* 1993) has lately been recognized for its significance within the Brazilian Modernist movement of the 1920s. Ercília Nogueira Cobra (1891–196?), who was active in the first wave of Brazilian feminism in the early twentieth century, also gave female sexuality, including lesbianism, representation in her work. What distinguishes Machado, however, is the exuberance and excess of female desire represented in her poems. What these other early twentieth-century writers seem to lack, and Machado's poetry offers, is a female *erotic* discourse and the affirmation and celebration of female sexuality.

Introduction

Thus, some pertinent critical questions that I address in the following chapters are: What constitutes female eroticism in works by Brazilian women writers? What is an appropriate definition of the erotic? What are the problems involved in the creation of a female erotic discourse? I discuss these issues in Chapter 2 and examine the production of some Brazilian women writers of the 1970s and 1980s, a period when a significant amount of female erotic poetry and fiction is published. I then focus my analysis on two novels: Marilene Felinto's *As mulheres de Tijucopapo* (1982; *The Women of Tijucopapo,* 1994), and Helena Parente Cunha's *Mulher no espelho* (1983; *Woman between Mirrors,* 1989). Both writers have been successful in representing female eroticism in these novels. However, important questions emerge from them: Can female desire be rendered in a way other than submissive to male desire, and to what extent can the dialectics of *domination* versus *subordination* be left out of the erotic exchange?

The female discourse that emerges in the last three decades of the twentieth century is varied in genre, in poetic and narrative strategies employed, and in tone. As the writers portray women's reality and address issues concerning the female body, sexuality, and desire, the tone they employ in their works can be lyrical, realist, assertive, or ambiguous. It can express rebelliousness and defiance against the dominant patriarchal ideology, or it can express guilt and uneasiness when women confront, on the one hand, the options they seem to have and, on the other, the traditions that for so long have alienated them from themselves and their bodies. Some female novelists have given expression to this alienation through the use of elements of the fantasy novel—more specifically, elements of the fantastic, the gothic, and the grotesque.

In Chapter 3, I examine how Telles and Lya Luft (1939) have made use of such strategies in order to represent their female characters' problematic relationships with themselves, their bodies, and their reality. And again in Chapter 4, I discuss the role the grotesque plays in Brazilian women's fiction. This time I examine its use by Coutinho in her short fiction, along with other narrative strategies she utilizes to represent the aging female body and to problematize aging as a social construct.

In Chapters 2, 3, and 4, as I discuss the construction of a female erotic discourse and the representation of the female body by Brazilian women writers, I consider how many of them convey the problematic relationship that may still exist between Brazilian women and their bodies and sexuality. Nevertheless, other authors are able to create a poetic voice, or a fictional character, who comes to terms with her own body, and experiences her sexuality and desire freely, both in heterosexual and in lesbian relationships.

In Chapter 5, I discuss the existence of a tradition of lesbian literature in Brazil, followed by an analysis of short stories by five contemporary Brazilian women that portray lesbian desire. They are: Van Steen's "Intimidade" (1977; "Intimacy," 1991); "A mulher de ouro" [The golden woman] (1980) by Myriam Campello (194?); Telles's "A escolha" [The choice] (1985); Denser's "Tigresa" [Tigress] (1986); and Coutinho's "Fátima e Jamila" [Fatima and Jamila] (1994). While some of the authors problematize the invisibility of the lesbian woman in society and in literature, others present lesbianism as a space in which the authentic expression of female desire is made possible.

In Chapter 6, I again focus on women's heterosexuality, addressing the questions raised in Chapter 2 of whether female desire can be rendered in a way other than submissive to male desire, and whether an erotic exchange that is satisfying for the female subject can take place outside, or in spite of, gender hierarchies. In order to address these issues, I examine some of Denser's short stories published in the mid-1980s and Colasanti's poetry published a decade later.

My aim in this book has been to present an assessment of what Brazilian women poets and fiction writers have accomplished in the twentieth century. At the same time, I point out some tendencies that can be identified in narrative fiction and in poetry by Brazilian female authors, particularly in the last quarter of the century. Some of the writers here discussed, as for example, Coutinho and Colasanti, are at the avant-garde of a new female discourse in Brazil, one that announces the "New Woman" of the twentieth-first century. Overcoming patriarchal guilt, successful in the deconstruction of old cultural myths, celebrating the female body, and giving authentic expression to women's desire, their works, at the beginning of a new millennium, constitute a counterideological discourse that also proposes the possibility of a new order, giving expression to what this new woman has to say about—and for—herself.

Chapter One

Female Body, Male Desire

Twentieth-century Brazilian women's literature constitutes a body of ideological discourse that stands in opposition to the work of male writers who typically have rendered female sexuality as subservient to masculine desire. The best example of this masculinist perspective of the female body is Jorge Amado's *Gabriela, cravo e canela* (1958; *Gabriela, Clove and Cinnamon,* 1962), perhaps the most widely translated novel by a Brazilian author. Gabriela, Amado's protagonist, is the stereotypical sensual mulatto girl, at the same time child and woman, naive and sexually experienced. Seen from a patriarchal viewpoint, Gabriela has come to embody the ideal image of the Brazilian woman, particularly after Sonia Braga, the popular Brazilian actress, portrayed the character on television and in the movies.

In this first chapter, I discuss the representation of women and female sexuality in four male-authored canonical novels published in Brazil in the nineteenth century. Beginning with an analysis of two important Romantic novels, Manuel Antônio de Almeida's 1853 *Memórias de um sargento de milícias* and José de Alencar's 1865 *Iracema,* I will examine two other canonical novels that have helped define and establish some Brazilian stereotypes about female sexuality: the sensual mulatto woman; the seductive, unfaithful woman; the pure, white, married woman; and lesbians as perverted and/or frustrated women. These novels are Aluísio Azevedo's *O cortiço,* published in 1890, and Machado de Assis's *Dom Casmurro,* published nine years later. By analyzing the representation of women and of female sexuality in these four novels, I hope to establish the type of cultural and literary stereotypes Brazilian female authors have responded to in their writings.

***

The literature produced in Brazil during the Romantic period gave expression to an ideology responsible for the creation of cultural myths still prevalent in Brazilian society throughout the twentieth century. For most of the next one hundred years, these Romantic cultural myths would inform what we may call the *mentalidade brasileira,* the Brazilian mentality or, in other words, the dominant worldview in Brazilian society, whereby all social relations are understood and defined. In my analysis, I rely on a concept of ideology as defined by Louis Althusser, for whom ideology refers to a system of representations that holds a historical function in the context of a given society. In other words, this system of representations fulfills a specific social function in a particular historical process. Such function can be understood as the very process of the production of meanings and ideas that, in turn, constitute "the expression of the special interests of some class or social group" (McGann 5). Myths, belonging to the same category as ideas, concepts, and images, are forms of representation that constitute a particular ideological system (Althusser 13), serving as vehicles for the transmission of said ideology. For the purpose of my analysis here, a definition of *myth* can be derived from that set forth by James George Frazer (1890). Myth should be understood as a basic narrative structure that is part of the imaginary of a group or society, which has an emotional appeal, and which has the purpose of explaining reality, the world, and its origins. In the case of the Brazilian Romantic myths, even as they carry on to the twentieth century, their purpose is, specifically, to explain and define the origins and identity of the nation.

Brazilian Romantic Myths: *Iracema* and *Memórias de um sargento de milícias*

Literary historiographers generally use the year of 1836, when Domingos José Gonçalves de Magalhães published in Paris his first book of poetry, *Suspiros poéticos e saudades* [Poetic sighs and longings], to mark the beginning of Romanticism in Brazilian letters and arts. The inception of the Romantic Movement in the arts coincides thus with the early years of Brazil as an independent nation, and with the political, philosophical, and cultural efforts toward a definition of a national identity. Within this context, Romanticism can be understood as an ideological discourse that establishes in Brazilian culture myths that only begin to be consistently undermined in the last three or four decades of the twentieth century, with the advent of a postmodern counterideological discourse. The Brazilian postmodern discourse, and specifically the discourse of female authors as counterideological, will be discussed later in this book.

For now, it should be noted that it is in the foundational literature of the nineteenth century that we find very clearly shaped the myths that will be used to define and explain the origins and identity of the nation. Nineteenth-century Brazilian writers, similarly to their Spanish American counterparts, "were encouraged both by the need to fill in a national history that would legitimate the emerging nation and by the opportunity to direct that history towards a future ideal" (Sommer, "Romance" 49). In the specific case of Brazil, this literature represents "a discourse of gendered politics" (Sommer, "Romance" 49) that attributes fixed roles to the white protagonist and to the native woman/land, thus engendering the myth of national foundation. In Brazil, José de Alencar and his Indianist novels serve as the best example of a mythmaking foundational discourse.[1]

The Brazilian Indian and landscape, as the most relevant "symbols" of the Romantic period, have been extensively discussed by Brazilian cultural critics such as Antonio Candido and Dante Moreira Leite, the latter elaborating on these symbols' relationship to the national psyche. According to Leite (1979), these are "symbols" that, still in the last quarter of the twentieth century, sustained nationalist feelings in the country. Reading them as symbols and not myths, the author expresses his belief that these images have become part of the national consciousness and represent the nation (Leite 44). However, he concedes that these symbols do become cultural myths when they "são empregados como recurso de mistificação, isto é, forma de impedir o aparecimento ou o triunfo de outras formas de vida social" (Leite 44) ["are employed as a strategy of mystification or, in other words, as a form of preventing the advent or triumph of other forms of social life"]. Thus I propose to read these images as myths or "ideological strategies," to use Terry Eagleton's (1991) expression. The Brazilian Romantic discourse, concerned with painting the portrait of the newly independent nation, constructs the national identity from a masculinist and ethnocentric perspective, utilizing ideological strategies that preclude the participation of certain social groups, namely, women and blacks, in the national cultural project.

Brazilian literature, from the time of independence in 1822, sought to respond to a newly perceived lack, that of "a clearcut, fully accepted racial and national identity," with the "conviction that a single, unifying identity can and must be found" (Haberly 7). After achieving political independence from Portugal, Brazilians rejected the Portuguese national myths that had helped define the identity of the colony. And if *Os Lusíadas* cannot be embraced any longer as our own "supreme national text" (Haberly 8), it becomes urgent to write the Brazilian national text and to create the myths that will define the new nation. Brazilian Indianist literature, most notably Alencar's novels, responded to this urgency by creating an idealized image of the Indian. The heroic Brazilian Indian that we find, not only in Alencar, but also in the Indianist poems of Antonio Gonçalves Dias (1823–64), established a noble ascendance of which Brazilians could be proud.

At the same time, while this false Indian aristocracy, created by the white, Eurocentric discourse, was the source of national pride, the participation of African blacks was minimized, or even erased from the dominant discourse on national identity. In fact, Antonio Candido recalls the practice, common in the nineteenth century, by which the somatic characteristics ensuing from the miscegenation of blacks and whites were attributed to the individual's Indian heritage (Candido 37). Thus Indianism also offered Brazilians the possibility of disassociating themselves from the African slaves. This form of ethnic misrepresentation, however, continued in the twentieth century and is illustrated, for example, in the short story "Viva la patria" by Otto Lara Resende (1975), among many other examples. Resende's protagonist is proud to be called "Indian" because it allows him to hide his African heritage, even though his enemies use the nickname in a derogatory way.

Chapter One

But it is the Indianist novel of Alencar, particularly his famous *Iracema*, that stands as the "supreme national text" of Brazil. *Iracema* presents the genesis of the people of Ceará, Alencar's home state, and by extension (and due also to the novel's wide circulation and impact) the genesis of the new nation. The novel effects a foundational myth that explains the origins of a new race. In it, Iracema, the Indian woman, is at the same time Eve and Mary, portrayed as seductive, on one hand, and, on the other, reduced to a maternal, nurturing role, submissive to male desire. Iracema is identified with the American landscape; in fact, the interpretation of the name *Iracema* as an anagram of *America* is now a commonplace, since Afrânio Peixoto pointed it out in 1931. Called the "daughter of the forests" (Alencar 5), Iracema is identified with the tropics, with the new land, an identification that becomes evident in the descriptions of the character and in the numerous comparisons the author makes between her and the local flora and fauna.[2]

As the landscape itself is exuberant, hot, and sensual, so, it is implied, is the Indian woman. Beautiful and graceful, Iracema is "naturally" seductive to the eyes of the white warrior, who sees her naked body for the first time when it is still resplendent with the "aljofar d'água" (48; "pearly drops of water"; 14) from her recent bath. To identify Iracema as a native Eve agrees with the general reading of the novel as a genesis of the people of Ceará (and Brazil) proposed by the author himself. The first encounter between her and Martim, the white warrior, narrated in chapter 2, parallels the biblical story of the first man and the first woman in the garden of Eden. Following this reasoning, many critics have characterized Iracema as the seducer, while Martim is the poor Adam who falls prey to the woman's charms. However, Alencar's text is more complex than that, as it tells the ambiguous story of love, desire, and seduction.[3]

In fact, "Who seduces whom?" is an important question that must be framed by the ideological standpoint from which Alencar writes, and which dictates the characterization of the two protagonists. Iracema is the beautiful "virgin of the forests" in complete harmony with nature, and reacts instinctively when she sees the strange white man. Purity, goodness, and instinct are qualities generally associated with her. Martim, on the other hand, while equally noble and good, personifies civilization, marked by the "Ignotas armas e tecidos ignotos [que] cobrem-lhe o corpo" (15; "Unknown weapons and unknown cloths [that] covered his body"; 4). He is clearly the man after the Fall who has come to cause the Fall also of the Indian Eve: for his sake, Iracema will transgress the laws of her people, will leave her original garden of Eden, and will (alone) be punished for that. Nonetheless, Martim's noble spirit and gentleman-like manner stem from his Christian upbringing that has inculcated in him a respect for women as "[símbolos] de ternura e amor" (15; "[symbols] of tenderness and love"; 4). In fact, he evokes his Christian beliefs more than once so as not to succumb to the "temptation" he sees in the Indian woman.

Iracema, in spite of being a savage, is characterized also by qualities associated with femininity in Western culture, including obedience and submission to the male. Her main function in the novel will be to give life to the new American (Brazilian) race, in the form of her and Martim's son, Moacir. In this primarily maternal role, the character's sexuality is described in contradictory terms. The first expression of her desire is depicted in terms of maternal feelings toward Martim: she wanted to shelter and protect him, and the image of Iracema embracing his head as he sleeps clearly evokes the *Pietà* (*Iracema,* trans. Landers 21). Her love and desire for the white man is manifested through her longing, but chaste, "bird-like" eyes (48 and others) and, more importantly, by the haste with which she submits or obeys each time she hears his voice calling her (17, 48, 49, 50, and others). The sequence of events in chapter 15, when Martim drinks from the *jurema* liquor, is a most eloquent example of her submission. Here Iracema is represented as a beautiful bird "fascinado pela serpente" (68; "fascinated by the serpent"; 48), Martim. Seduced by his smile, Iracema leans over to kiss him but is rejected: as a Christian, Martim would not in full conscience bring disgrace to the Indian virgin and to her father, who is Martim's host among the Tabajara Indians. Immediately, though, he asks her to bring him the *jurema* and insists when she tries to dissuade him from drinking the sacred liquor (trans. Landers 49–50). Submissive, she obeys, handing him the drink that will liberate his conscience and allow him the satisfaction of his desire. And again he is the one who calls her name, and she submissively obeys. Immersed in a fantasy state induced by the *jurema*, Martim can take pleasure from Iracema's body, without having to take responsibility. And in fact, after the effects of the drink have dissipated in the morning, he again rejects Iracema, who is now the "chaste" wife (50–51).

The lyricism of the language employed by the author, and the European Christian ideology that frames Alencar's narrative, relating Iracema to both Eve and Mary, have shaped the reading of the novel for many generations. It is fairly easy to accept Iracema as the seducer, an acceptance that, in turn, has softened the violence of the colonization process. As Ria Lemaire states: "[The novel] describes the Indian world, its nature and culture and its women in such a marvelous, fascinating beauty that readers unconsciously shut their eyes to the cruelty of the facts and visions that are narrated" (69). By conveying an image of Iracema as seducer or, at best, as submissive and willing, the author eases the pain ensuing from the ethnic and cultural conflicts between colonizers and colonized. And Alencar, who during his lifetime had already achieved distinction and authority within Brazil's intellectual and literary circles, not only creates the foundational myth of Brazil, but also "constructed its frame of interpretation . . . in his letters and literary discussions" (Lemaire 70).

The apparently conciliatory union between the two races hides the process of domination, making possible the myth of racial democracy (Duarte 199) associated with the origins of the new nation. Interestingly, in forging a myth of femininity, Alencar does not escape the dialectics of race and sexuality that seems to have been an intrinsic part of Brazilian literature since the arrival of the Portuguese in Brazil.[4] Later in the novel, after Iracema's chastity and purity of spirit have been well established, her sexuality is represented as "ardent" (in the original, "ardentes amores"; 68; in English, "ardent loves"; 48; the plural word implies sexual favors), in opposition to the "chaste affection" of the "blond maiden" that awaits Martim at home (48). The dialectics of race-sexuality is at work here, with the sexuality of the woman of color represented as passionate and exuberant, unlike that of the white woman. This dialectics will be developed to a much greater extent in works of literature that depict black Brazilian women, as will be discussed below.

* * *

Like the Indianist literature of Alencar, Brazilian Romantic urban literature also served as an ideological discourse, by creating myths of femininity that prescribed acceptable forms of behavior to women, established boundaries for the participation of women in society, and regulated women's bodies and desire. This Brazilian urban literature of the second half of the 1800s originates within a "heterosexual, reproduction-oriented mindframe," as Michel Foucault (*History of Sexuality. An Introduction* 3) has characterized Western cultures. Thus its ideological project is to curb or "to expel from reality the forms of sexuality that were not amenable to the strict economy of reproduction" (Foucault, *History of Sexuality. An Introduction* 36). Even works that depict Brazilian social reality critically, or with irony, such as Manuel Antônio de Almeida's popular novel *Memórias de um sargento de milícias,* fail to significantly deviate from a stereotypical portrayal of women. In reality, *Memórias* defines some of the myths of femininity that will be pervasive in Brazilian culture throughout the twentieth century. These myths are concerned particularly with the female body and sexuality, and with marriage as the institution that sets the boundaries for women's social actions.

Almeida plays up with humorous mastery the dichotomy between the "domestic woman" and the "public woman," through two equally adorable—but for different reasons— female characters, Luisinha and Vidinha. Luisinha is first described as "alta, magra, pálida; andava com o queixo enterrado no peito, trazia as pálpebras sempre baixas, e olhava a furto" (*Memórias* 75; "tall, skinny, and pale; she walked with her chin buried in her chest, kept her eyes aimed downward, and looked by furtive glances"; *Memoirs* 70).[5] In short, she was a timid adolescent who had "perdido as graças de menina" (75; "lost the graces of a girl"; 70), but whose budding body did not yet display any of the physical characteristics traditionally associated with female beauty. Later in the novel, after she has

Chapter One

been briefly—and unhappily—married, and meets the male hero again, she is an "elegant, young lady" who has lost her former "physical timidity" (164), but who still acts "cautiously" (165) and with propriety, with *ladylike* behavior. The character of Vidinha, on the other hand, is described from the outset in very different terms:

> Vidinha era uma mulatinha de dezoito a vinte anos, de altura regular, ombros largos, peito alteado, cintura fina e pés pequeninos; tinha os olhos muito pretos e muito vivos, os lábios grossos e úmidos, os dentes alvíssimos, a fala era um pouco descansada, doce e afinada.
>
> Cada frase que proferia era interrompida com uma risada longa e sonora, e com um certo caído de cabeça para trás. . . . (*Memórias* 118 [1])

Vidinha's physical attributes define her as eminently sensual. She displays a number of characteristics that seem to constitute the ideal female figure in various cultures, and the contrast of sizes and proportions are noticeable: "broad shoulders" versus "slim waist"; "salient breasts" versus "tiny feet." The qualities of her voice, her tendency to giggle easily, and her mannerisms contribute to a portrait of female sexuality as excessive. In addition, she is later described as also "movediça e leve" ("flighty and shallow") and "uma formidável namoradeira" (120; "a shameless flirt"; 119), jealous and hot-tempered. In sum, Vidinha is a kind of tropical *femme fatale* seen through the relative innocence of Almeida's Romanticism; she is the paradigmatic Brazilian sensual mulatto woman.

Another aspect complements this contrastive characterization of Luisinha and Vidinha, and that is the space that each one inhabits. Luisinha is seen mostly within the protected space of the home, and in the few occasions when she does go out, she is followed by the attentive gaze of her aunt and legal guardian, Dona Maria, and her entourage of adult friends, servants, and slaves. Vidinha, on the contrary, can go out on her own whenever she pleases and is seen on the streets in the joyful company of other girls and young men her age, without the supervision of an adult chaperone whose presence would have been expected then. Thus we can ascertain that Luisinha is mostly confined to the domestic space, while Vidinha has much more mobility, having free access to the public space of the streets. As Antonio Candido points out in "Dialética da malandragem" [The dialectic of roguery], *Memórias de um sargento de milícias* deals exclusively with the lower strata of Brazilian society, excluding both the upper classes and the slaves. However, one can distinguish a social hierarchy within the lower classes portrayed in the novel. Dona Maria and Luisinha, the latter being heiress to "some thousands of cruzados" (*Memoirs* 69), are at the upper end of this social group, while Vidinha and her family are at the other end. It is useful to emphasize here that race plays a major role in the identity of these two characters and in determining the spaces wherein each woman is allowed.

Almeida's delicious and, for this very reason, insidious novel introduces within our national consciousness myths of female behavior that later novels and other forms of cultural expression (such as movies, TV, and popular music) will reinforce within the Brazilian collectivity. Among these myths, those represented again and again in Brazilian literature and culture, are that of the "domestic woman," respectful, virgin, ready and willing to get married and be a mother; and that of the "public woman," not necessarily the prostitute, but the sexually free woman, aware of her own body and desires, who has control over her own sexuality. *Memórias de um sargento de milícias,* even if it does not inaugurate such dichotomy in Brazilian letters and culture, is the text to leave a deep mark in the Brazilian imaginary, therein weaving together the representation of the female body and a dialectics of race. In this way, we will have in Luisinha and Vidinha the incarnations of the marriage-appropriate woman and of the sexually free woman, juxtaposed to the "purity" of the white woman and the "uncontrollable" sexuality of the black woman. And so that the readers should have no doubts about the ideology the novel wants to convey, suffice it to recall which one of the two women is given the reward of marrying the hero: Luisinha, the well-behaved, proper, shy, white woman.

Vidinha, it should be noted, does not appear eager to marry, as marriage brings inevitable restrictions on a woman's freedom, which the character highly values. But even with all her independence and free behavior, much of Vidinha's identity comes from her position as an object of desire for the male voyeur. Vidinha is probably the first example in Brazilian fiction of a prototype Affonso Romano de Sant'Anna has identified in nineteenth-century Brazilian poetry as the "mulata cordial," or the "cordial mulatto woman" (Sant'Anna, *Canibalismo* 19), whose body is synonymous with parties, dancing, laughter, and pleasure. Seen as the locus for *male* pleasure, the "mulata" is in fact the mediating element between the white woman and the prostitute, as Sant'Anna has correctly asserted (*Canibalismo* 24), and between the domestic and the public space.

O cortiço and the Myth of the Sensual Mulatto Woman

The myth of the sensual mulatto woman is well defined in the Brazilian Romantic narrative, and we find similar representations in Brazilian poetry of the same period. Sant'Anna, for instance, has analyzed a representative number of works by male poets of the period in his book *O canibalismo amoroso* [Amorous cannibalism] (1984). Sant'Anna's analysis leads to some important conclusions, among them, that Brazilian Romantic poetry "dramatiza o jogo entre a mulher *esposável* (branca) e a mulher *comível* (preta)" (19) ["dramatizes the play between the (white) *marriageable* woman and the (black) *good to eat* woman"]. He also discusses how in this poetry the female slave's body becomes the *locus* for male pleasure, and how Brazilian Romantic poetry brings together violence and seduction (19). Later in the twentieth century, the association *women of color–food–pleasure* becomes the main axis in Jorge Amado's popular novels, *Gabriela,* mentioned here before, and *Dona Flor e seus dois maridos* (1966; *Dona Flor and Her Two Husbands,* 1969). Having been taken to Brazil as slaves, blacks were stigmatized also by the long-held view of slaves as sexual objects, pervasive in Western culture since before the Classical period. As Foucault states in the second volume of his *History of Sexuality,* "Slaves were at their master's disposition, of course: their condition made them sexual objects and this was taken for granted" (*Pleasure* 215–16). Interestingly, in *Woman: An Intimate Geography* (1999), Natalie Angier recalls how his-

Female Body, Male Desire

torians have established that in early times, slavery always meant the enslavement of women, used by their captors for sex and procreation, while men would be killed once defeated in a battle (279).

The stigma *slave/sexual object,* therefore, especially hurt black women in Brazil. Although slavery as an institution was officially eradicated from Brazil with its abolition in 1888, it has lingered within the dominant ideology, affecting the way blacks are regarded by society. In the twentieth century, Brazilian popular culture and the mass media continued selling the image of the sensual mulatto woman. In fact it brought from the page to the big screen Azevedo's Rita Baiana and Amado's Gabriela (*Gabriela* was also the basis for a popular TV soap opera), whose famous protagonist can be seen as a direct descendant of both Rita Baiana and Almeida's Vidinha. Many other examples could be mentioned here; suffice it to say that, still at the turn of the new millennium, the sensual mulatto woman is one of the images most commonly used to sell the country to foreign tourists.

* * *

Almeida's Vidinha, the paradigmatic sensual *mulata* of Brazilian fiction, is shown through the lenses of the Naturalist movement in Azevedo's *O cortiço*. Here the image of the sensual mulatto woman is fundamentally associated with a definition of national identity. The *cortiço,* which literally means a beehive, is presented as a live organism growing spontaneously, like larvae that multiply themselves (26). As such, it appears as a microcosm of Brazilian society, more specifically of a low segment of the society, men and women of the working classes, washer women, quarry laborers, factory workers, slaves, and other types of workers. Alongside the petit bourgeois household of Miranda, a textile merchant, the slum is the perfect background for the author to practice the philosophical and scientific ideas of the Naturalist school of literature *en vogue* then. Azevedo was particularly fond of the ideas relating to Materialistic Determinism, according to which human beings are moved by biological and/or social forces, and of the influence of the environment over the individual. Following the

Chapter One

directives of Naturalism, the novel offers a pathological view of the characters and emphasizes themes such as adultery, criminality, and mental and physiological disorders. As Foucault has made clear, this is the period when Western cultures see a proliferation of discourses on human sexuality. In addition, forms of sexuality considered "perverse" or "deviant," such as male homosexuality and lesbianism, are labeled and catalogued by the medical and juridical-legal discourses (Foucault, *History of Sexuality. An Introduction*). Azevedo utilizes the slum's inhabitants as case studies that illustrate several different social and or biological "anomalies," such as the "nymphomaniac" and adulterous Dona Estela, the weak homosexual Albino, and the prostitute Leónie. Others serve as exaggerated and grotesque representations of normal biological processes such as aging (for example, the old man Botelho).

Interestingly, exaggerated, if not pathological, portrayals of women seem to be more abundant than those of men in *O cortiço*. The characterization, both of men and of women, is achieved mostly by means of a process of reification that underlines the animal-like characteristics of the individuals. Female characters are often defined by way of their sexuality, and their sexuality, in turn, is inscribed in their physical attributes, as in "olhos luxuriosos de macaca" (Azevedo, *O cortiço* 38; "lustful eyes like a monkey's"; *The Slum* 24) that describes Florinda, a fifteen-year-old mulatto girl.[6] Others are characterized by a *lack*, as in the case of Pombinha (her name means "little dove") who, at the age of eighteen has not yet had her first menstrual period. Some of the female characters (Florinda, Rita Baiana) are described as erotic objects, others (Augusta Carne-Mole, Piedade) by their capacity for procreation and/or hard work, while others still (Dona Estela, Leocádia) by their uncontrollable sexuality.

In all, the level of sensuality or eroticism of a character seems to be in inverse relation to their capacity to procreate or to work. Thus, it is apparent that characters such as Rita Baiana, Firmo, her mulatto lover, and others, do not belong within the dominant capitalist mode of economic production. For example, Rita Baiana does work but goes through long periods of inactivity when she is involved in a new or passionate love affair. The best example of the inverse relation between work

Female Body, Male Desire

and eroticism is Jerônimo, the Portuguese quarry mason who comes to live in the *cortiço* with his wife and young daughter, and to work on the quarry behind the slum.

When Jerônimo and his family arrive, he is described as hardworking and industrious, "perseverante, observador e dotado de certa habilidade" (53; "determined and quick-witted"; 40), a man of simple habits and strong as a bull (53). Likewise, Piedade too is hardworking, healthy, honest, strong, and completely faithful to her man (54). They keep to themselves, living and working to build a better future for their daughter. They are the guinea pigs the author utilizes in a social experiment. Having fallen in love with Rita Baiana, Jerônimo undergoes a moral degradation described as a process of *abrasileiramento,* or of becoming Brazilian. He begins to enjoy everything that is Brazilian, and to show a preference for the local food, music, and *cachaça* over the food, *fado,* and wine from his native Portugal. Most importantly, Jerônimo becomes more sensual, more erotic, and at the same time, lazier, preferring to make love with Rita than to work. Piedade and, later, their daughter also suffer the impact of Jerônimo's *abrasileiramento* and the subsequent dissolution of their family, Piedade becoming an alcoholic and the young girl following the path to prostitution. In the novel, these processes are described as consequences of the inescapable influence of the social environment upon the individuals' helpless will, and serve to prove the social experiment the author set out to make. Through this social-literary experiment, the author seeks to demonstrate that the environment can shape and/or transform an individual, even the most ethical and moral.

O cortiço is structurally organized over a series of oppositions or parallels: between social spaces and social classes (the *cortiço* and Miranda's household; the working poor and the bourgeoisie) and between characters (João Romão and Miranda; Rita Baiana and Piedade; Jerônimo and Firmo, etc.). The most significant oppositions, that primarily define each of the characters, are those between *races* (whites versus blacks or mulattos) and between *nationalities* (Portuguese versus Brazilian). Attaching specific characteristics to each side of these oppositions, the author draws a critical profile of the Brazilian national identity, although he is no less critical of the

Chapter One

Portuguese characters in the novel. From this profile, which can be better understood from table 1, emerges a strong identification between the woman of color and the Brazilian land. The novel forcefully establishes a link between Brazilians, particularly those of African descent, the body, and other related attributes, such as instinct and sexuality. On the other hand, whites, for the most part, are moved by rationality and especially by a desire to ascend socially and economically. Thus whites, as for example, João Romão, Miranda, and Jerônimo, are all linked to work, and they express in different ways a desire to conquer Brazil.

Table 1
Profile of Oppositions in Azevedo's *O cortiço*

Portuguese characters	Brazilian characters
White	Black/mulatto
Work, greed, capitalist production	Indolence, laziness
Rationality	Instinct
Domination over nature	Nature
The controlled body	The sensual, hot, exuberant body
Sexual procreation	Sexual pleasure

There are, however, some presumable exceptions to the pattern that emerges from table 1. For example, Augusta Carne-Mole, one of the washerwomen at the *cortiço,* is a white Brazilian married to a mulatto policeman, with whom she has several children. Her name literally means "soft flesh," but also implies a person of slow movements, lazy and indolent, which is her most defining characteristic. As a Brazilian woman of the white race, she lacks the excessive sensuality that defines mulatto women in the novel. Augusta Carne-Mole is famous among her neighbors for her honesty and faithfulness to her husband. Nevertheless, the narrator immediately qualifies her honesty as "without merit," for it resulted from her "indolent character" rather than from any free will. Augusta, therefore, embodies one of the defining elements of Brazilianness, that of laziness. In addition, Augusta has several children, and thus her capacity for procreation follows one of the two or three possible patterns of female characteristics established in the narrative.

O cortiço typically relates excessive or uncontrollable sensuality to Brazilian women of color, who mostly belong to the lower classes. An exception to this is Dona Estela, Miranda's adulterous wife. She is a married white Brazilian woman, of Portuguese origin, and from an upper class, but with a strong sexual drive that she seeks to satisfy through adulterous relationships. Thus she obviously transgresses the limitations placed on women of her race and social status. She says at one point: "Desgraçadamente para nós, mulheres de sociedade, não podemos viver sem esposo, quando somos casadas; de forma que tenho de aturar o que me caiu em sorte, quer goste dele quer não goste!" (33; "Unfortunately for us society ladies, once we're married we have to put up with our husbands whether we like them or not!"; 19).

More than the adulterous relationships and her flirting behavior with her husband's employees, what is described as perversely transgressive is the violently erotic encounters between Estela and her own husband. These encounters take place after the couple had been all but separated from each other and combine hatred and lust, his shame and her scorn. The disparity of emotions involved in these sexual encounters lends them an element of the grotesque, since Estela reveals a dimension of herself normally hidden because socially unacceptable: the behavior of an experienced but passionate prostitute under the skin of a respectable, married bourgeois woman. The first two encounters are carried out because of Miranda's urgency to release his sexual desire, and from then on, Miranda and Estela alternate between hatred and moral repugnance toward each other during the day (6–7) and the most violent erotic desire at night. In a sense, Miranda ends up being his own rival, as if he were committing adultery with his own wife who, in turn, acts like a "whore," according to the dominant social norms. It is this intricacy of opposing sentiments that makes Estela a transgressor, and their sexual relationship repugnant even to today's readers.

The gallery of "abnormal" or "perverse" female behaviors in *O cortiço* includes a representation of lesbianism. The prostitute Leónie's passionate desire for Pombinha is satisfied

Chapter One

in a sequence of events that amounts to not much less than rape. It is lesbianism depicted from a masculinist perspective (Foster, *Sexual Textualities* 2), showing the innocent young virgin being forced to submit to the older, more powerful, and sexually experienced woman (cf. Mott 76–77), in a scene that might fulfill the fantasy of some male voyeur. In addition, lesbianism here serves another purpose, that of a rite of sexual initiation. The homosexual act, although violent, awakens Pombinha's sexuality, and soon after, she has her first menstrual period, which in turn makes her ready for marriage. If Azevedo initiates "a tradition that recognizes lesbian sexuality in Brazil and Latin America" (Foster, *Sexual Textualities* 2), it is a tradition that will have to be rewritten, for it shows the homosexual woman as violent and perverted and does not allow for the healthy expression of lesbian sexuality. As I discuss in Chapter 5, it will be necessary to examine literary texts by Brazilian female authors in order to find the authentic expression of lesbian desire or, in other words, to find homosexual female desire represented *not* from a masculinist perspective but, rather, from the perspective of the lesbian subject herself.

* * *

O cortiço, much like *Iracema,* displays a close link between Brazilians and the land (nature). Words such as *sensuality, instinct, hot,* and *exuberant,* may describe the landscape as they do some individuals, in particular, women of color. In Alencar's novel, the Indian woman, living within the exuberant American nature, acted *instinctively* and was capable of *ardent* love. In *O cortiço,* however, it is the *mulata* Rita Baiana who is compared to the Brazilian landscape, in a series of associations that evoke the heat, the colors, tastes, and smells emanating from nature. Seen by the Portuguese Jerônimo, Rita was the synthesis of all the elements of the Brazilian land that had left an unforgettable impression upon the European; she was:

> . . . ela era a luz ardente do meio-dia; ela era o calor vermelho das sestas da fazenda; era o aroma quente dos trevos e das baunilhas, que o atordoara nas matas brasileiras; era a palmeira virginal e esquiva que se não torce a nenhuma outra planta; era o veneno e era o açúcar gostoso; era o

> sapoti mais doce que o mel e era a castanha do caju, que abre feridas com o seu azeite de fogo; ela era a cobra verde e traiçoeira, a lagarta viscosa, a muriçoca doida, que esvoaçava havia muito tempo em torno do corpo dele, assanhando-lhe os desejos, . . . picando-lhe as artérias para lhe cuspir dentro do sangue uma centelha daquele amor setentrional. . . . (73 [2])

One could argue that the image of the *mulata* has come to represent the nation, but obviously this image is nothing more than that: an image or, in other words, an object for the enjoyment of the voyeur, be he foreign or native. Meanwhile, Brazilian black women—as well as Brazilian women in general—have been mostly reduced to the position of the Other, excluded from the dominant discourse. Of course, one should not be blind to the issue of women as oppressors of other women. This is certainly a problem in Brazilian society, and its most obvious example is the case of domestic servants and their relationship with the middle- and upper-class women they work for. The social oppression of women by other women results from forms of capitalist exploitation of the lower classes but is also a consequence of the slavery-patriarchal mentality that has shaped the dominant ideology in Brazil. As such, it is just another way Brazilian women of color are rendered passive objects by the dominant ideology.

Dom Casmurro and the Nineteenth-Century Domestic Woman

The novels of Machado de Assis are set mostly within the domestic space of the household, specifically those four novels commonly referred to as belonging to Machado's first phase, which follow more closely a Romantic narrative composition in the plot development and in the constitution of characters and their motives. These first four novels—*Ressurreição* [Resurrection] (1872), *A mão e a luva* [The hand and the glove] (1874), *Helena* (1876), and *Iaiá Garcia* (1878)—are centered on female protagonists, and the women in these novels seem to fit the Romantic ideal of femininity. As Ann Pescatello describes, they are "virtuous, beautiful, romantic" (18). Nevertheless, the careful reader will find that these early female

Chapter One

protagonists are more complex than the women characters of other Brazilian Romantic novels. In addition, each one of them serves to illustrate the social situation of nineteenth-century Brazilian women of the middle classes, and several critics have written exclusively on Machado's female characters.[7]

In the five novels that follow Machado's first phase, beginning with *Memórias póstumas de Brás Cubas* (*Epitaph of a Small Winner*, 1952; *The Posthumous Memoirs of Brás Cubas*, 1997), published in 1881, the narrative focus is on the male protagonists. Although women continue to be important as they relate to and help define the male characters, the female characters in this second phase play somewhat secondary roles in the novels, with the notable exception of Capitu, the famous heroine of *Dom Casmurro*. Here Machado again sets his story in the domestic realm, and makes of Capitu an excellent example of how Brazilian women of the middle—or intermediate, as John Gledson characterizes them (69)—classes lived in the second half of the nineteenth century. Capitu's struggles with love, the prospect of marriage, class distinctions, and life as a married woman, are illustrative of the kind of social expectations Brazilian women of that period had to face—and tried to fulfill. However, just as Capitu is a more complex character than some of her predecessors in Brazilian fiction, so is the author's perspective on women's social situation at the turn of the twentieth century. Indeed, not only does *Dom Casmurro* present a portrayal of Brazilian women's condition at that time, but it also problematizes that condition through the use of ambiguity and an unreliable narrator, thus inviting the reader to look at it in a critical way.

※ ※ ※

My title for this section about the "domestic woman" evokes the book by Nancy Armstrong on the emergence of the English-language novel. In fact, in *Desire and Domestic Fiction: A Political History of the Novel* (1987), Armstrong dedicates one chapter to the "domestic woman" that came to be shaped in England, and later in the United States, by the numerous "conduct books" published in those two countries during the eighteenth century. My concern here, unlike Armstrong's, has been with the literature produced in Brazil in the nineteenth century, particularly after the 1850s. However, some of Armstrong's findings are not totally alien to the situation of the nineteenth-century Brazilian "domestic woman," particularly in that the public discussion on women's education in England and in the United States will find parallels in similar discussions held later in Brazil. For example, Armstrong contends that the English-language conduct books

> . . . assumed that an education ideally made a woman desire to be what a prosperous man desires. . . . For such a man, her desirability hinged upon an education in frugal domestic practices. She was supposed to complement his role as an earner and producer with hers as a wise spender and tasteful consumer. Such an ideal relationship presupposed a woman whose desires were not of necessity attracted to material things. But because a woman's desire could in fact be manipulated by signs of wealth and position, she required an education. (59)

The "domestic woman," for whom these conduct books were written, represented women from a middle class, emergent in England in the eighteenth century and in Brazil a century later. As John Gledson asserts in his *The Deceptive Realism of Machado de Assis* (1984), *Dom Casmurro* deals with the ascension of the middle class and its interactions with the upper, landowning classes.

Up until 1808, when the Portuguese crown moved to Brazil in order to escape Napoleon's invasion of the Iberian Peninsula, Brazil was an extremely conservative patriarchal society. In the patriarchal family, the father (or a surrogate male figure) was the exclusive authority in charge of everything, including the household, the children, and the slaves. The woman held a very low status in the house, treated almost as one of the children, or even as inferior to the male children once they reached a certain age. According to many travelers' accounts, the women of the house were usually kept hidden from visitors. On the other hand, certainly no one looking from the outside would be able to see these women, since the interior of the house was protected by the *muxarabiê,* the traditional tall wood lattice of Arab influence.

Chapter One

The arrival of the Portuguese court brought a number of changes to the country, and particularly to the city of Rio de Janeiro, which underwent a series of structural changes and urban and cultural improvements. With the Portuguese, many foreigners also went to Brazil, among them women, introducing new habits and forms of behavior in the country. These changes in cultural practices were more noticeable in Rio de Janeiro after the 1840s, and later in other parts of Brazil. Nevertheless, with the upgrade in the political status of the country (from colony to Reino Unido de Portugal, Brasil e Algarve [United Kingdom of Portugal, Brazil and Algarve] in 1808, and to independent nation in 1822), the colonial woman turned démodé. The wife became then the one responsible for running the household, in charge of the children, domestic slaves, and other servants. She would also be called upon to receive and entertain the husband's guests, at times acting as a kind of unofficial public relations agent for him, helping the husband in business deals or in his political aspirations (Costa 119–20).

The importance of the woman's role within the family became an object of discussion in Brazilian intellectual and political circles, and this discussion eventually came to address the social function of women in regards to their contributions to the community and to the nation at large. The public debate about the women's role in Brazilian society is better understood if examined within the context, again, of the efforts to define national identity following Independence. While these efforts were heightened with the declaration of the Republic in 1889, by then a consensus already existed for women to be active participants in society, and supported their right to be so. Nevertheless, the consensus remained that women's realm of participation should be primarily within the limits of the family—or in the public arena, provided the needs of the family had received priority and had been properly taken care of.

Among the many improvements introduced by the Portuguese king after arriving in Rio de Janeiro were those made in the fields of culture and education, starting a trend that was followed by the two Brazilian emperors after Independence in 1822. In addition, the Enlightenment, even if arriving late in Brazil, reinforced the importance of education in general and disseminated among the public the idea of the importance of women's education. Thus the second half of the nineteenth century in Brazil witnessed a movement toward better education for girls, more comparable to that received by boys. At the same time, a woman's right to higher education was defended, and eventually the first woman to enroll in an institution of higher education in Brazil joined the School of Medicine in Rio de Janeiro in 1881. From the perspective of the dominant ideology, the issue of women's education was seen as part of a general understanding of a woman's role within the family and in society. The pervasive idea was that, responsible for the education and welfare of the children, an educated mother would be a better mother; and in preparing the country's (male) leaders of tomorrow, an educated woman would be better prepared to help shape the future of the nation. As an article published in 1897 in the women's journal *A Mensageira* [The female messenger] made clear, it was necessary for Brazil to realize that a major distinction existed between *criar* ("to raise") and *educar* ("to educate") a child (49), and the time had come for Brazilian women to do more than "just" raising a child.

This ideology survives into the twentieth century, as is attested by many publications, fiction and nonfiction. As an example, it may be sufficient to revisit here the preface to the first edition of the book *Perfil da mulher brasileira* [The Brazilian woman's profile], published in 1922 and reprinted in a second edition of 1938, authored by the medical doctor Antonio Austregésilo:

> ... como dirigente e guarda do lar, [a mulher] poderá sempre incutir no homem os princípios sólidos de um bem inestimável e essencial à nossa índole.
>
> A influência que a mulher exerce na formação, das nossas qualidades, e o muito que a Brasileira pode contribuir para a organização do caráter [nacional]. . . .
>
> As qualidades maternas influirão consideravelmente no bosquejo e na constituição do perfil moral dos homens, que delas precisam para construir solidamente as ações nacionais. (v–vi [3])

It should be noted that the Positivist ideology, predominant in Brazil throughout the nineteenth century and early part of the twentieth century, depicted women as morally superior beings

Chapter One

whose superiority ought to be preserved within the domestic space by the social institution of the family. In spite of her moral superiority, a woman was still legally inferior to the male figure, since the law determined that the husband was the head of the household. Legally, therefore, the expectations placed on a married woman were of submission, obedience, and faithfulness to the husband.

Interestingly, the law considered male adultery very differently from female adultery. During most of the nineteenth century, the *Ordenações Filipinas,* the Portuguese laws, according to which the husband would be legally protected if he killed his adulterous wife, ruled Brazilians. Even though these legal codes suffered a series of changes and amendments implemented by new codes in the late 1800s, it is well known that the practice went unpunished in Brazil for many decades of the next century. In fact, only in the 1960s and 1970s, did the unwritten law that had for so long protected the male murderer of an adulterous woman begin to suffer strong opposition.

* * *

Those familiar with Machado de Assis's novel *Dom Casmurro* know that the theme of adultery is at the very core of the novel. This is not to say that *Dom Casmurro* is about adultery. Since Helen Caldwell published her famous study *The Brazilian Othello of Machado de Assis* in 1960, in which she defends Capitu's innocence, several critics have pointed out that whether or not Capitu committed adultery is beside the point, since it is practically an insoluble enigma. Paul B. Dixon, in his book *Reversible Readings: Ambiguity in Four Modern Latin American Novels* (1985) asserts the impossibility of determining either Capitu's guilt or innocence, and states that, in fact, "the enigma of Capitu must remain unsolved" (29). In this way, what matters in Machado de Assis's *Dom Casmurro*—and what matters in all his novels—are not so much the facts, but rather, how they are narrated. The novel is about ambiguity itself, and it is this ambiguity that has come to be known as the writer's distinctive mark.[8] Nevertheless, many other critics have continued to insist on the issue of Capitu's alleged adultery, either to find her guilty or to defend her innocence.[9]

Female Body, Male Desire

The fact is that, still at the end of the twentieth century, Bentinho, or Bento Santiago, the protagonist/narrator of *Dom Casmurro*, was known in Brazilian culture as a "cuckold" (Bonassi 73), while the ambiguity involving Capitu's innocence or guilt conferred upon her the category of myth (cf. Mindlin 78). Capitu's eyes, described as "de cigana oblíqua e dissimulada" (38; "a bit like a gypsy's, oblique and sly"; 48), her famous "olhos de ressaca" (46), or "undertow eyes" (63), have become synonymous with mysteriousness and seduction, capable—we may conclude from the narrator's remembrances—of dragging one against one's will:[10]

> Traziam não sei que fluido misterioso e enérgico, uma força que arrastava para dentro, como a vaga que se retira da praia, nos dias de ressaca. Para não ser arrastado, agarrei-me às outras partes vizinhas . . . ; mas tão depressa buscava as pupilas, a onda que saía delas vinha crescendo, cava e escura, ameaçando envolver-me, puxar-me e tragar-me. (46 [4])

It is quite noticeable in this passage that, seen through Bentinho's emotions, Capitu appears as another version of the seductive Eve. In fact, if the reader pays attention to words such as *força, puxar, cava e escura,* and *ameaçando,* what emerges is really a sketch of the powerful Medusa with her dangerous, hypnotizing eyes or, as Sant'Anna has put it, the "castrating sphinx" (*Canibalismo* 77, 78–79). The fear of being swallowed up by this Medusa may be understood as describing the conflicting emotions of a romantic male adolescent in love. However, if we remember that the words are actually coming from an older narrator who writes his memoirs, and thus has a privileged authoritative position regarding his own past, it becomes apparent that what Bentinho, and later Bento Santiago, really feared was some kind of a mythical *vagina dentata*. Sant'Anna discusses the myth of the *vagina dentata* as a variation of the devouring sphinx, a recurring theme in Brazilian male-authored poetry of the Parnassianism, the poetic movement that was dominant in Brazil after the 1880s. The fear of the *vagina dentata* seems to originate in the trauma afflicting the male child of a "phallic mother" (Sant'Anna, *Canibalismo* 78).

Gledson discusses Dona Gloria, Bentinho's mother, as a kind of dominant/domineering mother. In fact, as a widow, she represents the patriarchal figure. She is the head of the household after her husband's death and, as such, she makes decisions concerning such items as the properties of the family, the slaves, and the household helpers, as well as Bentinho's future. Bentinho submits to his mother's desires, unable to stand up for what he truly wants, or even to express his wishes. The manner in which he reacts to Capitu, the portrayal he presents of her as someone who thinks, makes plans, and takes action, reflects his own passivity and submissiveness toward his mother.

In this regard, the reader should not ignore the adjective *enérgico* in the passage quoted above. The duality *activity* or *initiative* versus *passivity* is recurrent throughout the narrative and is used to compare and contrast Capitu and Bentinho. It would seem that the narrator Bento Santiago wants to characterize himself, from an early age, as somewhat passive, naive, and accepting of others' wishes, particularly the desires of women—first of all, his mother, and then, Capitu. Roberto Schwarz comments that Bento presents himself as a "venerador lacrimoso da mãe" ["weeping adorer of his mother"], as one of various strategies utilized by the narrator to obtain the reader's sympathy (Schwarz 10). By underscoring his adoration for his mother, whom he labels a "saint" (*Dom Casmurro,* trans. Gledson 236), the narrator finds himself a place within the Christian dogma of veneration for the Mother and, by extension, for women in general, much like Martim in *Iracema.* Thus Bento defends himself against any possible accusation of having done harm to his own wife, whom he would necessarily respect as a result of the Christian spirit in which he was raised (cf. Gledson 197–98).

Gledson proposes another way of understanding Bento's reaction to Capitu, an interpretation that complements what I have discussed above. According to the critic, "In order to marry Bento, Capitu has to manipulate and dominate him, a process which, reversing the traditional roles of man and wife, produces resentment and jealousy" (Gledson 8). The suggestion that Capitu in fact manipulates and dominates Bento springs from the narrative itself or, in other words, from Bento's own perspective. Nevertheless, what should be considered here is that Capitu seems intent on marrying Bentinho.

Marriage was at that time the only truly acceptable social end for a woman and the only form of social ascension available for women of the middle classes. Machado's novel portrays the dominant ideology at the time of Brazil's *Segundo Império* [Second Empire], the period following Don Pedro II's coronation in 1841; more specifically, it portrays Brazilian society in the late 1850s when most of the action in the novel takes place. Among the various social, legal, and political-economic codes that regulated social relations in Brazil then, was the social-religious code that concerned marriage and the social situation of women in the second half of the nineteenth century.

Capitu embodies this social-religious code, representing the social status of middle-class women at the time. Thus we see how the character inhabits primarily the domestic space, in her father's house, in Dona Gloria's, and in Bento's once they have married. We see also that Capitu receives the education typically available for Brazilian women then (*Dom Casmurro*, trans. Gledson 59), and we can understand her efforts to secure her marriage to Bentinho, since marriage was the only acceptable means a woman of Capitu's status had in order to ascend socially. As his wife, Capitu occupies herself with running the household efficiently and economically and with the care of their son. She also submits to Bentinho's whims, as we see, for example, when he insists that she should not show her bare arms at a ball, even when in his company (*Dom Casmurro*, trans. Gledson 183). In sum, she fulfills in many aspects the expectations of submission and obedience to the husband commonly placed on a married woman. However, as with some of Machado's other female characters, Capitu displays a strong and independent personality and, as was said earlier, often takes the initiative, rather than assuming a passive role. Here perhaps lies Capitu's flaw for, otherwise, she is practically the perfect domestic woman of late-nineteenth-century Brazil. Her independent thinking and initiative translate as signs of unfaithfulness for the jealous husband who then accuses her of adultery.

It is interesting that this split between tradition, on the one hand, and independence and initiative, on the other, that confronts Capitu in the late 1800s seems to follow Brazilian women throughout the next century. In actuality, it will become

Chapter One

a common topos in Brazilian women's literature, from Gilka Machado at the beginning of the twentieth century, to writers such as Helena Parente Cunha (1929) and Sonia Coutinho at the end of the millennium.

In *Dom Casmurro,* this split or duality of *tradition* versus *independence* is best illustrated at the end of the novel, when Capitu is faced with Bento's accusation and reacts with dignity, not as an accused woman (trans. Gledson 231). Taking the initiative again, she instead asks for "an immediate separation" (231), which would mean social ostracism. Within the limits society imposes on women, Capitu finds solace in religion and submits herself to her husband's desire: ("—Confiei a Deus todas as minhas amarguras, disse-me Capitu ao voltar da igreja; ouvi dentro de mim que a nossa separação é indispensável, e estou às suas ordens" (146; "'I confided all my bitterness to God,' said Capitu when she came back from church; 'I heard a voice inside me saying that our separation is unavoidable, and I am at your disposal'"; 233). Having shown throughout the narrative a preference for dissimulation, Bento sends Capitu to exile in Switzerland under some pretense, in order to "delude public opinion" (235).

As the memoirs of Bento Santiago, *Dom Casmurro* obeys the single perspective of the male narrator who seeks to write and to rewrite, reorganize the past, and to construct not only a portrait of Capitu but mainly of himself. Capitu's voice is never heard in the novel, except through the voice of Bentinho/Bento, and *her* story is never told. Only a hundred years later does it appear, as a palimpsest, in the 1999 novel by Ana Maria Machado (1942), *A audácia dessa mulher* [This woman's audacity].

In Ana Maria Machado's novel, the protagonist, Bia, an independent and self-sufficient woman living in Rio de Janeiro at the end of the twentieth century, is presented with a notebook that had belonged to a young housewife a hundred years earlier.[11] In it, the young woman wrote her diary among cooking recipes, grocery expenses, and home remedies. As Bia finds out, this woman is no one else but Capitu herself, and her secret diary tells her version of the events that led to her exile. The title of the book thus refers to Capitu's audacity, as well as to Bia's and to another female character's in the novel who, like

Capitu, has to face her partner's extreme jealousy. These *fin-de-siècle* women dared stand their ground and not submit to masculinist desire. The female voice—of Capitu, of the author, and of the characters who tell Capitu's and their own stories— is raised in opposition to the discourse of the male narrator of *Dom Casmurro*. Hence Ana Maria Machado aligns her work with those of other Brazilian women writers who counteract the masculinist ideology. This ideology had for a very long time enacted a kind of social-literary "ventriloquism"—to borrow an expression used by Sant'Anna (*Canibalismo* 39)—by which the body is female but the voice—and the desire—male.

Exerting its power to regulate the female body, the dominant ideology has created a number of cultural myths catering to a masculinist form of desire: the reification of the female child and adolescent; the childish woman as a synonym for "being feminine"; the invisibility of the middle-aged and elderly woman; the sexuality of the working-class woman and of the woman of color as being easily negotiable; and similar devices. Whether or not all these representations of the feminine originate in cultural manifestations prior to the advent of Romanticism in Brazil, they generally become part of our national discourse thanks to the artistic expressions of the Romantic and of the Realist-Naturalist periods, when culture becomes more accessible to the middle classes. Later, with the advent of the mass media, literature will find in the movies, radio, television, and in various forms of popular culture, most notably Brazilian popular music, vehicles for the widespread propagation of these myths.

In this regard, we should remember that these nineteenth-century novels discussed here have been adapted to the cinema and/or television, and that Almeida's *Memórias de um sargento de milícias* became a popular samba in the hands of Paulinho da Viola, a well-known Brazilian composer and singer.[12] Certainly, one factor has played an important role in the process by which these literary characters became widely accepted myths of cultural behavior, and that is what Foucault calls the "author function." The "author function" has a classificatory effect, as the author's name confers a particular status to the literary work in a given society (Foucault, "What Is an Author?" 107–08). In addition, the author's name may indicate,

Chapter One

or even dictate, a particular way of approaching the text. Thus, Alencar, for example, having achieved early in his lifetime great recognition among literary critics and the general public, was called the "Father of Brazilian Literature." His public authority, along with letters and other writings he produced before and around the time he published *Iracema,* certainly exerted an influence upon his readers.

The same could be said of Machado de Assis, the founder of the Brazilian Academy of Letters, who held the status of a literary authority, enjoyed great prestige among his peers and the reading audience, and is considered the greatest Brazilian writer of all times. During their lifetimes, Almeida and Azevedo perhaps did not hold quite the same level of prestige as did Alencar and Machado de Assis. This is quite understandable in the case of Almeida, who wrote *Memórias de um sargento de milícias* when he was only twenty-three years old and died prematurely in a shipwreck. Nevertheless, during his time Azevedo was called "the first national novelist" by some critics (Viveiros de Castro, in Mott 77). By the time he published *O cortiço,* Azevedo had already been a literary success, with the publication some years earlier of *O mulato* (1881; *Mulatto,* 1990; 1993). Furthermore, both he and Almeida had an influential instrument at hand: the newspapers, for which they both wrote satire and social commentary, and Azevedo, in addition, worked as a cartoonist.

In sum, the four nineteenth-century novelists discussed here constitute literary authorities whose influence extends into the culture and the entire nation's way of thinking, while some of their female characters represent myths of feminine behavior that have become part of the Brazilian imaginary. It is against the literary authority of Alencar, Almeida, Azevedo, Machado de Assis, and other names in a male-dominated canon that Brazilian women authors in the twentieth century have produced their works. These women have attempted to find an authentic expression for the social and psychological reality of Brazilian women, for their desire, their bodies, and their sexuality, and have often succeeded, although not without problems. In the chapter that follows, I will examine the expression of female desire and eroticism in the poetry of Gilka Machado, who is considered a pioneer in the tradition of Brazilian women's literature, specifically in female erotic discourse. I will then discuss how some late-twentieth-century Brazilian women writers have continued this tradition by seeking to give expression to female eroticism, and the problems of literary representation that have emerged.

Chapter Two

Brazilian Women Writers
The Search for an Erotic Discourse

The Transgressive Eroticism of Gilka Machado's Poetry

As I discussed in the previous chapter, canonical Brazilian literature by male authors often represents the female body and sexuality as subservient to male desire, and has shaped myths of femininity that originate in, and help maintain, the dominant masculinist ideology. However, these stereotypical representations of the female body are not exclusive to the pages of Brazilian literature. Rather, they have left a deep mark within the larger frame of Brazil's national culture and have impacted the social relations between men and women, between blacks and whites, and between elements from different social groups and social classes. Within this context, the dominant ideological voice has belonged to the white, heterosexual man of the upper classes who, as I mentioned before, acts "like a ventriloquist: the body belongs to the Other, but the voice is his" (Sant'Anna, *Canibalismo* 10).

Only after the last quarter of the nineteenth century, with some isolated exceptions in the periods before, do Brazilian women have a visible presence in society as producers of literature who seek public recognition. At the beginning of the twentieth century, two female authors had already achieved significant critical recognition in Brazil: the poet Francisca Júlia (1871–1920), and Júlia Lopes de Almeida (1862–1934), a journalist, fiction writer, and author of children's books and of didactic literature aimed at a feminine audience. During their lifetimes both writers were already considered part of the literary canon and, later, they were seen as precursors of women's literature in Brazil. Francisca Júlia was in fact among the most significant poets of the Parnassian School in Brazil. Her poetry showed a concern with the poetic craft, with art for art's sake, with an ideal of beauty to be created by the poet-artificer that seemed to preclude the poet's subjectivity, not to mention her desire. Lopes de Almeida, in turn, wrote extensively about women's issues and, in some of her fiction, criticized with light humor gender relations in Brazilian society then. Nevertheless, she generally fit within the dominant ideological patterns that affected her, as a woman, and as a female author.

Francisca Júlia and Lopes de Almeida were not by any means the only women who took up the pen in a rather conservative society, but for many decades, they were among a very small female group "given entrance" to the literary canon. I propose that the reason they were accepted in the canon is that their literature was deemed "safe" or even "masculine" enough by those who set the literary and ideological standards of the time. Something similar happened in the 1930s with Rachel de Queiroz, whose literature was characterized as "virile" by one critic (Silveira 89). That is not to say that Queiroz and other Brazilian women writers in the first part of the twentieth century did not raise issues relating to female sexuality and desire, or did not care to give representation to the female body. Indeed Queiroz herself was brave enough to write about issues such as sex outside the marriage and abortion in her 1939 novel *As três Marias* (*The Three Marias,* 1963).

However, if these women writers wrote about the female body and desire in their works, these issues were clad in layers of metaphorical language, actual clothes, and proper behavior. A female author who attempted to speak frankly of a woman's desire and to depict her sexuality would run against social censorship, but was most likely stopped by self-censorship and the fear of being labeled inappropriate, pornographic, or obscene. Eroticism, and particularly female eroticism, can be rather disturbing when brought into the public space of literature or the arts, because of its intrinsically private quality. As Lynn Hunt states in *Eroticism and the Body Politic* (1991), eroticism is "the intrusion into the public sphere of something that was at base private" (5). Blurring this distinction, the woman writer who attempts to bring such a private affair into the public arena becomes herself identified with the public. In other words, *she*

Chapter Two

becomes the public woman, the prostitute: "The prostitute was *the* public woman, and any woman pretending to act in public . . . risked being identified as a prostitute" (Hunt 10).

Nevertheless, at the beginning of the 1900s, one Brazilian female poet was daring enough to take this risk, following her urge to speak of her self, of a woman's body, and of her desire. Gilka Machado caused a very strong reaction among the literary public and critics with the publication in 1915 of her first book, *Cristais partidos*, followed by *Estados de alma* [States of the soul] two years later. Machado's subversion lay in her claims of women's subordination in society and, mainly, in her erotic poems. These were cause for scandal, fed in part by the sensationalist treatment the author received in the media at the time. This early negative encounter with the literary establishment had a great impact upon the way that Machado was perceived in Brazil vis-à-vis the poetic canon. For several decades since the publication of these two early volumes, Machado was often ignored in literary histories and manuals, or simply mentioned in passing without any in-depth assessment of her work. Many times her name appeared alongside her more famous contemporary Cecília Meireles (1901–64), the works of both seen as examples of "feminine poetry." Machado's poetry, however, seems to be more in opposition to that of Meireles. The poetic voice in Meireles's poems frequently masquerades under the masculine gender or seeks a neutrality that denies gender as a mark in the literary discourse. In Machado's poems, on the contrary, the female subject explicitly sings of her woman's body and sexuality, either in a celebratory way or with regret for being a female in a patriarchal world.

In this regard, Machado was rather innovative in her discourse. In fact, many feminist critics credit her with inaugurating a female erotic discourse in Brazilian literature, and thus set her work in opposition to the repression of the female body and desire that was common in Brazilian women's poetry of the period (cf. Paixão, "À sombra de eros" 115). Only in the 1930s do women writers in Brazil begin to let their female protagonists speak without denying their femaleness while, at the same time, questioning the dominant gender constructions. This change is noticed first in the works of Brazilian women fiction writers, as for example, in novels by Rachel de Queiroz, Lúcia Miguel Pereira (1901–59), Telles, and others. In her

The Search for an Erotic Discourse

expression of female sexuality and desire through the voice of a female subject, Machado remains alone and isolated within the national literary canon for many decades. Following the slowly growing influence of feminist literary studies in Brazil after the late 1970s, Machado's poetry becomes the focus of a renewed critical interest. Like her, however, other women poets have only very recently been the subjects of critical study, as for example, Narcisa Amália (1852–1924), whose life and poetry Christina Ramalho discusses in *Um espelho para Narcisa: Reflexos de uma voz romântica* (1999), while others, like Colombina (1882–1963) and Adalgisa Néri (1905–80), still await critical recognition.

Before the late 1970s and the 1980s, when critics such as Fernando Py (1978), Nádia Gotlib (1982), and Joyce Carlson-Leavitt (1989) began to reexamine Gilka Machado's work, the poet's critical recognition was quite uneven. The often-brief mention of her name in literary histories, manuals, or anthologies represented an example of "the 'roll call' courtesy" (Berkin 44) that, for a long time and in many different cultures, placed "exceptional" women writers at the end of a long line of male names. These women had been found to somehow fit within some preestablished (masculine) parameters, and their inclusion would reiterate the idea that the only acceptable critical parameters were those already in place. Different critics read Machado under different labels: as a Symbolist poet, as a Neo-Parnassianist, as a Pre-Modernist, or as an example of the "*Nova Poesia*," a new kind of poetry that critic João Ribeiro understood was being produced in Brazil then.[1] Indeed, Machado's poetry is characteristic of a period of transition in Brazilian letters and displays influences both of Symbolism and Parnassianism. At the same time, the poet also begins to make use of some poetic elements that will be proposed by the Modernist poetry of the 1922 Generation; specifically, varied metrics, free verse, the use of colloquial language, and the representation of aspects of everyday life.

However, the importance of Gilka Machado's poetry for this study lies in the fact that she initiates a female erotic discourse in Brazil and, by doing so, transgresses all social expectations placed upon women then. Her first two volumes of poetry were perceived as scandalous, while the poet was regarded as extremely audacious, but at the same time naive, for thinking

Chapter Two

that she could grant her poetic voice the same kind of agency that had always been a male prerogative. In these two early volumes, *Cristais partidos* and *Estados de alma,* we find the most powerful expression of female sensuality and eroticism:

> Sensual
>
> Quando, longe de ti, solitária, medito
> neste afeto pagão que envergonhada oculto,
> vem-me às narinas, logo, o perfume esquisito
> que o teu corpo desprende e há no teu próprio vulto.
>
> A febril confissão deste afeto infinito
> há muito que, medrosa, em meus lábios sepulto,
> pois teu lascivo olhar em mim pregado, fito,
> à minha castidade é como que um insulto.
>
> Se acaso te achas longe, a colossal barreira
> dos protestos que, outrora, eu fizera a mim mesma
> de orgulhosa virtude, erige-se altaneira.
>
> Mas, se estás ao meu lado, a barreira desaba,
> e sinto da volúpia a escosa e fria lesma
> minha carne poluir com repugnante baba . . .
> (*Cristais partidos* [5])

Machado constructs here, as in several other poems, an "eroticism of memory." The object of desire is absent, but it is recalled through memories, and its evocation is sufficient for the sexual arousal of the female poetic voice. The poet also plays with the dialectics of *chastity and sin, purity and guilt,* as the female "I" depicts herself in the acceptable position of the passive woman, fearful, hesitant, or in other words, submissive to the other's desire.

Reading the sonnet as a "fervent confession," we see the interference of an old form of social control over human sexuality, that of religion, in this case, Catholicism. Introduced by the Portuguese in Brazil, the Catholic Church left a deep mark upon Brazilian culture in matters related to human sexuality, marriage, and procreation, from the time of the first visits of the Holy Inquisition at the end of the sixteenth century. However, confession is also the transformation of desire into discourse and, as such, constitutes a mechanism for replaying and increasing pleasure (Foucault, *History of Sexuality. An Introduction* 21, 22). Thus, in "Sensual," the female subject also portrays herself as the sensual woman, who lets her guard down to live the satisfaction of her own desire. The ambiguity present in the play of chastity versus guilt carries over into other levels of ambiguity. First, desire (hers? the Other's?) is both an abstract entity and a very concrete experience, represented in an image evocative of male sperm ("sinto da volúpia a escosa e fria lesma" ["I feel the thick and cold slug *of voluptuousness itself*"]; my emphasis).[2] Second, the reaction of the poetic voice is one of fascination and repugnance, both feelings represented in the image of a slug.

Considering the strong imagery of Machado's poems, it is not difficult to understand the reaction her poetry caused. Even today, some might find it embarrassing to discuss such vivid images of human sexuality in a classroom. Such audacity continues in Machado's second volume of poetry, in poems such as "Volúpia" [Voluptuousness], wherein the strong imagery is enhanced by a sensually rhythmic metric:

> Volúpia
>
> Tenho-te, do meu sangue alongada nos veios;
> à tua sensação me alheio a todo o ambiente;
> os meus versos estão completamente cheios
> do teu veneno forte, invencível e fluente.
>
> Por te trazer em mim, adquiri-os, tomei-os,
> o teu modo sutil, o teu gesto indolente.
> Por te trazer em mim moldei-me aos teus coleios,
> minha íntima, nervosa e rúbida serpente.
>
> Teu veneno letal torna-me os olhos baços,
> e a alma pura que trago e que te repudia,
> inutilmente anseia esquivar-se aos teus laços.
>
> Teu veneno letal torna-me o corpo langue,
> numa circulação longa, lenta, macia,
> a subir e a descer, no curso do meu sangue.
> (*Estados de alma* [6])

Again we find an object of desire that is not clearly marked but that could, rather, be understood as "volúpia" itself. In this case, the poem could be read as another expression of autoeroticism. However, the poet makes use of biblical images, specifically the serpent and its poison ("veneno"), but inverting the scene of the original seduction: while the serpent is the seducer, the female I, carrying her "alma pura," tries to repudiate the Other and is finally seduced. The "serpent" becomes, in turn, a phallic symbol ("minha íntima, nervosa e rúbida serpente" ["my intimate, nervous and ruby serpent"]) whose movements ("coleios") reproduce the sexual act. Most notable in this poem as in the one below, is the sensuality the poet is able to convey through the very rhythm of her verses:

> Invocação ao sono
>
> Sono! da tua taça brônzea e fria
> dá que eu possa esgotar o éter, a anestesia . . .
> Eis-me: corpo e alma—inteira,
> para essa tua orgia.
> Busco esquecer a minha hipocondria
> na tua bebedeira.
> Quero sentir o teu delíquio brando
> apoderar-se do meu ser
> e cochilando,
> bamboleando,
> ir, lentamente, escorregando,
> pelo infinito do prazer.
> . . . .
> Vem! — já de mim se apossa um sensual arrepio,
> todo meu ser se fica em total abandono . . .
> Dá-me o teu beijo frio,
> Sono!
> Deixa-me espreguiçar o corpo esguio
> sobre o teu corpo que é, como um frouxel, macio.
> . . . .
> Eis-me, lânguida e nua,
> para a volúpia tua.
> . . . .
> Faze a tua carícia,
> como um óleo, passar pela minha epiderme;
> essa tua carícia, humectante e emoliente,
> que no corpo me põe coleios de serpente
> e indolências de verme.
>   (Fragments; *Cristais partidos* [7])

The Search for an Erotic Discourse

Machado's poetry allows the female subject to express her desire for an Other whose body is made present through the sensations the poetic voice recalls and describes. In the three poems quoted above, the object of desire is not gendered: it could be a male lover, it also could be another woman, or desire could be embodied in an abstract category. In "Invocação ao sono," for example, the female subject addresses herself to "Sleep" in a poem that depicts a scene of autoeroticism. Thus in Machado's poetry, female desire is experienced outside of the binary *male* versus *female*. In other words, female desire is autonomous, not submissive to male desire, and the erotic experience may take place between the female subject and her environment.

Indeed, eroticism in Machado not only expresses the satisfaction of sexual desire, but also is a way of *being in the world*. The poet gives expression to the female subject's aspiration for unity—with the Other, with nature, and with the Cosmos. In fact, this desire for unity, particularly with the Cosmos, reflects a desire for spiritual elevation and for perfection, and is a common element in poetry of the period. As a poetic motif, it may be found in poems by the Nicaraguan Ruben Darío (1867–1916), the Portuguese Fernando Pessoa (1888–1935), and the Brazilian Augusto dos Anjos (1884–1914). In Machado, however, it constitutes another dimension of eroticism made very carnal and explicit. For some critics, Machado's eroticism is an attempt to reconcile the flesh and the spirit (Paixão, "A fala-a-menos" 140). This attempt can be comprehended in the context of a socially imposed conflict between female sensuality and guilt, as Nelly Novaes Coelho has proposed ("Eros e Tanatos" 55–56). It is best understood, however, in light of Georges Bataille's theoretical work. For Bataille, eroticism responds to human beings' nostalgia of a primal continuity and their need to connect. Thus eroticism is necessarily transgressive and exuberant (Bataille 11); it *trans*-gresses, *ex*-ceeds: "It is a state of communication revealing a quest for a possible continuance of being beyond the confines of the self" (17).

Machado's erotic poetry creates the possibility of a space in opposition to the social space that renders women submissive to male desire. While Machado spoke up against the social repression of women in poems such as the anthological "Ser mulher . . . ," from *Cristais partidos,* her sense of disconnection, isolation, and marginality finds full resolution in the poetic satisfaction of female eroticism. In this regard, the five senses play an important role in her poems, as they give expression to the sensuality and desire of the poetic voice. As I stated above, her desire is channeled toward a nongendered object, or it may be expressed as autoeroticism. Therefore, Machado's poetry achieves another level of transgression; for in her depiction of female sexuality, she fulfills the challenge proposed some sixty years later by feminist thinkers like Hélène Cixous (1975) and Luce Irigaray (1977). Says Cixous: "you can't talk about *a* female sexuality, uniform, homogeneous, classifiable into codes—any more than you can talk about one unconscious resembling another. Women's imaginary is inexhaustible, like music, painting, writing" ("The Laugh of the Medusa" 280). A woman's sexuality is "cosmic" (Cixous, "Medusa" 293), fluid, not fixed or centered. She "*has sex organs more or less everywhere*" (Irigaray 28; emphasis in original), and her pleasure and her eroticism flourish everywhere. This female sexual fluidity is present in much of Machado's poetry and is emphasized in her playing with the five senses, particularly the senses of touch and vision. Thus rugs, suede gloves, a peach, and her own hair take the female subject to erotic desire and to sexual ecstasy.

Likewise, the sense of vision is central in "Impressões do gesto" [Impressions from the motion], from *Mulher nua* [Naked woman] (1922), a poem Gilka Machado dedicated to a "bailadeira" ("female dancer"):

> Danças . . . teus gestos são carícias mansas,
> a tua dança é um tateio vago,
> é o próprio tato dedilhando
> as melodias do afago . . .
>
> Danças, e fico, a quando e quando,
> presa de gozo singular;
> e sonho que me estás acariciando,
> e sinto em todo o corpo o teu gesto passar.
>
> (Fragment [8])

The Search for an Erotic Discourse

Here the poetic voice takes the place of the *voyeur*, and this visual experience awakens other senses, particularly the sense of touch, and leads to an erotic experience. Dedicated to another woman, the poem conveys a homosexual desire made explicit in the second stanza above (stanza 8 of the poem).

As Irigaray maintained in her book *Ce sexe qui n'en est pas un* (1977; *This Sex Which Is Not One,* 1985), lesbian desire opens up yet another space for the affirmation and celebration of women and femaleness, while breaking away from sexual binaries. In Adrienne Rich's words, "lesbian existence" allows for "the rejection of a compulsory way of life" (157), the rejection of compulsory heterosexuality that does not mean necessarily the condemnation of all forms of heterosexual relationships. As proposed by Rich and, more recently, by Teresa De Lauretis (1994), lesbian desire allows for a kind of relationship wherein an ideal reciprocity and identification between two individuals becomes possible, and "binary oppositions become nonpertinent" (Suleiman 125).

"Impressões do gesto" emphasizes the identification between the two women, the poetic subject and the dancer, which is made clear in the last part of the poem, in stanzas 11–13:

> Danças, os membros novamente agitas,
> todo teu ser parece-me tomado
> por convulsões de dores infinitas . . .
> e desse trágico *crescendo*
> de gestos que enchem o silêncio de ais,
> vais
> *smorzando,* descendo,
> como que por encanto,
> presa de um místico quebranto . . .
> danças e cuido estar em ti me vendo.
>
> Os teus meneios
> são
> cheios
> dos meus anseios;
> a tua dança é a exteriorização
> de tudo quanto sinto:
> minha imaginação
> e meu instinto
> movem-se nela alternadamente;

Chapter Two

> minha volúpia, vejo-a torça, no ar,
> quando teu corpo lânguido, indolente,
> sensibiliza a quietação do ambiente,
> ora a crescer, ora a minguar
> numa flexuosidade de serpente
> . . . .
> . . . nos teus membros leves, quase etéreos,
> eu contemplo os meus gestos interiores,
> meus prazeres, meus tédios, minhas dores!
>
> . . . .
> A tua dança para mim é infinda,
> vejo-me nela, tenho-a dentro em mim,
> constantemente assim! [9]

In the last stanza (stanza 14), the poetic subject reaffirms the identification between the dancer and the poet, announcing their union, their embodiment as one, in verses that recall a marriage ceremony:

> No mais alto prazer, no mais fundo pezar,
> ativa esteja, esteja embora langue,
> tenho-te na loucura do meu sangue
> para o Bem, para o Mal, a bailar, a bailar! . . . [10]

Dancing stands here as a metaphor for the act of writing, as the entire poem may be read as a metapoetic representation of Machado's work, the recurrent images she employs, the rhythm of her verses, the effect she seeks to achieve, and the subject she commonly depicts: a woman's body and desire. Again Machado portrays female desire as autonomous of the masculine figure. The male body is not the object of desire and is totally excluded from the poetic space. This exclusion posits Machado's poetry as a transgressive discourse within a social context centered on male power, as was the case in Brazilian society during the first part of the twentieth century.

Eroticism, Pornography, and the Woman Writer in Brazil

Gilka Machado paid a high price for transgressing the social and literary norms of her time, as the audacity of her poems

The Search for an Erotic Discourse

tarnished her own reputation. She was often labeled "immoral," was made fun of, and, with her supporters, spent much time trying to show that there was a wide difference between the real-life Machado and the poetic voice who spoke so openly of female desire in her poems. Machado's transgression consisted of the invasion of a space from which women had been excluded and that, still today, does not quite belong to them: the erotic space, in which sexuality and desire are made explicit, not hidden and not disguised (Castello Branco 101). For many decades, the aggressive negative reception to Machado's erotic poetry obscured the value of her work and placed her in a marginal position within the literary canon. While it is true that Machado experienced some kind of recognition, the public attacks she suffered made her opt for a form of self-exile, choosing to lead a very private life away from the public eye. Thus her case serves to illustrate the censoring power of the dominant ideology upon female discourse. If before Machado no other Brazilian woman writer had challenged the established rules in society and literature, in such a daring manner, she is also the precursor of a female eroticism that cannot again be found in Brazilian letters until the 1970s and 1980s.

The reception of Machado's poetry, discussed by Gotlib and other critics, is an expression of the dominant ideological discourse attempting to silence the individual, while working at the same time as a potential warning for other women writers. The dominant ideology "speaks" through social institutions such as religion, marriage, institutionalized medical literature, and the literary and artistic canon. Its goal is to control human sexuality, and specifically the female body, and one of the mechanisms it employs is the use of labels such as "pornographic" and "perverse." Thus censorship is played out not only against one particular writer—in this case, Gilka Machado—but also against a whole group, leading often to self-censorship.

Self-censorship, the fear of being marked with the scarlet P of pornographic, can silence the expression of female eroticism. Behind this fear lies the dominant cultural perception of what is acceptable. First, the perception is that pornography and eroticism can be easily differentiated from each other and that the latter is acceptable while the former is not. In reality, the line between eroticism and pornography can be rather thin, and the distinction between the two categories depends a great deal on the audience or on the reader's personal history and perceptions. For this reason, critics such as Jesus Antônio Durigan (1985) in Brazil and Linda Williams (1989) in the United States stress the need to historicize the production and the reception of eroticism/pornography, since it is a representation contingent upon the period, values, social groups, particularities of the writer—in sum, upon the specific characteristics of the culture that produced it.

Maurice Charney in his *Sexual Fictions* (1981) surveys different definitions of "pornography" and "eroticism," opening with a definition offered by French writer Alain Robbe-Grillet (1922) who claims that "Pornography is the eroticism of others" (qtd. in Charney 1). This idea is, incidentally, echoed by Brazilian cinema director and critic Jean Claude Bernardet, in an essay entitled "Pornografia, o sexo dos outros" [Pornography, the sex of others] (1979). In turn, Charney confronts numerous and often disparate definitions of the terms and concludes: "'pornographic,' 'obscene,' 'erotic' and 'sexual' can be seen as synonyms depending upon the value judgment and class orientation of individual users" (2). Therefore Charney chooses to employ the general term of "sexual fiction" to describe narratives that depict human sexuality and eroticism or that otherwise sexualize reality.

Nevertheless, a distinction can be useful in understanding the position of the female writer vis-à-vis her society and the literary canon (which includes expressions of male-authored "sexual" literature). In this regard, two main considerations should be made. One concerns the primacy of the aesthetic experience in the erotic discourse. Gabriela Mora (1991) has pointed out the relationship between eroticism and the poetic word (132), a connection also stressed by Cunha (1999) in an article that discusses Brazilian women's erotic poetry. On the other hand, for Mora, pornography relies on crude and even demeaning representations of the body. She also recalls the frequent presence of violence in pornography and the relationship that exists between the pornographic work and the tendency within mass culture to commercialize the human body (cf. Mora 130).

The Search for an Erotic Discourse

For Brazilian sociologist Carlos Roberto Winckler (1983), pornography is centered upon the phallus and its domination over the Other:

> O Falo é símbolo do poder capitalista patriarcal, insaciável em seu desejo de expansão e domínio sobre seres humanos, aos quais atribui características na fantasia pornográfica, reflexo de relações efetivas da realidade social, vistas apenas sob o prisma da sexualidade e da excitação: continuidade do domínio do homem sobre a mulher . . . , reiteração do racismo . . . , permanência de relações sociais desiguais. . . . (81 [11])

In his discussion of pornography, which he categorizes as either "branda" ("soft") or "forte" ("hard core"), Winckler allows for an understanding of the phallus as a symbol for the white, heterosexual, masculine domination of the Other—women, homosexuals, blacks, and members of the lower classes (73–76, 81). Thus, pornography works on a dialectics of domination versus submission and, as Rosalind Coward (1985) has asserted, "constantly [sustains] male power and privilege and female subordination" (29). Other cultural critics have emphasized that pornography represents a masculinist desire for mastery over the female Other, rendering through violence a cultural male fear of the female body. Susan Griffin (1981) has called this the "pornographic imagination," which she places within a Western Christian tradition.

I generally concur with Mora in her association of violence and domination of the Other and pornography. However, violence can take different forms besides the explicit display of physical brutality. It may be present as a subtext within the sexual relationship between two individuals, and may take the form of implicit economic, political, or social coercion. For this reason, I find Winckler's and Coward's critical constructions of pornography more helpful because they stress the domination of the Other as the core element of pornography. Eroticism, in turn, celebrates the body and works on a notion of consensuality, in addition to showing the aesthetic concern as a distinctive element. This notion of eroticism, on the one hand, and, on the other, the notion of an existing link among pornography, violence, and domination of the Other are generally recognized in Brazil and in other Western cultures. Nonetheless, the problem of defining eroticism and pornography as exclusive categories does not stop here.

Considering the male-authored canonical texts examined in Chapter 1, or Amado's famous novel *Gabriela* and its cinematic version, not one reader would say that those texts are pornographic, and yet they all portray examples of sexual relationships that function as vehicles for the domination of the female Other. Therefore I prefer to use the term *phallocentric* or *masculinist* eroticism, for it better characterizes the erotic exchanges represented in these texts, exchanges that objectify women, limiting them within specific social roles, and reducing them to cultural myths that have become part of the Brazilian imaginary. In other words, these texts privilege masculinist desire, and the typical reader—male or female—accepts such privileging as the "norm."

A related matter of cultural perception has to do with what is and is not acceptable for a woman in a society such as that of Brazil. At the end of the twentieth century, critics and public alike still react negatively toward erotic expression in works by women writers, not with the same kind of aggression suffered by Gilka Machado, but rather through silence. Colasanti, for example, has commented on the general silence on the part of critics toward her and other Brazilian women's erotic poetry, while the "virile" eroticism of male poets is ostensibly and widely well received.[3]

Poet and fiction writer Hilda Hilst (1930) has experienced similar reactions to her work. In fact, her situation within the literary canon at the end of the twentieth century was somewhat like that of Gilka Machado's in the early 1900s. Hilst has been labeled a "difficult" author, is still read very little in Brazil, and has also been generally perceived as a "peculiar" writer and a somewhat "odd" person. Her latest fictional production—*O caderno rosa de Lori Lamby* [Lori Lamby's Pink Notebook] (1989), *Contos d'escárnio: Textos grotescos* [Stories of derision: grotesque texts] (1990), and *Cartas de um sedutor* [Letters from a seducer] (1991)—has been considered pornographic. Indeed the author makes use of pornography and, by doing so, takes on the position of transgressor in national letters and culture. While some Brazilian critics have recognized the high level of aesthetic and formal realization in her work, they have yet to assess Hilst's pornography as a strategy to problematize gender roles in the country. Interestingly, this assessment has been made in the United States (Foster, *Sexual Textualities*) and in France, where critics have been positive in their evaluation of Hilst's poetry and narrative, specifically of her "pornographic" fiction. For example, after the prestigious French press Gallimard published a translation of her *Contos d'escárnio,* critics there stated that Hilst "had raised pornography to the level of art" (qtd. in Mayrink 139).

Hilst represents the case of a woman writer who has appropriated a type of writing traditionally seen as the prerogative of a male author. In addition, male-authored pornography has only been widely accepted outside of the literary ghetto of "popular fiction" in the late part of the twentieth century. As examples, one could think of the short stories by Dalton Trevisan (1925) and the 1999 novel by João Ubaldo Ribeiro (1941), *A casa dos Budas ditosos* [The house of the fortunate Buddhas]. While in the present day Hilst may still be considered transgressive because of her daring use of eroticism/pornography, the expression of female eroticism by contemporary Brazilian women writers is not altogether uncommon.

As I mentioned here previously, as early as the 1930s other Brazilian female authors, such as Rachel de Queiroz and Pagu, addressed issues relating to the female body in their literature. Likewise, beginning in the 1940s, Lispector and Telles have treated themes relating to female sexuality, such as adultery, masturbation, a young woman's first menstruation, and lesbian desire. These themes are portrayed as part of the authors' representation of female characters and their search for an identity and self-realization. Eroticism thus plays a part in a larger process of self-development and self-affirmation. In addition, in early works such as *Perto do coração selvagem* (1944; *Near to the Wild Heart,* 1991) by Lispector and *Ciranda de pedra* (1954; *The Marble Dance,* 1982) by Telles, these issues are either veiled by a highly abstract and symbolic language (Lispector) or framed in such a way that they do not appear to challenge the dominant ideology (Telles).

Only after the late 1960s does eroticism appear more frequently in literature by Brazilian female authors. By then, women had gained a wider access to and more participation in the socio-political sphere, and a larger number of women writers had begun to achieve public recognition. Brazilian women poets and fiction writers began to explore female sexuality as an intrinsic part of their characters' lives, identity, and self-realization, and eroticism as "a source of power, change and creativity," to quote Audre Lorde, the Afro-American poet (285). In her 1978 essay "Uses of the Erotic," Lorde emphasizes the link among eroticism, self-knowledge, and power, characterizing the erotic experience as a space for female self-empowerment. Recognizing the importance of this link, late-twentieth-century Brazilian women writers recurrently address issues relating to the female body, desire, and sexuality: many works of fiction portray female eroticism as a significant part of their characters' life experience, while it is often the main focus of poetry.

In the 1970s, Brazil saw the publication of novels like Piñon's *A casa da paixão* [The house of passion] (1972), and anthologies of women's poetry such as *Mulheres da vida* [Public women] (1978), edited by Leila Míccolis (1947). Míccolis is one among four Brazilian women to appear in an English-language anthology of erotic writings by Latin American women, *Pleasure in the Word* (1994). She was a member of the "Geração Mimeógrafo" (Mimeograph Generation), a "Pós-Vanguarda" [Post-Avant-Garde] poetic movement that during that time produced and sold their poetry through alternative channels. In his book *Música popular e moderna poesia brasileira* [Popular music and modern Brazilian poetry] (1978), Sant'Anna recognizes a new tonality in Brazilian women's poetry as a distinctive feature of the "Pós-Vanguarda" movements of the 1970s. He states: "A mulher assume uma linguagem realista, descobre seu corpo, descreve as relações eróticas num tom totalmente avesso ao de Cecília Meireles e outras autoras típicas da 'lírica feminina'" (165) ["Women assume a realist language, discover their body, describe erotic relationships in a tone completely opposite to that found in the poetry of Cecília Meireles or of other typical authors of 'feminine poetry'"].

Mulheres da vida includes poems by Norma Bengell, Gloria Perez, Míccolis herself, and others. Beginning with the title,

The Search for an Erotic Discourse

the collection displays an overall attitude of rebelliousness by the participating female poets as representatives of a new woman— braver, more daring, and more in touch with reality. Says Míccolis in her introduction to the volume: "Ontem talvez temêssemos as conotações eróticas e ofensivas da expressão; ontem talvez pensássemos duas vezes antes de ousar viver e escrever. Hoje nós e nossas poesias nos jogamos nos bares, calçadas, ônibus, boates, prisões, trabalhos, manicômios, casas, bordéis" (5) ["Yesterday we might fear the erotic and offensive connotations of our expression. Today we and our poetry are out in bars, on sidewalks, in buses, clubs, prisons, workplaces, mental clinics, homes, brothels"].

Bengell, in a brief introduction to her own poetry, addresses other characteristics of many of the works in the anthology—a solidarity among women and a concern for the liberation of women in art as well as in real life: "Os meus trabalhos foram feitos em favor das mulheres violentadas, presas dentro de prisões ou dentro de casa. . . . Esta minha participação fica como continuação na luta pela emancipação da mulher na arte" (in Míccolis, *Mulheres da vida* 61) ["My poems were written for raped women, prisoners in prisons or in homes. . . . My participation in this anthology is a continuation in the struggle for the emancipation of women in art"]. This new woman has left the protected space of the home to be immersed in the public space, where she is as active and participative as she is in touch with herself, her body, her desire. Therefore, the reality sung by these women poets is complex and multidimensional: female hetero- and homoeroticism, the family, mother-daughter relationships, unsatisfying marriages, and the political moment.

In these poems, the female poetic voice accepts marginality as a way of challenging or even rejecting the dominant masculinist ideology, similarly to what is seen in some of Coutinho's short stories that I discuss in Chapter 4. For example, in this fragment from the poem "Na vida" [In life], Míccolis defends her right to define herself as she pleases:

> Não sou comportada.
> Puta e lésbica
> e o que mais me der na telha,
> pareço um pássaro maluco
> procurando espantalhos e alçapões,

Chapter Two

> querendo me expandir como sono
> em pálpebras cansadas,
> explodir como violência
> no silêncio dos acomodados.
> Puta e lésbica
> e o que mais me der na telha
> sou a seqüência
> do que o primeiro gesto desencadeia.
> (Mulheres da vida 44 [12])

The Portuguese title of the poem has a double meaning. In addition to the literal meaning translated above, "na vida" evokes the expression "cair na vida," which means to prostitute oneself. This latter meaning is present in the verse "Puta e lésbica" ["A whore and a lesbian"] wherein the poet defiantly embraces her marginality. Moreover, in linking these two locutions, Míccolis is appropriating a homophobic representation of the lesbian woman that stereotypically portrays her as a whore. The poet illustrates here the problem of the social and literary representation of the lesbian in Brazilian society, a problem she has addressed in her 1983 essay "Prazer, gênero de primeira necessidade" [Pleasure, an item of prime necessity] and which I discuss in Chapter 5.

Other anthologies followed, of both poetry and fiction, some with wider circulation. Many of the works anthologized spoke of gender relations and of women's dissatisfaction with hierarchical relationships and the lack of communication between men and women (cf. Coelho, "À guisa de posfácio" 242). Others sought to give expression to women's eroticism. Denser, a journalist and fiction writer, edited two important anthologies of female erotic short stories: *Muito prazer* [Pleased to meet you / Much pleasure] (1980) and *O prazer é todo meu* [The pleasure is all mine] (1984). The two anthologies were well received and considered groundbreaking, or perhaps as novelties by some readers and critics. And it was from this perspective that the publisher marketed the volume: "Escritores que falam de sexo é a regra, escritoras falando de sexo já vira exceção. . . . o resultado aí está: . . . as mulheres sabem (e muito bem) falar de sexo" ["Male writers who speak of sex constitute the rule, female writers speaking of sex, however, becomes an exception. . . . here is the result: . . . women can speak (and

The Search for an Erotic Discourse

speak well) of sex"] says the back cover of *Muito prazer.* In her preface, Denser reiterates this idea, stating that, previously, the theme of sex had seemed to be a masculine prerogative, and that her objective in editing the anthology was to show otherwise.

Other important ideas are conveyed in the short preface: one, that each woman has her own way of "feeling" [*sic*] sex, and it is not necessarily the way male writers have portrayed female desire; two, that women had been kept from talking of their own eroticism, and of their partners'; and three, that each woman has her own individual way of representing sex and eroticism. Denser points to the aspect of individuality and difference among women writers in their treatment of eroticism, an aspect revealed through the heterogeneity of narrative styles and perspectives that characterize the stories in both *Muito prazer* and *O prazer é todo meu.* In fact, the heterogeneity is such that the subtitle *Contos eróticos femininos* [Female erotic short stories] may not seem to fit all the narratives.

For example, the opening story in *Muito prazer,* Cristina de Queiroz's "A chave na fechadura" [The key in the keyhole], is less about eroticism than it is a fictional analysis of gender relations and marriage in Brazilian society. And Denser's own "O vampiro da alameda Casabranca" ("The Vampire of Whitehouse Lane," 1992) represents an excellent example of the author's cynical, antiromantic, and even *antierotic* eroticism. Both Cristina de Queiroz's and Denser's stories exemplify the different narrative strategies Brazilian female fiction writers employ in order to problematize gender relations and examine social hierarchies and power struggles within a society centered upon masculinist desire.

In 1984, poet Olga Savary published *Carne viva* [Bare/living skin], subtitled the first Brazilian anthology of erotic poems, including both male and female poets. The expression of female eroticism by some thirty women poets represented then a new phenomenon in Brazilian literature, possible only after the linguistic and thematic rupture evidenced in the 1970s "Pós-Vanguarda" poetic movements, particularly in the female-authored poetry that emerged during that decade. In addition, Savary's anthology appeared after the dark years of censorship of the Brazilian military dictatorship. In fact, some seven years before, the Department of Censorship in Brasília was still very active, especially censoring works that portrayed human sexuality and the human body in a manner deemed "offensive" or "obscene." The strict censorship that had begun around 1970, however, declined by the early 1980s due not only to political developments, but also to the social action of several liberal segments of the middle class who sought to establish a new socio-sexual hegemony (Winckler 72). While in the mass media these efforts seemed to have (again) favored male desire, in literature, women writers attempted to construct a space for the authentic expression of female sexuality and eroticism, and poetry proved to be an almost boundary-less space.

Nevertheless, Brazilian women fiction writers were also striving to find a new language to give expression to female sexuality, eroticism, and desire within the more confining limits of the narrative genre. In this regard, a noteworthy book published during that time is Joyce Cavalccante's *O discurso da mulher absurda* [The discourse of an absurd woman] (1985). Cavalccante presents here a collection of erotic short stories in which the female protagonists occupy the position of subject of desire, "aggressively" (according to the dominant patterns of female behavior) seeking sexual pleasure. In the story "Luta livre" [Wrestling match], for example, the protagonist is a single woman from the middle class who goes out at night looking for sexual partners. To each lover she finds, she introduces herself with a different name: Míriam, Cleide, Leila, Cláudia. Her various names represent the evasive nature of her identity before the men with whom she has sex and, at the same time, the elusive nature of female sexuality, not localized, but rather fluid and multiplied. In addition, her position as a woman not easily defined is made even more threatening to her male lovers (and perhaps even to some male readers then) by the fact that she is sexually experienced. Thus Cavalccante, in this and other stories, makes use of the disturbing nature of female sexuality. It is disturbing because both the author and her characters disrupt the dominant patterns of gender behavior: the characters, because they take the position of subject of their own desire; and the author, for speaking so explicitly about female eroticism.

Eroticism and the Search for Self-Identity:
Mulher no espelho and *As mulheres de Tijucopapo*

Eroticism has also played an important role in novels by Brazilian women that focus on female characters and their search for an identity and self-realization. Marilene Felinto's *As mulheres de Tijucopapo* (1982; *The Women of Tijucopapo*, 1994) and Helena Parente Cunha's *Mulher no espelho* (1983; *Woman between Mirrors*, 1989) each focuses on a female protagonist engaged in a process of self-examination and redefinition of her identity. Such a process entails revisiting and confronting the past, going back to their origins so as to understand who they are, and therefore rebuilding a sense of identity free from the constraints imposed by their society. In the last quarter of the twentieth century, this is the same Brazilian patriarchal and Eurocentric society that gave rise to such myths of femininity as those discussed in Chapter 1. For, as Roberto Reis has explained, "despite Brazilian modernization, certain myths and patriarchal legacies still impregnate the social imagination in regard to sexuality" (109). In other words, some one hundred years after the publication of *Memórias de um sargento de milícias, Iracema, Dom Casmurro,* and *O cortiço,* Felinto and Cunha were writing within and about a social context still structured upon a masculinist and "whitened" form of desire. In fact, gender and race are the main cultural categories scrutinized in *As mulheres de Tijucopapo* and *Mulher no espelho,* as these are the categories that, along with class, intersect in the societal construction of each protagonist's identity.

The position that each woman holds in this society, however, is not identical. Rísia, Felinto's protagonist, is a young woman of color, in her twenties, from a poor northeastern family, living in São Paulo; the unnamed protagonist in *Mulher no espelho,* on the other hand, is a forty-five-year-old, upper-middle-class woman from Salvador, the capital city of the State of Bahia who, at middle age, awakens to the reality of the subordinate position she has held within a male-dominated social environment. Nonetheless, *Mulher no espelho* and *As mulheres de Tijucopapo* hold in common several important elements, most relevant among them the fact that both novels represent one's "search for the origins," as Marilena Chaui has characterized Felinto's book (Chaui 9, 10). Both first-person narratives tell of the protagonist's search for her origins, in order to understand where she comes from and who she is, and therefore reconstruct a sense of identity. In this way, both novels can be read as female-authored examples of autobiographical fiction, or even as postmodern examples of *Bildungsromane*. In fact, in "Marginality in the Contemporary Female Brazilian Bildungsroman," Kimberle S. López and Alice A. Brittin discuss Felinto's novel as such. It should be noted that both the autobiographical genre and the *Bildungsroman* represent literary models that traditionally have not taken gender into account. Rather, the traditional critical concept of these two genres, or subgenres, of the novel assumed the presence of a male protagonist from the dominant culture, portrayed as an organic entity, whose "view of the life history is grounded in authority" (Benstock 9).

Such a model is problematic for the Brazilian female author, given women's subaltern status in Brazilian society. Therefore, in *As mulheres de Tijucopapo* and *Mulher no espelho,* the authors are engaged in a twofold deconstructive project. One, they write against a literary model that had excluded women protagonists and female life experiences; and, two, through their women characters, they seek to deconstruct cultural myths of female identity created by masculinist desire. Consequently, the characterization of these two novels as "narratives of search" is most appropriate: the phrase describes not only each protagonist's search for her origins and the process of reconstructing her self-identity, but also each author's search for her own language, a language suitable for the expression of a woman's life experiences, particularly her sexuality and eroticism. Hence, another important aspect that Felinto's and Cunha's novels have in common is the experimental nature of the language employed.

* * *

Formal experimentation has been a distinctive element in Helena Parente Cunha's literature since the publication of her first volumes of poetry and short stories, but is most notable in later works such as *Cem mentiras de verdade* [One hundred true lies] (short stories; 1985) and *As doze cores do vermelho* [The twelve colors of red] (novel; 1988). *Mulher no espelho,* her first novel, also presents the formal concern the author displays elsewhere, as it is marked by a strong metafictional component, and by a very innovative narrative strategy that underscores both the question of authorial power and the status of the self as a split entity. The novel, which achieved a renewed success after its English translation came to light in 1989, tells the story of a woman who, standing between the facing mirrors on the doors of an armoire, sees her image multiplied ad infinitum.

Confronted with these multiple images of herself, the woman embarks on a journey of self-discovery and rediscovery, of defining and redefining her own identity. From the successive images staring at each other in the mirrors, two stand out and are represented by the alternating narrative voices that speak to each other, in a dialogue, a battle of sorts or, as the narrator-protagonist states, a "jogo eu-ela" (28; "game of I-she"; 18).[4] One voice belongs to the protagonist herself, a repressed woman who has always been submissive to her traditional, patriarchal culture. The other voice belongs to "a mulher que me escreve" ("the woman who writes me"), an alter ego of the first woman, a liberal and rebellious female image who embodies everything the protagonist always wanted to do and be like, but never dared. These two narrative entities, who speak to each other through alternating fragments, represent at a structural level the psychological conflict of the female self, split between her own desire on the one hand and, on the other hand, her society's masculinist desire and the demands and expectations it places on women. Throughout the novel, the two narrative voices recount the protagonist's life story, the "I" trying to see her past and her present life positively, and the "woman who writes me" pointing out the repressed life the woman has led so far. As the narrative evolves, the two switch positions: the protagonist becomes more aware of her own desires and aspirations, and of how she has been repressed by a patriarchal system; she becomes more liberal, and begins to free her self, her body, and her sexuality from the previous constraints. The "woman who writes me," on the other hand, begins to take more conservative stances, afraid of the threat

Chapter Two

that the truly liberated and thus subversive female body poses. Therefore, as the protagonist begins to display the behavior of a liberated woman, the discourse of "the woman who writes me" seeks to tone down the other's bold attitudes and claims.

The protagonist's confrontation with her plural "images" (Cunha, *Woman* 1), a crisis elicited by the departure of her husband, leads her to revisit her past and her childhood, when she felt abandoned by her father after the birth of her baby brother. In fact, the protagonist-narrator acknowledges: "É verdade que o meu pai havia querido um menino quando eu nasci, em vez de menina" (59; "It's true that my father had wanted a boy when I was born, instead of a girl"; 42). Thus the narrative juxtaposes two spaces dominated by phallic desire. One is the space of the father's house, wherein the patriarchal power passes from father to son while silencing the females. For example, the daughter (the protagonist) is constantly neglected and unfairly punished as a child and, as an adolescent and a young woman, seriously repressed, particularly in her sexuality. Her mother is the image of the "perfect" woman, the "angel of the house," who seldom, if ever, speaks—she certainly never speaks up against the father—and whose voice is heard only as she whispers or sings "em voz baixa" (21; "under her breath"; 12). And the black nanny is repressed as a woman, as a black—thus a member of "anOther" culture—and as a servant or, in other words, as a member of an economically dependent class. As Gayatri Chakravorty Spivak states in her essay "Can the Subaltern Speak?," "if you are poor, black, and female you get it in three ways" (294), and this statement is most applicable to the Brazilian case, no matter how intertwined race and social class may be in the country.

The second space of masculinist desire is the protagonist's home, wherein her husband and three sons represent similar patriarchal values; there, as in her father's house, "um homem é um homem e a mulher deve saber o seu espaço" (15; "a man is a man and a woman must know her place"; 8). In a sense, the triangle formed by the protagonist and the images she encounters in the facing mirrors constitutes a space in opposition to the spaces centered upon masculinist desire, where a woman's social function is defined by her roles in the family, primarily as a wife and mother. Through the protagonist's mother and the protagonist herself in her domestic roles, *Mulher no espelho*

The Search for an Erotic Discourse

exposes the types of myths of female behavior Brazilian women have assimilated. For example, the protagonist states: "... meu marido gosta de me ver bem arrumada. Boniteza no vestir, cabelos bem obtidos, leve pintura concedida" (29; "... my husband likes to see me all dressed up. Nice clothes, my hair all fixed, just a touch of make-up"; 19). In this apparently encouraging behavior on the part of the husband, one may read a not-so-subtle form of repression: he desires her as a doll on display, with "just a touch of make-up" lest the wife—the private woman—look like a prostitute. At the same time, the passage above reminds the reader, as it surely reminds the protagonist, of her mother and the "perfect" relationship between the mother and the father. For example:

> Minha mãe repetia certas frases. Normas de vida. Em primeiro lugar, o marido, em segundo, o marido, em terceiro, o marido. Depois os filhos. Sim, ela era muito feliz. Toda cheirosa, à espera de que meu pai voltasse do trabalho. Ela o esperava. Perfumes, silêncios, sussurros. (21 [13])

The space marked by the facing mirrors constitutes the space "of one's own," wherein the protagonist will engage in an ever shifting process of self-questioning, self-definition, and, eventually, self-knowledge. The mirrors are the starting point of the narrative and, at the same time, complement the narrative act: seeing and narrating (speaking), the sight and the voice, are mutually complementary instruments of self-liberation that lead the female subject through her past and toward the future, toward the possibility of a new woman. In a section of the novel where the complementarity of sight and voice is most clear, female sexuality appears as the key component of the character's life that must be rescued, liberated, and satisfied. Alone in her room, away from the rigid stares of male desire, it is in front of the mirrors that she allows her body to come to life and her voice to rise from the low tones of the maternal whispers. Her body, her voice, her sexuality emerge in pleasure amidst the music from her record player and the rhythm of the author's language:

> Nos momentos em que estou realmente sozinha em casa, tranco-me no quarto, ligo o toca-discos e me ponho a dançar. Onda e som. Pulo para a outra margem, liberada dos

> nós e dos sinais. Balanço marcado, corpo inteiro enredado no ritmo profundo. Gosto de vestir um dos meus vestidos proibidos. . . . Sorrio cúmplice de mim mesma. . . . Quem é a mulher provocante no espelho? (37 [14])

Music, sensuality, self-pleasure, the mirrors become the doors, the "cracks through which [she escapes]" (26) to the space where female sexuality is not bound by the phallus, but is rather satisfied through self-love. The satisfaction of her sexuality represents at the same time the realization of the multiplicity of the self: "Estou muitas" (38; "So many of me"; 26). Later on, the female character will step in her newly invented independence, and taking on the demeanor of a sensual, provocative, and seducing woman, will seek her own pleasure in intercourse with different men.

In Cunha's novel, autoeroticism has been the transgressive act that, once realized, allows for other transgressions to take place, foremost among them narrating/writing. Laura Beard, in an article on Latin American metafiction authored by women, points out the relationship that exists between writing and sexuality. She states about *Mulher no espelho:* "Para la protagonista, escribir es un acto sexual, secreto y transgresor" (Beard 301) ["For the protagonist, to write is a transgressive, secret, sexual act"]. The phallocentric discourse has rendered both writing and sexual pleasure forbidden to women, and this is made vivid in the protagonist's dialogue with the "woman who writes me," as they remember the sad episode from her adolescence when the father reads and misinterprets her secret diary, reacting with physical aggression toward the daughter (55–57).

Years later, as a middle-aged woman, she will react against her father's violent repression, her husband's debasing behavior, and her sons' mockery by adopting a new form of behavior that stands as the antithesis to the phallocentric model of female behavior. She starts to venture out of the domestic space, and to bring men she meets on the streets to her home. In this way she rejects the clearly marked myths of the housewife and mother on one hand, and, on the other hand, of the "public" woman, blurring also the distinction between the public and the private. However, her sexual body, subversive of patriarchy, does not go unpunished, and the violent death of one of her sons will mark the end of the narrative and the failure of her search for independence and satisfaction.

The Search for an Erotic Discourse

Mulher no espelho is a novel still written under what we may call *the sign of sexual-cultural ambiguity*. This ambiguity stems from the conflicts faced by Brazilian women, particularly those who lived through the Cultural Revolution of the 1960s or grew up in its aftermath, torn between the traditions of patriarchal ideology and new lifestyles and forms of behavior disseminated by the mass media in an ever-shrinking world. Cunha has not been able to resolve such ambiguity for her protagonist. Rather, she represents it through the "fragmentação do sujeito, oscilando entre o aprisionante 'destino de mulher' e o repentino desejo de libertação do jugo" (Cunha, "Desafio" 155) ["the fragmentation of the subject, who oscillates between the entrapping 'woman's destiny' and the desire for liberation"]. As a consequence, guilt (cf. Cunha, "Desafio") dominates the female subject, while the woman writer is unable to finally represent her character's sexuality outside of the boundaries of male desire. In Cunha's novel, this is seen in the protagonist's search for sexual satisfaction in heterosexual relationships that turn out to be unsatisfactory. Interestingly, the most beautifully constructed passages of erotic discourse describe moments of self-love, when the protagonist experiences full satisfaction. For example:

> As minhas mãos percorrem o meu corpo, de alto a baixo. Detêm-se na nuca e se misturam aos cabelos para soltá-los, livre, sobre os ombros. As minhas mãos descem, contornando os seios, levemente sobre as pontas endurecidas, que somente conheceram as mãos balofas e suadas de um homem. Sinto que haverá um prazer à espera dos meus seios solitários. As minhas mãos descem pela cintura, pelas nádegas, se afundam no sexo, polpa madura e úmida aconchegada ao abrigo de vôos e mergulhos....
> ...
> Saio dos espelhos à procura do tapete de pele. Deito-me no chão e os meus poros conhecem a aspereza macia deste pêlo. O vento que vem do mar me traz o cheiro de manga madura. Encolho-me, estendo-me, rolo. (109–10 [15])

The sensuality experienced by the character is echoed in the writer's language. The passages above exemplify the use of some linguistic elements that distinguish the experimental style of *Mulher no espelho,* and that are even more striking in the Brazilian original text. For example, one may find the use of very short sentences, repetition of one or more syntactical elements, alliteration, and the careful construction of the sentence's rhythm. Throughout the novel, Cunha also employs truncated sentences, oxymora and parallelisms, and syntactical constructions that defy the rules of standard Portuguese language.

One of the novel's most important themes is the protagonist's attempt to recover her African heritage, which is vital in her process of reconstructing her identity. Therefore, the narrative abounds with images that relate to Africa and to Salvador's Afro-Brazilian culture, particularly the Candomblé religion. Afro-Brazilian gods such as Xangô, Iansan, and Oxum are evoked often, and in many passages the text reproduces the rhythm of the Candomblé drums in its syntax and through word choice. Images such as mangoes, the mango tree, the sea, seashells, and the wind are recurrent, and often come together by way of synesthesia. Africa and related images appear associated with the character's sexual awakening and satisfaction, as "o cheiro de manga madura" in the passage quoted above. In fact, the protagonist's sexual encounter with "the good-looking black man" is depicted as the most satisfying of her heterosexual encounters, and leads her to experience a sense of wholeness: "Preenchimento e totalidade. Estou aqui. Inteira e múltipla. Completa" (162; "Fulfilled and total. I'm here. Whole and multiple. Complete"; 125).

Standing on the other side of the Atlantic Ocean or, in other words, on the opposite side of the father's house, Africa, and by extension Afro-Brazilian culture, represent a space of freedom, pleasure, and self-realization. Nevertheless, just as the sense of totality is transitory, and even though she takes pride in her "pele queimada" ("tanned skin"), and in her "cabelo crespo" (158; "curly hair"; 121), the character can only temporarily experience this space of freedom. She has been removed from it by centuries of cultural whitening and by her standing in the class structure of Brazilian society. Consequently, she remains divided, her self forever split, fragmented as the images of her face reflected on the multiple fragments of the broken mirrors (132).

In this way, as Maria José Somerlate Barbosa argues, "os espelhos estilhaçados fragmentam a noção de uma identidade coesa" (147) ["the broken mirrors fragment the notion of a

The Search for an Erotic Discourse

cohesive identity"], also undermining the essentialism that the text and the character's search might have implied (cf. Barbosa 147). The concept of the subject as inherently split is an accepted premise in Lacanian and post-Lacanian psychoanalysis and cultural and literary theories. However, this concept entails a sense of failure or defeat, for the subject does require some conviction of his or her own stability and unity that, once reached, will be immediately questioned by the subject. It is the implication of failure and defeat that lies at the conclusion of *Mulher no espelho,* as the protagonist and "the woman who writes me," "feet gnawed at by rats," come together, driven by guilt (132).

* * *

Cunha's protagonist's search for an identity is a process that necessitates the creation of a new, more authentic language, and that unfolds *through* language, through the act of narrating and writing. These acts allow the subject—male or female—to revisit the past, and by way of revisiting, to relive, replay past experiences. In this way, narrating and writing are strategies of *repetition*, which leads the subject to mastery over past events and situations. In *Mulher no espelho,* narrating takes shape through the dialogue established between the "I" and the "woman who writes me," but writing is also an important component of the protagonist's development, from adolescence to maturity, and from there to self-awareness. She writes a diary when young, later writes in her room, hiding from her husband and sons, and eventually comes to write and publish a book of narrative fiction.

In Felinto's *As mulheres de Tijucopapo,* writing and narrating have a similar function. In fact, they take place concurrently, as Rísia, the protagonist-narrator, writes a letter addressed to her mother while going on a nine-month journey back to her place of origin. In fact, Rísia goes beyond her original birthplace to reach Tijucopapo, where she hopes to find a strong female lineage to which she lets herself be reborn. Her journey represents a "process of reverse gestation" (Matthews 125), a process through which she searches for a sense of a new identity. In Felinto's novel, as in Cunha's, the protagonist must devise her own language in order to narrate/write her childhood, her past experiences, what she encounters along her journey, her thoughts and emotions. In order to achieve a language that authentically represents her character's life experiences, Felinto weaves together different linguistic registers to form a fragmented narrative with often unusual syntax. These registers include an English-language song by the Beatles, verses from a Brazilian children's rhyme, references to a psalm from the Bible, poetic prose, and regionalisms. Throughout the novel, the author also uses repetition of sounds, words, phrases and sentences, and repeatedly breaks the traditional structure of Portuguese grammar. Moreover, Felinto transgresses the social and literary expectations regarding how a woman should speak or write by using crude language, making explicit sexual allusions, and employing a distinct tone of violence to mark her protagonist's discourse. In this regard, Felinto's novel is truly innovative within Brazilian women's fiction, for she openly gives expression to female violence and anger.

Rísia's journey is then a reconstruction of her past as well as of an identity: addressing the mother, she recounts her childhood, her family relations, her feelings, lacks and desires; she searches for her origins and searches for a *new* origin, a new identity. This is carried out through language, and becomes at the same time a most pressing search for a new and authentic language. Nevertheless, this authentic language sometimes proves to be elusive or not sufficient to convey the protagonist's feelings. In these moments, the character wishes to express herself through other means: "Ah, se pelo menos eu pudesse falar em língua estrangeira. Ah, se eu pudesse somente grunhir. Ah, se eu pudesse ser um bicho" (36; "Oh, if I were at least able to talk in a foreign language. Oh, if I could only grunt. Oh, if I could be an animal"; 23).[5]

Grunting, growling (97), stammering, silence (41), and the desire to be an animal, to be a mare (97), not only reflect the character's problematic relationship with language, but also her determination to break away from the dominant sociolinguistic system and be heard. Her position vis-à-vis the dominant system could be thus summed up: "Everything in me joined forces to forbid me to write [or speak up]: History, my story, my origin, my sex. Everything that constituted my social and cultural self. To begin with the necessary, which I lacked, the material

The Search for an Erotic Discourse

that writing is formed of and extracted from: language" (Cixous, "Coming to Writing" 12).

Rísia is socially and culturally displaced because of who she is: a woman, of color, poor. In addition, her family follows a Protestant faith in a country where Catholicism is the official religion; and she is a Northeasterner, standing out, because of her accent and her ethnic physical attributes, in São Paulo, a large, wealthy, cosmopolitan and Europeanized city in the Southeast region of Brazil. Rísia's voice, therefore, echoes those of marginalized groups in Brazilian society, voices often silenced, seldom heard. In fact, Rísia's narrative replays to a certain extent the story of generations of Brazilian Northeasterners who migrate, alone or with their families, to cities in Southeast Brazil, like São Paulo and Rio de Janeiro. They go looking for a better life, but typically find themselves, instead, culturally, socially, and economically marginalized.

Felinto recounts this story, made famous in Brazilian literature by novels such as Graciliano Ramos's *Vidas secas* (1938; *Barren Lives,* 1965) and Lispector's *A hora da estrela* (1977; *The Hour of the Star,* 1986). Like Lispector, Felinto focuses specifically on the plight of a woman, underscoring, throughout her narrative, the signs of Rísia's difference that make of her a social and cultural Other. Moreover, Felinto's novel reverses the usual path of the *retirante* (the Northeastern migrant) by depicting Rísia on her way *back* to the Northeast. In this way, Felinto portrays her character's rejection of the society's dominant values; at the same time, the author is able to disrupt the false notion of Brazil as a racial democracy, and free of gender, class, and religion-based discriminations (cf. Penna 218, 223–24). Such forms of discrimination are not always open and physically violent; rather, they often take the guise of tolerance and interaction among different groups, an interaction that maintains "a dominação de um sobre o outro, no caso sempre predominando a cultura e etnia branca européia sobre as outras" (Penna 223) ["the domination of one over another, in this case always prevailing the white European culture and ethnicity over the others"].

Furthermore, Rísia's displacement is also of a psychological nature, as a consequence of her conflicting relationships with her mother, who failed to nurture and protect her; with her father, who was frequently unfaithful to her mother, and verbally and physically aggressive to his children; and with her siblings, who were over dependent and abusive. At the heart of these conflicts is the subject's relationship with the mother—the primary Other—which can determine to a large extent the individual's later relationships, with herself and with others. Rísia's social, cultural, and psychological displacement begins thus in the mother, in her emotional absence, her inability to nurture her daughter. The mother becomes for Rísia a synonym of passivity, weakness, and the worst of the reality wherein they live—poverty, dirt, adultery, broken marriages, lack: "Mamãe, sua cara de cu" (21; "Mama, your shitty face"; 9).

Many psychoanalysts have asserted that the process of female identity formation necessitates a separation from the maternal figure. In Rísia's case, however, the process of individuation is framed by strong and conflicting feelings of rebelliousness and guilt toward the mother. Both sentiments are conveyed in her narrative, wherein she expresses the need to rebel against the mother and what the mother stands for, the necessity to reject identities imposed from the outside. "Jamais vou admitir que me definam" (24; "I'll never let anyone define me"; 11), Rísia states. Instead, she will construct a new sense of identity on her own terms, in her own language. At the same time, her narrative is born out of desire; it seeks to compensate for a lack, the lack left by her mother's emotional absence.

Rísia's journey, therefore, is threefold: it is the actual geographic displacement from São Paulo to the Northeast; it is psychological, as she reinvents herself in her own discourse addressed to an absent mother; and it is mythical, revisionist, mythmaking. In order to satisfy her desire for the maternal body, Rísia becomes her own mother, and creates not one mother figure, but rather a group of women with whom she can identify, the women warriors of Tijucopapo who will mother and nurture her. Thus she establishes a new genealogy for herself, a heritage of strong women to replace the passivity and weakness associated with her mother and other women of her childhood.

In seventeenth-century Brazil, the women of Tijucopapo used their own weapons—i.e., their cooking and washing utensils—to fight against the Dutch who had invaded Pernambuco;

these women had been, however, only a footnote in the male-centered Brazilian historiography. By foregrounding them, Felinto is interpolating two different chronological planes: the colonial and the contemporary periods, which confers upon the novel a mythic quality. Felinto is a mythmaker, as her character claims for herself a strong lineage of female fighters. In this way, the author is rejecting cultural myths and assumptions such as those that populated Rísia's childhood: passive women, like her mother; unfaithful and violent men, like her father; adultery, alcoholism, and promiscuity as the norm, as Rísia had seen in her neighborhood. In addition, Felinto questions Brazilian society itself, and social divisions along class and racial lines.

The character of Lampião, whom Rísia meets upon approaching Tijucopapo, advances the mythic dimension of Felinto's novel. Another chronological period thus intersects with the previous two, for Lampião was a real-life *cangaceiro* ("bandit") who terrified the population in the backlands of Brazil's Northeast region from the mid-1910s until his death in 1938.[6] Throughout the twentieth century, however, he became a cultural icon, famous for his bravery as well as his cruelty in dealing with his enemies, and admired as a symbol of rebellion against the status quo. As such, he underscores Rísia's desire for rebelliousness and Felinto's deconstruction of the Brazilian society's dominant values.

Interestingly, many women joined Lampião's group, including Maria Bonita, after the two fell in love. For these women, life with the *cangaceiros* represented an opportunity to escape the social restrictions typically imposed on women in the first decades of the twentieth century, and to live freely a life of adventures (Schumaher and Vital Brazil 171, 373–74). These *cangaceiro* women, some of whom carried small guns with them, certainly defied the accepted standards of behavior, by breaking away from the typical and stable family life. However, the idea that they participated equally with the men in armed struggles against the police is erroneous. In fact, during fights, they were generally kept in a defended hideout, protected by the men. Moreover, while many of them followed the *cangaceiros* of their own free will, others were kidnapped and forced to go along, serving the men as good wives and lovers,

Chapter Two

bearing children and doing typically "feminine" work, such as sewing.

Consequently, Rísia's encounter with Lampião in Tijucopapo, in the last chapters of the novel, signals a conflicting and ambiguous denouement. Her identification with the women of Tijucopapo emphasizes the characteristics of bravery, strength, and self-sufficiency "as desirable and indispensable for women seeking to create a new place for themselves in society" (López and Brittin 22). Nevertheless, while Lampião embodies the social revolution erupting in poor Northeastern Brazil against the dominant social and cultural values represented by the wealthy and Europeanized São Paulo, women's roles in such a revolution still seem to be those of followers. As Rísia states at the novel's very conclusion, in the letter to her mother: "eu posso no máximo seguir Lampião. Por uma causa justa" (133; "at the most I can follow Lampião. For a just cause"; 120). It is here that Felinto's novel seems to fail in its attempt to devise a new path and a new identity for the female protagonist.

Likewise, the expression of female desire and eroticism conveys a similar ambiguity. Felinto represents her character's desire and sexuality through an explicit and unashamed language, in a manner that reflects her self-awareness. Rísia *feels* sexual: "Mas hoje meu corpo precisou de um homem. Meu corpo estava insolarado e labirintítico [*sic*], meu corpo estava bêbado. *Eu queria ser seduzida*. . . . eu falei a um jovem montando um jegue. Não sei se falei coisa com coisa. Só sei que ele me seduziu" (110; my emphasis; "today my body needs a man. My body was sunstruck and labyrinthinine [*sic*], my body was intoxicated. *I wanted to be seduced*. . . . I talked with one virile young man mounted on a donkey. I don't know if I talked about anything in particular. I only know *he seduced me*"; 95; my emphasis). The use of passive voice by the female protagonist is telling of her stance toward her own sexuality: she is aware of her sexual desire, but will remain passive and allow the male to take the active role in the game of seduction and love. In the sexual act that follows and that is described as "quase a perfeição" (110; "almost perfect"; 96), the narrative portrays Rísia and Lampião as models of transcending femaleness and maleness joined in the millenarian act of love. This is achieved through the omission of their names and the repeti-

The Search for an Erotic Discourse

tion of words, particularly "man" and "woman," and through their implied identification as animals, horses and mares:

> ... os sons que se juntavam numa ária que era nossa, dele homem e de eu mulher cruzando uma noite de raríssima lua melada. O homem e eu apeamos no estábulo das éguas e entramos. O homem e eu deitamos no capim onde as éguas deitam. Foi no capim que eu amei um homem como era raríssimo aquela lua estar melada como estava. Eu senti que, com aquele homem, eu deitava com todos os atos que deitara antes com outros homens. Eu viera com todos os atos e aquele meu ato eu sentia que seria quase a perfeição. (110 [16])

In the passage above, Rísia claims her agency: she loves, she is, she stands equal with the man. Nevertheless, female agency is lost as the description of the sexual act continues in terms that progressively privilege the male's actions:

> O homem me tocava como se nenhuma parte do meu corpo sobrasse, eu era inteirinha do homem, ... eu estava sendo varrida e invadida como só a água salgada do mar pode me varrer e invadir até a exaustão. Eu estava sendo mergulhada e molhada. O homem me imprensou contra as paredes do estábulo das éguas e me penetrou num membro . . . , me invadindo, me varrendo de gosma, me mergulhando e me molhando até que gritei exausta e ele gritou exausto e nós caímos na beira dum mar de capim. (110–11 [17])

Again the author uses repetition, creating with it an effect that suggests the couple's movements during the love act. The use of the same or of corresponding verbs—to void, to invade, to exhaust, to saturate, to submerge—in the passive and, then, in the active voices, renders the woman subject to the active male. Despite the author's efforts to depict Rísia as equally participative in this erotic scene, and the sexual act as an act of unity and harmony—"O homem e eu nos movemos em todos os atos" (111; "The man and I moved together in every act"; 96)—in actuality she reproduces a traditional heterosexual relationship. While Lampião plays the active role, Rísia's agency in the love act alludes to the traditionally female functions of mothering and nurturing: "quando eu quis coroar o membro do homem com minhas mãos e ele se excitou, e quando eu o quis acalmar na minha boca e ele se molhou como uma criança se molha, eu chorei" (111; "when I tried to enwrap the man's member with my hands and he got aroused, and when I wanted to appease it in my mouth and he wet himself like a child wets itself, I cried . . ."; 96).

In conclusion, with *As mulheres de Tijucopapo* Felinto has been successful in the construction of an innovative discourse that authentically expresses a woman's emotions and life experiences, and is particularly effective in its expression of her anger and inner violence. The author has also succeeded in creating a female character aware of her own body, sexuality, and desire. Nevertheless, as noted above in relation to *A mulher no espelho,* like Cunha, Felinto fails to rethink female sexuality outside the frame of male desire and the dominance of the phallus. This is not to say that heterosexuality is not a valid expression of female desire, but rather that Felinto's novel points to the need to problematize how we think heterosexuality. Her erotic discourse is revealing of how twentieth-century Brazilian women writers, for the most part, have been unable to rethink it, and to disassociate the heterosexual act from a heterosexually hierarchical ideology privileging of male desire and penetration. Thus, it is not "the act of intercourse itself which [constitutes] the problem, but rather the way in which heterosexuality is institutionalized and practised under patriarchy" (S. Jackson 176), as a reflection of gender relations in a given society. In this way, even if Felinto's protagonist engages in a search that leads her to redefine her sense of an identity, by finding her own voice and means of self-expression, and by reidentifying her origins, she does not fully claim her agency. Rather, she adheres to a form of erotic expression that "has been culturally constructed around an eroticization of power" (S. Jackson 176). Eroticism in *As mulheres de Tijucopapo* has in fact been deemed disturbing and even pornographic by some readers, as it perpetuates male aggression over female passivity. The issue Felinto and other Brazilian women writers face, therefore, is that of crafting an erotic discourse through which the female body and sexuality are not rendered submissive to others' desire, but find, rather, authentic self-expression and satisfaction.

Chapter Three

Representation of the Female Body and Desire
The Gothic, the Fantastic, and the Grotesque

While many twentieth-century Brazilian women authors have attempted to give expression to female desire in a way that is liberating for the female subject, often they seem to have failed, falling into the old pattern of conceiving female sexuality and the female body as subservient to, or dependent upon, male desire. As I discussed in the previous chapter, this failure is illustrated in Felinto's *As mulheres de Tijucopapo* and Cunha's *A mulher no espelho*. Cunha herself, in her essay on Brazilian women's writings from the 1970s and 1980s, claims that women poets and fiction writers of that period accomplish different things in their works (Cunha, "Desafio"). She argues that, while Brazilian women poets are able to express female eroticism in a liberating way, our fiction writers have succeeded only in their critique of gender relations in Brazil. Their characters, however, are not liberated from the dominant patriarchal discourse, because they succumb to guilt. This guilt originates in the split experienced by the female subject, torn between patriarchal traditions and the desire for self-fulfillment—social, psychological, intellectual, and sexual. As presented in my discussion of Gilka Machado's poetry, this split is manifested also by a female poetic voice faced with the expectations placed on her by society and, at the same time, with her own erotic desire.

It would be safe to affirm that few women in Brazilian culture are totally free from guilt. Throughout the twentieth century, the biblical guilt laid on Eve and her descendents often haunted the female subject and influenced the way a woman saw herself and approached her own body and sexuality. The guilt with which women may regard their sexuality has its

Chapter Three

counterpart in a masculine fear of the female body, a fear that has been theorized by many and diverse critics, such as Griffin in the United States and Sant'Anna (*Canibalismo*) in Brazil. On the other hand, the masculinist fear of the female body has generated a number of different forms and institutions of control over women's bodies, as Foucault (*History of Sexuality. An Introduction*) explains, and as I have pointed out in Chapter 1. The frightening female body is represented in male-authored Brazilian literature in a variety of forms, such as the woman-statue, the *femme fatale,* the Medusa, or the sphinx that threatens to devour the man (Sant'Anna, *Canibalismo* 63, 78 ff.). In all, a composite characterization of female sexuality and desire is conveyed either in the physical depiction of the female as a grotesque or even monstrous body, or in the ambiguity involving male and female desire within the act of seduction attributed to the *femme fatale*. The characterization of female desire and sexuality through ambiguity and the grotesque may function as yet another form of censorship. Impacting the way women see their own bodies, social censorship may translate as *self-censorship* in female-authored texts, through the use of some strategies of self-representation that highlight the female body as socially and/or psychologically problematic for women.

Among the strategies of self-representation that Brazilian women writers employ is the use of subgenres of the fantasy novel, such as the gothic, the fairy tale, and the utopian novel; or the use of elements that may be found in these genres, such as the grotesque and the fantastic mode. Dinah Silveira de Queiroz (1911–82), with *Margarida La Rocque: A ilha dos demônios* [Margarida La Rocque: The Demons' Island] (1949); Coutinho, with *O jogo de Ifá* [Divination: Ifá's game] (1980), and *O caso Alice* [The Alice file] (1991); and Denser with *A ponte das estrelas* [The bridge of stars] (1990) are a few examples of this literary tendency. This chapter will focus on the use of the gothic, the fantastic, and the grotesque in two novels by two of the most prominent Brazilian female writers of the late twentieth century: Luft's *O quarto fechado* (1984; *The Island of the Dead,* 1986), and Telles's *As horas nuas* [Bare hours] (1989).

The Gothic, the Fantastic, and the Grotesque in Women's Literature

The gothic can be understood as a subgenre within fantasy literature and, as Rosemary Jackson points out, it in fact constitutes the more "immediate roots" of fantasy, while the genre's more remote origins could "be traced back to ancient myths, legends, folklore, carnival art" (95). However, what distinguishes the gothic within the fantasy genre is its "preoccupation with the domestic realm" (K. F. Ellis ix), which is constructed as an oppressive environment, wherein a sense of terror or imminent danger looms over the protagonist. The gothic novel shows a "topography of enclosures, wastelands, vaults, dark spaces, to express psychic terrors and primal desires" (R. Jackson 108). Since its inception, it has been characterized by elements of horror and violence and by supernatural effects. It emerges at the margins of the bourgeois culture, while at the same time representing a form of commentary and pressure against this culture. As the gothic undergoes changes in the early nineteenth century, with the novels of Mary Shelley and others, it becomes more concerned with psychological problems, often expressing the subject's conflicts within an inimical social situation. The modern gothic then is an enactment of the split of the subject, and an expression of the subject's desire for unity (R. Jackson 97, 99–101). In this way, the gothic is used by contemporary authors, particularly women, who have made effective use of the genre, developing and extending a tradition that has come to constitute "a literary form capable of more radical interrogation of social contradictions" (R. Jackson 97).

In the modern and contemporary gothic, "the object of fear can have no adequate representation and is, therefore, all the more threatening" (R. Jackson 112). Fear emanates, not from physical characteristics, but rather from antagonistic social values thereby represented. Yet, the source of fear is barely perceived by the subject, never fully articulated through language. The object of fear, as Rosemary Jackson says, is "unnameable" (112); it escapes language and therefore appears frequently as a grotesque construct, for the grotesque is "beyond the reach of language," it defies "our conventional, language-based categories" (Harpham 3, 5).

Chapter Three

At the same time, the grotesque represents the physical and/or psychological distortion of human or animal forms and can be seen also as a strategy, not only in fantasy novels, but especially in the literature of the fantastic, since exaggeration is one of the features that constitutes the fantastic figurative discourse (Todorov 77). In fact, there is a close association between the grotesque and the fantastic, for "Like the grotesque, with which it overlaps, the fantastic can be seen as an art of estrangement, resisting closure, opening structures which categorize experience in the name of a 'human reality'" (R. Jackson 175). The grotesque appears often as a metaphor that heightens the paltriness and absurdity of our lives; the fantastic, on the other hand, is the vehicle par excellence that allows for transgression, questioning—if not subverting—the value system supported by the dominant ideology (cf. Guerra-Cunningham 84). In addition, the fantastic mode "problematizes representation of the 'real,' . . . [by drawing] attention to difficulties of representation and to conventions of literary discourse" (R. Jackson 84).

The fantastic, as Tzvetan Todorov explains, deals with the same subjects all literature deals with, but brings to this subject a *different intensity,* the superlative and the excessive. It represents "an experience of limits" (Todorov 93) and the transgression of these limits. The use of elements of the fantastic mode in women's literature has another function as well, for it serves to highlight the ambiguous position of women in a male-centered order, to underline their marginality. By the same token, contemporary female authors, from Brazil and elsewhere, have also favored the gothic novel as the vehicle for "an increasingly insistent critique of the ideology of separate spheres," male and female (K. F. Ellis xv). Gothic novels bring together "fantastic occurrences," cases of madness (either real or perceived), "ghostly images, eerie voices, . . . ethereal figures" (Quinlan, *Female Voice* 97), constructing thus a troubling portrayal of the inequalities and frustrations faced by contemporary women. In the gothic novel, the supernatural threatens to invade the boundaries of the "natural," and in this way serves the "purpose of journeying into the psyche" of the female subject but is also "a way to dissect the silent, mad places of a collective consciousness" (Quinlan, *Female Voice* 83).

The Gothic, the Fantastic, and the Grotesque

* * *

The fictional works of Telles and Luft present many common aspects, in spite of the generational difference between the two authors (Telles was born in 1923, and Luft in 1939). Perhaps the main common factor in their fiction is that both writers probe into the lives of middle-class and upper-middle-class women, and thus their works constitute fictional studies of the female subject in her relations with the Other within the context of Brazilian society. This society, in turn, is seen as inherently patriarchal, in spite of some relative freedoms that women from the upper classes have achieved in Brazil during the twentieth century. In addition, in their novels, as well as in Telles's short stories, the reader often encounters a gap between the expected, common logic and the characters' actual lives. Such a gap leads the reader to share the characters' feelings of ambiguity caused by the merging of two worlds—"that of the real and that of the fantastic" (Todorov 26). The focus in Telles's and Luft's fiction on contemporary, middle-class, and most often urban, women leads to the questioning of the human condition within a society in transition, in a crisis "gerada pela desorientação de homens e mulheres diante de uma avalanche de interrogações impostas pelos novos tempos, pós-teológicos" (Coelho, "Presença da mulher" 13) ["generated by men and women's bewilderment when faced with an avalanche of questions raised by the new, post-theological order"].

A recurrent theme in Telles's and in Luft's novels is precisely the decadence of the bourgeois order and, within it, the decadence of the family institution as representative of and as a vehicle for the dominant ideology. Nevertheless, within this context of ideological changes, women still experience conflicts resulting from the clash between their desires and aspirations, on the one hand, and, on the other, the demands and obstacles imposed by the social order. From such conflicts derive the ambiguity and absurdity experienced by the characters, and highlighted by the use of the gothic novel, by elements of the fantastic, or metaphorized through the use of the grotesque. The gothic, the fantastic, and the grotesque therefore constitute strategies of estrangement, which lead to the exposure of a different kind of logic that rules the lives of these otherwise ordinary women—or, as it may turn out, the lack of any logic altogether. In this respect, Telles's and Luft's narratives can be read as Kafkaesque, in the sense that the everyday, ordinary middle-class lives of the female protagonists are shown to obey an absurd order.

Lya Luft's *O quarto fechado*

The intrusion of the supernatural into the daily life of the woman protagonist can be seen in Luft's *As parceiras* [The partners] (1980), which Susan Quinlan discusses as a contemporary example of the gothic novel in *The Female Voice in Contemporary Brazilian Narrative* (1990). *As parceiras* serves as a paradigm for the author's later novels, introducing many of the same thematic and formal elements present in *O quarto fechado*. Madness, death, the repression of desires and aspirations, and the absurd logic of human life all come to light as the middle-aged female protagonist delves into the absurdity of her own life, in a reassessment of her past, her frustrations, and her failures. Death is the starting point of these two novels, as the narrative compensates for the void left by the absence of the dead (in both novels, the protagonists' sons). But while the narrative—in the form, mainly, of the characters' thoughts and memories—serves the function of filling in the space left by a loss, it will also reveal other losses and absences, the *death in life* experienced by each character in her or his daily existence.

In *O quarto fechado,* death is at the core of the text in several different ways. First, it is identified with one of the characters, Ella, whose strange name in Portuguese allows for this ambiguous identification: Ella, a woman's name; and *ela, a Morte,* "she, death" (cf. McClendon and Craige xi). Death is a character in its own right, referred to as the "Lover" and the "Bride," whose presence in the house is first acknowledged by the external narrative voice. Death "holds the symbolic center for the narrative" (McClendon 24) and is also at the center of the text in a structural way, in the form of a casket holding the body of Camilo in the center of a room, around which sit the various characters. Death is finally a central theme in the text, a leitmotif intertwined with the life of each character as the characters' existences are examined through the narrative.

The Gothic, the Fantastic, and the Grotesque

In *O quarto fechado,* Luft manipulates elements of the grotesque, the gothic, and the fantastic in order to expose the conflicts of the characters and, by extension, the disintegration of the bourgeois family unit. In an interview with Judith Payne, Luft herself states that the novel is about "the conflict of a woman who wants to have a career . . . , and also wants to have the joys of a married life, of being a mother. . . . [and] how difficult it is to conciliate" (qtd. in Luft, "Fiction" 113). Having given up a satisfying and yet incomplete life as a famous pianist to become a wife and mother—roles that she does not find self-fulfilling— the protagonist, Renata, is portrayed as psychologically split. The meaning of her name, Renata, is easily recognized ("re-nata," "born again," "reborn") and seems at first to point to the eventual mending of the character's subjectivity. As the novel progresses, however, the reader finds the name's denotation to be ironic: what we witness is not the character's rebirth to a new self, with the positive implications usually associated with "the beginning of a new life," but rather her slow death, as Renata's aspirations are, little by little, left unfulfilled.

As a counterpoint to Renata is Martim, her husband, whose attachment to the traditional male role of *material provider–emotional absentee* does not allow him true self-realization or a satisfying relationship with his wife and children. His clinging to a traditional, patriarchal order clashes with Renata's aspirations and her inability to submit to social expectations. Renata's conflicts, her sense of being incomplete, are thus similar to the split we see in Martim and also in the other characters, each one torn between roles he or she has to accept and desires that remain unfulfilled. In fact, although the novel centers on issues that are most pertinent to middle-class women in Brazilian society, a profound affinity exists between the protagonist and the other characters. The narrative presents the inner turmoil, frustrated expectations, and hidden selves of each family member and thus underscores the main thematic concern Luft addresses in this and in other texts. This concern refers to the inner split experienced by every human being, the desire for connection and unity each individual seeks to achieve in different—and most often failed—ways, and how women, specifically, experience these issues. Most interestingly, while the author focuses on a female protagonist in a novel that

Chapter Three

presents multiple narrative viewpoints, it is Camilo, Renata's son, who in fact incarnates his mother's and the other characters' conflicts, becoming himself an embodiment for repressed female desire and sexuality.

The narrative opens with Camilo's body in a casket. His presence/absence in the center of the room, and in the center of the text, creates the possibility for each family member to rethink his or her own process of destruction, and each one's path toward death. Brazilian critic Ruth Silviano Brandão states: "É diante dele [Camilo morto] que todos revivem suas fantasias, fazem retornar seus fantasmas, penetrando mais na própria loucura, pois a loucura é a outra face da morte. Para todos, ele começa a ser uma ausência que deve ser preenchida por palavras . . ." (34) ["It is in front of Camilo's body that they all relive their fantasies, bring back their ghosts, delving more and more in their own madness, for madness is the other face of death. For everyone he becomes an absence that must be filled by words"].

Camilo's casket in the center of the room/text, his slow "death" within death, marked by subtle but regular changes in his face and appearance, the presence of death itself as a character in the narrative—all this makes María Luisa Bombal's *La amortajada* (1938; *The Shrouded Woman,* 1948) an unavoidable reference for the reader of Spanish American literature. In many of Bombal's works, reality becomes an ambiguous concept, oscillating between what we usually call "real" and a dreamlike, fantastic, or imaginary dimension, which defies a fixed definition. This ambiguity serves to highlight—in both Bombal's and Luft's works—the female problematic within a male-dominated order, as Lucía Guerra-Cunningham has asserted (82). In *O quarto fechado,* however, it is also used to underscore Camilo's quest for wholeness, his desperate search for unity, which becomes a troubling representation of every individual's search for him/herself. Camilo is the transgressive element, the one who dares search for the true meaning of existence beyond existence itself. He is aware of life's meaninglessness and seeks to fulfill it, as he is attracted by the other, definitive emptiness/absence—death. Death is the ultimate answer, the only possibility of achieving totality, the integration of the self with the self. It is by actively seeking death that

The Gothic, the Fantastic, and the Grotesque

Camilo becomes the transgressor. His death—actually his suicide—is the transgressive and epiphanic moment, the instant of knowledge:

> Cavalgando o demônio, o cheiro do próprio sêmen misturado ao de suor e emanações brutais, ele urrara de prazer e medo, ódio e vitória. Expelira fezes e urina, e despencara enfim naquele abraço, onde seria unicamente Camilo: dissolvido em beleza, liberado numa água sem margens. . . . (118 [18])

Camilo's suicide is described as a moment of liberation, exuberance, excess—elements that also characterize eroticism as Bataille has shown (11). The description of Camilo's encounter with death as sexual is not unintentional, precisely because death is here the culmination of Camilo's search, a search that earlier had taken him to other borders, to other possible transgressions, such as the possibility of incest with his twin sister. Death is thus a dimension of the erotic experience, both as transgression and as a moment of integration, when the subject feels complete, whole.

Camilo is also the transgressor in that he is an androgynous figure. In fact, his characterization, particularly through his father's eyes, implies the possibility that he is homosexual, or bisexual, for that matter. But his sexual orientation is not precisely the point. Rather, as an androgynous figure, Camilo represents the very totality he searches for. Furthermore, his androgyny and his excessive sexuality confer upon him a grotesque quality if we understand the grotesque as a juxtaposition of elements that normally belong to different realms or are isolated. These elements are, obviously, his masculinity and his femininity. His body, his desire, is both male and female. Moreover, as a young man who is "different,"[1] who may be perceived as "effeminate" (Luft, *Quarto fechado* 36), he represents female excess, and as such, he is a challenge to the patriarchal order the father stands for. And, finally, in the characterization of Camilo we find an example of authorial manipulation, which lends the narrative a tone of ambiguity and mystery.

This ambiguity is achieved through an abundance of certain locutions, such as "maybe," "perhaps," "it seemed," "as if," and the recurrent use of the imperfect tense as well as of questions

Chapter Three

that remain unanswered. The passage below clearly exemplifies the use of such narrative strategies:

> Clara saberia talvez das incursões ao quarto de Ella, mas Renata não tinha coragem de indagar. A cunhada olharia, sorrindo, que mal tinha isso? Um quarto de doente, apenas. Ella não era um bicho. *Ou era?* diria Clara, com seus olhos bem abertos, de criança, de louca, de sábia? (84–85 [19]; emphasis in original)

The use of the imperfect tense and modalization are identified by Todorov as narrative strategies that contribute to the construction of the fantastic. The imperfect tense, in particular, "introduces a further distance between the character and the narrator, so that we are kept from knowing the latter's position" (Todorov 38–39). The reader is kept "suspended" between everyday events and the supernatural and therefore is in doubt as to what is actually taking place. The intrusion of mystery into everyday life constitutes a break in the common, acceptable order and thus discloses some hidden dimensions of "normal" life. As I have noted previously, the fantastic produces an effect of estrangement and thereby serves to highlight and address the incongruities of the established social order. Likewise, the grotesque (perhaps from the influence of German writers such as Thomas Mann and Günter Grass, whose works Luft has translated into Portuguese) is also used as a social commentary. *O quarto fechado* contains several examples of what we may characterize as the grotesque masks of femaleness. Ella's huge and lifeless body, Mamãe's grotesquely made-up face, and Clara's daily routine of making up and dressing up in order to wait for a date that never arrives, are all caricatures that hide a hollow body of unfulfilled desires, destitute of meaningful life. The three women are metaphors for everyone's hopeless and absurd wait: they all wait or have once waited for happiness, self-realization, and wholeness, when the one who *has* come indeed is death.

O quarto fechado offers examples of Luft's taste for the fantastic and the supernatural as vehicles for denouncing the failures and frustrations of the contemporary individual within the chaos and uncertainties of a social order in crisis. Although Luft's social commentary concerns everyone, regardless of sex, we cannot ignore the author's own remarks about the novel's theme (i.e., the conflicts of a female protagonist). Nor can we ignore the fact that, of the only two male characters in the book, one, Martim, serves as a counterpoint to Renata's conflicts, while, at the same time, representing the very patriarchal order that engulfs her. The second male character, Camilo, as an androgynous figure, represents, at the same time, the duality of human life, of male and female, and everyone's desire for unity. The articulation of elements of the fantastic and the grotesque, the themes of death, suicide, madness, and transgression, along with the imagery of spider webs, closed spaces, and the fog that threatens to invade the house, create a contemporary gothic novel "to demonstrate the author's contention that the norms of . . . [that society are] in and of themselves abnormal" (Quinlan, *Female Voice* 81). As in some of her other novels, Luft illustrates the difficulties faced by the female subject, divided between her own aspirations and the demands of a patriarchal social order within which self-realization and integration are nearly impossible. Death, then, may seem to be the only answer.

Lygia Fagundes Telles's *As horas nuas*

The obstacles faced by women in conflict with an inimical society is also a recurrent theme in Telles's fiction. In *As horas nuas,* her fourth novel, the author once again places the female subject at the center of the narrative, from which point she raises pressing issues for the contemporary subject, male and female. The use of the fantastic and the supernatural in *As horas nuas* serves similar purposes to those seen in Luft's *O quarto fechado,* however with different results. This is in part due to the fact that, while *O quarto fechado* leaves the reader with a deep sense of the powerlessness experienced by the characters, irony and a somewhat humorous sense of the absurd permeate Telles's novel.

Telles's use of the fantastic, the magical, and the supernatural has long been recognized and studied by the critics, but mostly in reference to her short fiction. Her novels, nevertheless, have also shown the author's skill in creating an atmosphere wherein the boundaries between the real and the supernatural are broken. In her novelistic work, Telles often reveals her "strong inclination for exploring the manifestations of the unconscious" (Lucas 288), with dream fragments playing an important part in the narrative and character development.[2] Telles utilizes dreams to create a sense of discontinuity in the characters' reality and thereby leads the reader to question the integrity of such reality. Likewise, the recurrence of omens, signs, visions, and memories, and the characters' pursuit of their meaning and echoes in real life, produce an effect of ambiguity: did it happen or was it a subjective impression on the part of the character, an impression the reader is led to share? In fact, the reliance on memories in the construction of the narrative, as in *Verão no aquário* [Summer in the aquarium] (1963), points to the very fragility of any categorization of what may be termed "real."

In the three novels published before *As horas nuas,* the most obvious sign of the fantastic is the ambiguity that results from the identification between reader and protagonist, as the reader follows the characters in their hesitation before the probable occurrence of a dream or vision and its possible meanings. In addition, Telles's first two novels—most notably *Ciranda de pedra*—are set in a gothiclike oppressive environment. However, *As horas nuas* represents a departure from the earlier novels, in the sense that the fantastic is now fully developed, constituting a main element in the narrative structure.

As horas nuas reworks the general conventions of the gothic novel, if we consider it, with Fredric Jameson (1989), a genre "in which the dialectic of privilege and shelter is rehearsed: your privileges seal you off from other people, but by the same token constitute a protective wall through which you cannot see, and behind which, therefore, all kinds of envious forces may be imagined . . . preparing to give assault" (528). In Telles's novel, the protagonist hides in the confines of her upper-class apartment, protected and cared for by an elderly maid who also serves as a channel of communication with the outside world, bringing her reports about the weather or the day's patron saint read on the wall almanac. Ironically, however, the "envious forces" threatening the protagonist are signs of the collapse, not only of her personal life—abandonment by her lover, aging, idleness—but also of the dominant social order—sexual liberation, feminist agendas—and of society in general—AIDS, urban chaos, violence. It is here that *As horas nuas* is able to give a "more substantive and formal leap" as a gothic novel, for, despite the protagonist's reactionary mentality, she nevertheless represents the crisis confronted by the individual within contemporary society. As the "victim" in this late-twentieth-century gothic, she is but a metonym for the collectivity assaulted by similar problems (cf. Jameson 529).

As horas nuas has three main focuses, just as it has three narrative voices. The central focus is occupied by the protagonist-narrator, Rosa Ambrósio, an aging, alcoholic, and decadent actress who struggles with the specter of old age. The world she sees around her is equally decadent, a society in crisis. The two other focuses of the text are centered on two strange characters that function as Rosa's alter egos. The first, Ananta, a psychoanalyst and feminist, is not a narrator, but the external, omniscient narrative voice lets the reader share her thoughts, uncovering desires and motives normally hidden behind her mask of aloofness and self-control, characteristics that contrast with Rosa's alcoholism and excess. As the protagonist's alter ego, Ananta serves as a voice to express opinions that are rebuffed by Rosa, thus establishing a dialogue that examines issues such as women's roles and feminism in Brazilian society.

Rosa's second alter ego, who is also a narrator in the text, is Rahul, a cat. Here the fantastic comes into play, no longer as "an uncanny event . . . [that appears] following a series of indirect indications, as the climax of gradation" (Todorov 171), but as a "reality" the reader has to accept without any seemingly reasonable explanation: a cat who thinks and remembers, an ironic, cynical, "Machado-de-Assis-like" observer who critically watches Rosa, making her and the others into characters in his own narrative. The creation of a cat who thinks as a human being represents a grotesque construct, for it fuses in one character both animal and human traits. At the same time, Rahul evokes the fable, also a subgenre within fantasy literature, not only because he thinks and narrates, but also because his observations and remarks seem at times to convey a moral.

Rahul, a cat with a man's name, is a lucid but marginal voice, an outside observer in the tradition of Machado de Assis's Brás Cubas.[3] In fact, Rahul's detachment from his human "fellows"

Chapter Three

is very much the same attitude that comes to characterize Brás Cubas in his "life" after death. A comparison between the last lines of *Memórias póstumas de Brás Cubas* and the following excerpt from *As horas nuas* reveals an unexpected intertextuality:

> ... Não alcancei a celebridade do emplastro, não fui ministro, não fui califa, não conheci o casamento. Verdade é que, ao lado dessas faltas, coube-me a boa fortuna de não comprar o pão com o suor do meu rosto. ... ao chegar a este outro lado do mistério, achei-me com um pequeno saldo, que é a derradeira negativa deste capítulo de negativas: —Não tive filhos, não transmiti a nenhuma criatura o legado da nossa miséria. (Machado de Assis, *Memórias póstumas de Brás Cubas* 144 [20])

> A única vantagem do bicho sobre o homem é a inconsciência da morte e da morte eu estou consciente. Resta-me o consolo da morte sem bagagem, deixo uma coleira antipulga. Duas vasilhas e uma almofada. (Telles, *As horas nuas* 114 [21])

Rahul holds a privileged position as observer/narrator/commentator of the lives of those who inhabit Rosa Ambrósio's world, because of his double marginality, as a cat living among humans, and as a cat who does not participate in a feline mode of economic exchange: since he is declawed and castrated, Rahul neither hunts nor procreates.

As one of the narrative voices, Rahul allows the author a greater distance between herself and the events and issues involving the female characters. In addition, Rahul is an obvious parallel to the protagonist, for as a cat he has nine lives to live, just as Rosa, an actress, has had several previous lives, having played different roles. The memories of their previous lives are a common point between Rosa and her cat. In a world that seems decadent and, in Rosa's existence, whose fragility is made obvious by the approach of old age and of death itself, memories are a recourse for postponing the inevitable. Memories serve to relieve the characters—as well as the reader— from a bleak reality, by bringing into it seemingly better and happier times. But the cat narrator will take away from the reader the possibility of relief when he begins to interpose within his own remembrances the painful doubt as to whether

The Gothic, the Fantastic, and the Grotesque

the memories he has been narrating are anything but fiction (see *As horas nuas* 53, 54–55, 59). According to Nancy A. Walker, it is not uncommon to find that, in writings by women, "the validity of the author's or the narrator's own perceptions is called into question and revised or reconstructed" (186). In a similar manner, Rahul questions the authenticity of his own discourse by shattering the "suspension of disbelief" that had been the contract established between the text and the reader.

This fantastic dimension of the novel, constructed around the figure of Rahul, is augmented by his narrative of having had visions, ghosts from recent times and from other lives (other incarnations) he had lived before. All this is narrated in a matter-of-fact tone that demands that the reader accept the supernatural as normal. So we may say of *As horas nuas* what Todorov did of Kafka's *Metamorphosis* (*Die Verwandlung*, 1915): "the most surprising thing here is precisely the absence of surprise" regarding events that affect the character (Todorov 169).

The reference to Kafka here is not casual, for the Jewish writer was one of Telles's favorite readings at the beginning of her career and has been an influence on her work (see Silva; Telles, "Baroness" 30). Kafka's influence may be seen in the use of metamorphosis as a means to achieve a fantastic effect. The fantastic centers now on the character of Ananta and is used to shed a new light on such trivial things as somebody coming home after a workday to an empty room, or somebody disappearing in a big city without anyone ever knowing his or her whereabouts. We come across facts like these, through the newspapers or in our own lives, with such frequency that we stop paying attention to them. Telles, however, makes clear that, while common, they are not "normal," but rather a reflection of the chaos of contemporary life. Likewise, Ananta's Spartan and orderly lifestyle is revealed to be a mask hiding the fear of the outside reality (*As horas nuas* 78). It is in this light that we can read the metamorphosis of Ananta's neighbor in the upstairs apartment:

> [Ananta] ouviu os passos circulares na ronda da fatalidade, ainda o espanto. Ainda a contenção toda feita de cálculo, ele se preparava. Quando a respiração se acelerou, vieram os espasmos, o corpo crescendo intenso com a música . . .

> até estourar em focinho, cascos, crinas. . . . O úmido resfolegar soprando furioso por entre os dentes, as veias saltadas, os olhos. O latejamento crescendo na acomodação das carnes, peles. . . . (70 [22])

Undressing upon coming home, the man takes off clothes as well as skin, removing the human mask worn on the street in order to become a horse and thus liberate himself, within the confines of his lonely apartment, as energy, strength, fury.

In Telles's novel, the horse symbolizes the unconscious and the liberated female desire. It thus presents here the same archetypal meaning Cunha has verified it to hold in erotic poetry by Brazilian women, in which animals are often used to represent the male lover (Cunha, "Desafio" 164). Through images of animals and others associated with nature, women writers give expression to female desire freed from the phallogocentric Law, and so Eros may follow its libidinal course (Cunha, "Desafio" 166). Although Cunha discusses the use of such archetypal imagery in poetic works only, it appears also in narrative fiction, as *As horas nuas* exemplifies.

Both Cunha and Mora call attention to the close relationship between eroticism and the poetic word, proposing that the poetic language may be a more welcoming vehicle for the expression of female erotica. Nevertheless, Telles is able to achieve a similar result in narrative prose by making use of the fantastic and the grotesque. Embodied in the man-horse, the grotesque stands also for female desire, as the invisible man's movements in his apartment parallel the nightly ritual Ananta enacts in her own home, of listening in fascination to her neighbor's routine (71). Later in the novel, when Ananta disappears at about the same time as the upstairs apartment is vacated, there is a suggestion that she and the man-horse had in fact achieved some kind of authentic communication, breaking the isolation that is the norm in postmodern society. In this manner, here, as in Kafka, the fantastic object is the normal, everyday human being, and the supernatural (the physical transformation of the man, Ananta's mysterious disappearance) becomes both a consequence of, or rather, a reaction to the dominant logic, and a way of highlighting the absurdity of our existence.

The Gothic, the Fantastic, and the Grotesque

* * *

Both Telles's *As horas nuas* and Luft's *O quarto fechado* offer examples of the use of the gothic novel, as well as elements of the fantastic and the grotesque, in the representation and problematization of the female body and desire by contemporary Brazilian women writers. While Luft's novel concludes on a much more pessimistic tone in regard to the perspectives (or lack thereof) that await the female subject in contemporary Brazilian society, both authors, nevertheless, find a common ground in their use of the gothic, the fantastic, and the grotesque. As Anne Cranny-Francis points out, "fantastic elements or conventions . . . disrupt the realist surface of narrative," and the lack of final resolution or explanation for events perceived as supernatural or "unnatural" maintains the disruption of the dominant discourse, which otherwise would have been reasserted, had a resolution been achieved (100, 102). The fantastic mode and the gothic genre, therefore, constitute effective vehicles to denounce the failure of traditional logic and the incongruities of the dominant value system.

Focusing on problems affecting Brazilian women of the middle classes, Telles and Luft have been successful in exposing the many ways in which late-twentieth-century society has failed to provide for the self-realization of the female subject in Brazil. Even in Telles's ironic and sometimes humorous novel, the reader witnesses the feelings of nonaccomplishment, failure, and meaningless anticipation that involve the protagonist. In Telles's Rosa, as in Luft's Renata, Clara, and Mamãe, we find well-characterized examples of how women have been alienated from their own bodies, an alienation that has often created a schizophrenic relationship between the female subject and her self; in Cixous's words: "We've [women] been turned away from our own bodies, shamefully taught to ignore them" ("Medusa" 289).

One key element contributing to what may be called a female "schizophrenia" is aging. Telles explores this issue in her novel, and much of the sense of failure and decadence that affects Rosa, and her inability to come to terms with her own body, results from her realization that she is getting old. In the next chapter, I will address the problem of aging vis-à-vis the

Chapter Three

female subject as represented in Coutinho's short fiction. Coutinho also makes use of the grotesque in the representation of the female body, achieving through it, however, a much more positive expression of female sexuality and desire. While Telles as well as Luft portray the problematic relationship between women and their bodies, many of Coutinho's women characters are able to come to terms with their sexuality, their desire, and their bodies, however imperfect. And if these women wear the grotesque mask of the Medusa, they do it defiantly, laughingly, as Cixous has proposed.

Chapter Four

Sonia Coutinho's Short Fiction
Aging and the Female Body

Cixous, in her famous essay "Le rire de la Méduse" (1975; "The Laugh of the Medusa," 1983), in which she celebrates women's sexual, erotic, and linguistic differences from men, urges us to take a new look at the Medusa. She encourages us "to look at the Medusa straight on to see her" (289) and look beyond the Freudian male fear of women's bodies, thus seeing not the scary and deadly female figure, but rather recognizing a kind of feminine beauty that is self-assertive and self-celebratory. The Medusa is "beautiful and she's laughing" (289), and Cixous invites women to laugh along.

The laugh of the Medusa resonates in Coutinho's short fiction, as her female protagonists are able to move away from the guilt that alienates women from their bodies, to a state of self-assurance and even defiance of patriarchal ideology. Coutinho seems to contradict the findings Cunha presents in her article "O desafio da fala feminina ao falo falocêntrico": guilt is certainly an element with which Coutinho's protagonists struggle, but they are often able to overcome it, coming to fully experience their sexuality. The author deconstructs various cultural myths of femininity and points toward new possibilities of self-realization for Brazilian women. Thus Coutinho, in her short stories as well as in her novels, illustrates a common element found in literature by women: the appropriation and deconstruction of cultural myths. In the process, female authors also expose the existing tension between social expectations placed on women and how much (or how little) they are willing to submit (Pratt 6–12).

Having begun to publish fiction in the late 1960s, Coutinho is considered by critics to be one of the most interesting and

Chapter Four

original fiction writers in Brazil. She has been praised for the formal aspects of her fiction, as well as for her feminist critical analysis of gender relations in Brazilian society. Since her 1971 book of short stories *Nascimento de uma mulher* [Birth of a woman], the writer has focused on the problems of women from the middle classes, showing in this early book an awareness that hers was a *female* literature: "forming a private territory, different from—but not inferior to—the male's" (Coutinho, "Sobre a escrita feminina"). Coutinho has also been striving to create a language adequate to the representation of women's social and psychological realities, and to the representation of the female body, sexuality, and desire. In her novella *O jogo de Ifá,* which I mentioned in the previous chapter, she presents a counterideological discourse that specifically deconstructs the Brazilian Romantic myths of gender, race, and national identity that I discussed in Chapter 1. Here she constructs a complex and polyphonic novel that utilizes various narrative strategies associated with an antimimetic postmodern discourse, such as metafiction, intertextuality, and historical and mythical references. In *Ifá*, the author's main proposition is to question traditional gender roles in Brazilian society and therefore to create a locus wherein the expression of the female voice as agent of the historical process, and as subject of desire, becomes possible. A strategy the author employs in *Ifá* is the use of two protagonists, Renato and Renata, who are two different projections of the same being, one masculine and the other feminine. In this way Coutinho weaves an androgynous form of writing that disrupts traditional sexual binaries and, at the same time, allows for the textual inscription of female experience.[1]

The same proposition that informs the complex narrative structure of *Ifá* will generally inform Coutinho's body of fiction. In seeking to give authentic expression to female desire and subjectivity, she makes use of different thematic elements, narrative strategies, and genres. These elements include the representation of lesbian desire, which I discuss in the next chapter; the adaptation of the detective novel genre; and the utilization of the grotesque as a strategy for the representation of the female body. As I discuss later in this chapter, Coutinho employs the grotesque allied with irony and humor in a way that celebrates the female body, in an appropriation of a literary image traditionally used by male authors to represent the threatening, devouring, monstrous, uncontrollable female.

* * *

Born in the town of Itabuna, in the northeastern state of Bahia, Coutinho moved to the capital, Salvador, while still a child, and in 1968, to Rio de Janeiro. Her novels and short stories constantly place these two cities in opposition: Salvador, more provincial and conservative, and with a strong African heritage, and Rio de Janeiro, a large cosmopolitan city where one experiences all the problems common to a big urban center, among them loneliness, isolation, and anonymity. Her protagonists, with very few exceptions, are middle-class women whose backgrounds are similar to hers, having also moved from a provincial town to Rio de Janeiro. As women they seem to suffer twice the problems commonly associated with urban life, because they find themselves split between the patriarchal tradition within which they grew up, and the new social values of the cosmopolitan city, with its promises of freedom, independence, and self-realization.

Examining the social and psychological obstacles faced by these urban women, Coutinho is rather critical of relationships between the sexes and deconstructs cultural myths of femininity, particularly those concerning female sexuality and aging. Her paradigmatic female character is a single woman, either divorced or never married, who, at middle age or approaching it, becomes aware of her social situation, of the obstacles she will have to overcome in order to achieve self-realization, and of the drawbacks that come with this achievement. Most typically, Coutinho's women characters end up rejecting marriage, as the author portrays this social institution as patriarchal and repressive for women. A cultural myth Coutinho sets out to deconstruct in her fiction is the association of physical beauty and youth with an ideal image of femininity. Aging, the passage of time, the loss of youth, has been a recurrent theme in Coutinho's fiction since her first publications. In the three volumes of short stories that follow *Nascimento de uma mulher,* the problematics of aging appear in about 60 percent of the

Chapter Four

narratives. In this regard, the stories present some common elements: the figure of a middle-aged protagonist, the realization by the characters of the passage of time, or the sudden self-awareness of the aging body. In her 1998 novel *Os seios de Pandora—uma aventura de Dora Diamante* [Pandora's breasts—A Dora Diamante adventure], Coutinho again addresses the issue, showing how aging affects a woman's sense of self.

Aging as a Social Construct

In her short stories, Coutinho generally focuses on female protagonists, some of them already at mid-life. Her characters live a historical moment when, from the 1970s on, Brazil experiences some important social and political developments that occasion changes in behavior and social practices, including sexual practices. Brazilian women then become increasingly aware of their social condition and begin to question their roles in society, seeking more mobility and participation in the public arena. This phenomenon takes place first in the large urban centers like Rio de Janeiro and São Paulo, while other regions of Brazil, like the Northeast, remain rather conservative, patriarchal societies. Nevertheless, Coutinho's female characters represent, for the most part, a new woman, "urban, free, protean and contradictory" (Helena, "Perfis" 96). Much like Coutinho herself, her characters are often women who have abandoned the limiting social roles afforded them by a conservative society in the interior of Bahia, in order to seek a new life in the cosmopolitan and (supposedly) liberating space of Rio de Janeiro. Says Coutinho in this regard: "A transformação que presenciei no Rio foi significativa para mim pelo fato de ter nascido numa cidade do interior do Estado da Bahia. De Itabuna ao Rio foi como fazer uma viagem no tempo. Ter passado parte de minha infância lá foi como viver num enclave de passado, no século dezenove" ("Sobre a escrita feminina" 22) ["The transformations I witnessed in Rio were important to me because I was born in a small town in the interior of Bahia. From Itabuna to Rio it seemed like a journey in time. Having spent part of my childhood there, in Itabuna, was like living in a pocket of the past, in the nineteenth century"].

Likewise, her female characters experience the double reality of two opposing social spaces, different not only in geographical terms but also, most importantly, ideologically different. These women, too, embark on a journey in time through memories, through recollections that confront past and present and, therefore, various dimensions of the same subject. Thus, in many stories, the narrative is centered on the protagonist who reminisces in a Proustian fashion, "with the I unfolding ideas and images, recalling flavours, smells, touches, resonances, sensations" (Kristeva, *Proust* 6). From the weaving of memories, thoughts, and sensations, the subject is able to reorganize her past and thus reach a new understanding of her present.

In the story "Uma certa felicidade" [A certain happiness], from the volume of the same title (1976; 1994), memories are juxtaposed to recent events and to present sensations, and from this juxtaposition emerges a portrait of the protagonist in the present: a lonely woman, living in Copacabana in the solitude typical of a big urban center, as she realizes her youth is behind her. "Uma certa felicidade" is paradigmatic of Coutinho's fiction as it presents several elements that characterize the author's body of work, such as the female character who leaves a conservative and repressive life in a small town to try an independent life in a large city; loneliness as the price paid for that independence; the sense of loss as a woman realizes she is not so young as she once was; and the notion of old age as a threat one tries to evade. As is characteristic of literary works that deal with the issue of aging, many of Coutinho's stories are structured around memory and recollections from the past and, at the same time, are informed by a feeling of nostalgia. Nevertheless, aging can also represent the opportunity for a new process of learning and development, if the subject is willing to redefine her (or his) sense of identity.

Aging, middle age, old age, is usually associated with loss of physical attributes, with social alienation, and with physical and mental decadence, especially when contrasted with an idealized image of beauty and youth (Woodward 98). For Coutinho's characters, however, the fundamental conflict is that between the aspirations one has when young and the realization later that those aspirations have not been fulfilled, while realizing too the dwindling opportunities one may still have of fulfilling them.

In order to understand the conflicts experienced by Coutinho's protagonists, it becomes necessary to evaluate the very definition of concepts such as "maturity," "middle age," and "old age," and to examine the expectations society has concerning the aging process. Most psychologists, sociologists, and other theorists agree today that aging is not so much a biological process, but rather a process influenced by many different factors, while "old age" represents a socio-cultural category: "Aging is much more a social judgement than a biological eventuality" (Sontag 36). The social status of an old person thus varies according to the society in which she or he lives. In traditional or primitive societies, old individuals are respected for their experience and wisdom; modern industrial and capitalist societies, in turn, privilege youth, physical appearance, and sensual pleasures. These societies value productivity measured in terms of economic profit, while "age will be devalued, making it more difficult for the elderly to have a positive self-image" (Hendricks and Leedham 9). For this reason, and because most individuals, male and female, are deeply influenced by this ideological rendering of success (youth) and failure (old age), aging is experienced as a very difficult process, and old age becomes a disease one must avoid.

But not only does the older individual hold a different status within different cultures, he or she may be considered old or still young, depending on various factors: the cultural context within which one lives; the social class; the access to medical resources; and, particularly, the sex of the individual. In Brazil, as in other Western cultures, the youth-privileging ideology is assimilated by the dominant patriarchal ideology. Together these two forms of ideological discourse establish cultural myths that define what is acceptable and desirable in a man—types of behavior, social roles, and models of physical beauty—and in a woman. Women, thus, are constantly subject to a double form of discrimination: age and sexual discrimination. These cultural myths are promoted especially by the mass media and are useful in explaining why in the movies a sixty-plus-year-old male actor can easily find his romantic counterpart in a woman half his age or younger. Susan Sontag states:

"Getting old is less profoundly wounding for a man, for in addition to the propaganda for youth that puts both men and women on the defensive as they age, there is a double standard about aging that denounces women with special severity" (32).

    This double cultural pattern responds to the different expectations society places upon a man and a woman. Masculinity is defined in terms of independence, self-confidence, and authority; femininity, in turn, is defined by such qualities as passivity, fragility, and dependence (Sontag 33). In this way, while men can develop or increase the qualities that make them "masculine," the same cannot be said of women and the characteristics that make them "feminine." In fact, in Brazil, women are able to achieve a certain authority as they get older, an authority that is linked to women's roles within the family and to their experience as mothers and grandmothers. But this form of authority grows in indirect proportion to those characteristics associated with femininity: sexual appeal, beauty, and youth. Indeed, the social value of women is still very dependent upon reproductive capacity and ability to attract the male. In other words, a woman's value in society derives in large part from marriage, from the husband, and from the family she might be able to have. Notwithstanding the scientific advances in the field of reproductive medicine, advances that in Brazil benefit only a minority, once a woman has grown older than her years of fertility, her social roles are drastically reduced, and she definitely loses her sexual "status." For most women, therefore, "aging becomes a humiliating process of gradual sexual disqualification" (Sontag 34).

Aging in Sonia Coutinho's Short Stories

The female protagonists in Coutinho's short stories live a similar reality when they suddenly become aware of the loss of youth and of their "sexual disqualification." The awareness takes the form of a painful epiphany, occasioned by the individual's experiencing a psychological disjunction. This disjunction results from the conflict among her chronological age, her emotional or subjective age (i.e., the image she has created of herself), and her social age (in other words, how society sees her). Normally, it is the recognition of her social age that elicits

Chapter Four

the epiphanic moment when the subject is made aware of the passage of time and her own aging. Therefore, the consciousness of how "old" or "young" we are depends much on the image society holds of us: "[The] recognition of our own age," says Kathleen Woodward, "comes to us from the Other, that is, from society" (104). Society thus functions as a mirror that reflects the individual's social value:

> [We] usually don't discover that we are getting old from internal clues; our first messages are liable to come from the outside. We feel no real diminution of capability, strength, or sexuality, but we are simply put into another category by the eyes of others. What these eyes tell us is that they will no longer mirror us. The eyes make no contact; they glance and slide off as if they had seen an inanimate object. (Melamed 75)

The protagonist of "Uma mulher sem nenhuma importância" [A woman not at all important] (from *Uma certa felicidade*) comes to a similarly painful realization:

> Ao se deter na esquina da Rua Bolívar, à espera de que o sinal mudasse, reparou que o rapaz guiando o grande automóvel vermelho, ali parado, olhava exatamente para a mocinha loura à esquerda, e não em sua direção. Foi quando, numa bofetada, soube que os sonhos dourados, os sofrimentos atrozes e os grandes projetos haviam ficado para trás. (121 [23])

This epiphanic moment reveals to the protagonist her somewhat new inability to arouse male desire, thus revealing her new "invisibility." At the same time, sudden images from her past come to highlight the fragility of the aspirations held in her youth, as well as the failure of any illusion of personal and social realization. What is left her is only a deep feeling of being useless, of being nobody in the consumer society in which she lives, a society of which Copacabana, its crowded streets, shops, and boutiques, is a symbol (see "Uma mulher" 122, 123).

Copacabana is the supreme representation of a bourgeois society that buys and sells the illusion of youth, beauty, and social status. The protagonist buys into this kind of delusion,

Aging and the Female Body

bearing alongside her husband the existential tediousness of her petit-bourgeois life in an apartment full of questionable symbols of status. The realization that she is getting old forces the woman to recognize her present mediocrity, while memories from her past offer little or no consolation. Few are the notes of distinction left from her youth—a passing lover, French classes at the Alliance Française—and little is equally left from her adult life. She is but a woman from the middle class, married and childless, who occupies her time worrying about her looks. Contrary to what may take place in a traditional society, where old people are valued for their knowledge and wisdom, the protagonist has no social status as an aging woman in the context of Copacabana:

> ... não tinha lição nenhuma para dar, como se acreditava, outrora, que os velhos fossem capazes de fazer. Outrora, ah, outrora, pensava-se serem os velhos depositários de mil saberes e de poderes mágicos. Agora, tudo mudava depressa demais, Copacabana era um torvelinho onde ela se sentira, hoje, uma preciosa, inútil e patética ave rara, ... ah, meu Deus, estava ficando velha e não sabia de nada. (125–26 [24])

Lost among the crowds in Copacabana, the protagonist perceives the presence of young people around her as an aggression to her self (122). However, if on one hand she feels like a victim confronting the conspicuous youth of others, on the other hand, she also feels guilt (121). The feeling of guilt and inadequacy comes from not knowing how to stop her own aging or not knowing, at least, how to disguise it under the young-looking masks offered by the cosmetics industry.

The pretense of youth is closely associated with the idea of femininity promoted by consumer societies: "To be a woman is to be an actress. Being feminine is a kind of theater, with its appropriate costumes, *decor,* lighting, and stylized gestures. From early childhood on, girls are trained to care in a pathologically exaggerated way about their appearance" (Sontag 36). In Brazil women also learn from an early age to be the focus of attention for the male gaze, while men learn to openly look at women. Such cultural patterns of behavior are reinforced by the mass media that offer cosmetics, clothing, plastic surgery,

Chapter Four

and a number of other products as a means of attaining youth, physical beauty, and sexual appeal, while these characteristics become synonymous with social power. The vehicles that recurrently sell these images—the press, cinema, television, and advertisement—most often have women as their target. The mass media thus work like "mirrors" reflecting the dominant myths of femininity as defined by a given culture. In Brazil, the ideal images of women are necessarily young looking. Thus even ads that purport to portray middle-aged individuals will show women with little or no exterior signs of aging. "Grandmothers," in turn, are generally portrayed as happy and young looking, and the only sign of aging they display is well-styled gray hair.[2] These idealized images are in conflict with the image the subject recognizes as her own, and from this conflict, in turn, results a psychological split of the subject in three entities: the inner I, or how the individual sees herself; the I in the mirror, the real but almost always unsatisfactory image the person finds in the mirror; and the idealized image conveyed by the mass media, which the consumer industry holds up as an attainable promise.

Sontag notes that women are much more prone to look at their image in the mirror than men are (36). A woman learns at an early age to be seen by the Other and learns too to look at herself in the mirror in an attempt to *verify* her own existence and to assure that the image she projects is acceptable to the dominant cultural patterns. This female dependence on the looking glass seems to be cross-cultural and is reflected in the recurrence of the mirror in female-authored literature, as Jenijoy La Belle discusses in her book *Herself Beheld: The Literature of the Looking Glass* (1988).

Mirrors are a recurrent image in Coutinho's short stories. In "Uma mulher sem nenhuma importância," the mirror exposes the first sign of the passage of time marked on the character's face: "diante do espelho, reparou que sob seu queixo, à luz implacável da cabine da loja, havia uma dupla ruga desprendendo a pele e tornando imprecisa a linha até recentemente nítida do pescoço" (121) ["standing before the mirror, under the fitting room's unforgiving light, she noticed under her chin a double wrinkle that loosened the skin and turned imprecise the until recently well-defined line of her neck"]. Her aging

Aging and the Female Body

and, therefore, her new status as a nonsexual, undesirable woman, are confirmed by the social mirror—in other words, by the male gaze that ignores her. This revelation sets her on a journey through memory, finally leading her to realize how mediocre her life has been, and how it holds no opportunities for change. As a result, the middle-aged protagonist of "Uma mulher sem nenhuma importância" arrives at a stage of self-awareness that precludes a sense of realization and integration. On the contrary, the woman is left with feelings of failure, despair, and fragmentation.[3]

* * *

Mirrors again play a significant role in the process of self-awareness associated with aging in the story "Uma certa felicidade" mentioned before. They appear numerous times in this somewhat long (forty-six pages) narrative, but are particularly important in two specific instances. One is a moment of crisis, when the female protagonist does not recognize the fragments of her image seen in several mirrors that appear to her in a dream (23). And the second moment is one of self-integration, when the character, older and more mature, is able to accept herself without conflicts or feelings of guilt:

> Nua diante do espelho, a escovar o cabelo diante do espelho, observo—minha carne macia e perecível, como uma carne que o tempo trabalhou. Não estou mais tão jovem, mas isto tem um gosto de mel e de vinho tinto, numa branda manhã de maio, no Rio de Janeiro.
> . . .
>   Corpo bronzeado e fresco e ardendo por dentro, rindo diante do espelho, dentinhos pontudos—vampira. . . . olho-me agora ao espelho e me designo: puta, que puta és. (55–56 [25])

The sense of integration the protagonist achieves comes mainly from her acceptance of her mature body and from her sexuality that she is now able to experience, freely and guiltlessly. The liberation of her sexuality is possible only after a long and painful learning process that begins with the juxtaposition through memory of past and present. This is a process of

Chapter Four

coming to terms with her past, her youth and, as a consequence, of lending new meaning to what she had been as well as to her present reality. The woman's journey through memory brings to the narrative a series of thematic elements that are paradigmatic in Coutinho's fiction. They are: the female character's previous life in a patriarchal town in the interior of Brazil; the conservative education she had received; a jealous or otherwise domineering fiancé or husband; the prospects of a "perfect" but unhappy marriage; the character finally breaking away from the repressive environment; the move to the big city and the loneliness she encounters there. These elements form the background of various female characters in many of Coutinho's short stories and in her novels.

As she grows older, the protagonist of "Uma certa felicidade" goes through a process of self-development and learning that is also sexual in nature. Gradually she learns to overcome her negative feelings toward sex by having sexual relations with different men. At the same time, her perception of her surrounding reality—the streets of Copacabana, the sounds, the bodies, the beach—becomes more and more sensual. This sensuality then spreads onto the text, lending the story an erotic quality in several different passages; for example:

> ... o homem com uma perna nua em cima da nua perna da mulher, ela falando você parece uma pantera negra, uma grande pantera calma lambendo as grandes patas negras, o homem virando-se para pegar um cigarro, é muito bonito as costas nuas de um homem, as nádegas, uma carne sólida, dura, forte e curvilínea, ao mesmo tempo, um homem feio com uma cara de felino ... (42 [26])

Eroticism will be, therefore, not only an expression of the character's sexuality, but also an important factor in the woman's self-awareness. At the same time, the use of eroticism here underlines the important role it can play in women's lives as it enables self-knowledge and self-empowerment. Thus, in Coutinho's story, the crisis that began with the realization of the passage of time and the loss of youth eventually leads the female protagonist to a sense of integration—psychological and sexual. However, the final integration of the self does not imply the crystallization of female subjectivity. Similarly to the novel *Mulher no espelho* that I discussed in Chapter 2, "Uma certa felicidade" presents a textual circularity that takes the reader from the last paragraph back to the beginning. In this way, the character is continuously engaging in her assessment of past and present, and in her redefinition of her own self. Female subjectivity, therefore, is for Coutinho a "process, a becoming, . . . an ongoing discursive practice" (Butler 33).

The conclusion of "Uma certa felicidade" clearly contrasts with that of "Uma mulher sem nenhuma importância" discussed above. In "Felicidade," the protagonist is able to break away from the patriarchal order in which she grew up and learns to live in the instability and loneliness of the big city as a form of freedom. At the same time, she is able to accept her aging body, and guiltlessly experience her sexuality. As for the character in "Uma mulher," the realization of her own aging does not lead her to self-development or to personal integration, as she is not able to change her unsatisfactory reality. While one woman takes on an active role in life, as a "vampira" ("Felicidade" 56) who looks for her own sexual and personal satisfaction, the other is unable to act, but is rather resigned to her tedious and unfulfilling married life, waiting, melancholic ("Uma mulher" 129), for old age and death. Not by chance does the author point to a connection between marriage and a woman's dissatisfaction in this story. In fact, in her fiction, marriage represents a hierarchical relationship, following the dominant gender relations that submit women to male desire. Coutinho often denounces an ideology according to which a woman's self-worth comes not from herself, but from a male figure—the father, the husband, a fiancé, or boyfriend. Marriage represents thus, as Gary Lesnoff-Caravaglia points out in "Double Stigmata: Female and Old," a path women follow because of social expectations or for the lack of other acceptable options (17).

Coutinho's protagonists, however, are most often single or divorced women. Some may still long for the sense of "security" that comes from marriage or from a stable relationship with a man. And if they have not found such a relationship by the time they are no longer young, these women look for ways of escaping from the marginal position in which society places the older single woman. This situation takes place, for example,

Chapter Four

in the story "O dia em que Mary Batson fez 40 anos" [The day Mary Batson turned forty] from *O último verão de Copacabana* [Last Summer in Copacabana] (1985). Here the female protagonist, in order to minimize the sense of isolation and loneliness, "se transformou numa mulher de constantes novos amores, não sabe como isso chegou a lhe acontecer, a ela, a maior vocação para o amor e a fidelidade eternos, entre as amigas de sua geração" (68) ["became a woman of constant new lovers, who knows how this happened to her, who had the greatest vocation for eternal love and fidelity, among the friends of her generation"]. Passing lovers, "superficial" and "provisory" ("Mary Batson" 71) friendships, help her bear the "burden" of living alone, a condition worsened by society's demands upon women. As Lesnoff-Caravaglia would explain: "Living alone is a radical change in lifestyle for many women, but the difficulties of single life are compounded by the fact that in our society women have been led to believe that they require a man to fulfill their existences" (16).

Single middle-aged women are numerous in Coutinho's fiction, but they are often portrayed with humor and irony in their attempts to disguise their age. For example, in another story from *O último verão,* "Josete se matou" [Josete killed herself], we find such a portrait: "uma mulher no início da casa dos 40, queimada de praia, os cabelos pintados de acaju, passeando na calçada com seu cachorrinho pequinês ou *poodle-toy* [sic]" (17) ["a woman in her early forties, tanned, her hair dyed red, strolling down the sidewalk with her little Pekinese dog or toy poodle"]. This image appears in Coutinho's stories with slight variations and one constant element: the dyed-red hair trying to hide the first signs of old age.

Nevertheless, perhaps more typical in Coutinho's fiction are the characters who *choose* not to marry or those who leave their unhappy marriages after becoming aware that leaving would be necessary in order to attain personal realization. The protagonist of "Uma certa felicidade," which I examined above, falls into this category. She and other characters like her break away from the patriarchal ideology in favor of self-realization—professional, emotional, and sexual. The woman able to go against this ideology can, as a result, accept her own maturity, her sexuality, and independence. However, this acceptance necessitates a certain degree of rebelliousness and marginality, which are represented in images such as "vampira" and "puta." We can infer from this that, in Coutinho's view, the self-realization of Brazilian women (including their sexual liberation) is possible only at a mature age, and it implies the deconstruction of conventional female roles and of cultural myths of femininity.

The Female Grotesque: "Cordélia, a caçadora"

The short story "Cordélia, a caçadora" [Cordelia, the huntress], from the 1978 volume *Os venenos de Lucrécia* [Lucrecia's poisons], corroborates what I have discussed concerning women's aging in Coutinho's short fiction. At the same time, it serves to illustrate the appropriation of the grotesque by the author in order to represent a transgressive and disruptive female body. As Geoffrey Harpham explains, the grotesque implies "a confusion of language categories. The word itself is a storage place for the outcasts of language" (xxi); in other words, the grotesque typifies those bodies that, because they juxtapose elements or characteristics that normally do not belong together, occupy "multiple categories" or fall "between categories" (Harpham 3). In this way, the grotesque lives at the margin of the dominant discourse and calls into question fixed categories defined by such discourse. The grotesque is thus the transgressive body par excellence.

In addition, the grotesque is profoundly associated with the female body because of the name's connotation: *grotto-esque,* cave, cavern, vessel, womb. However, while the grotesque has been used to represent the female body from a masculinist perspective, the "female grotesque" may be appropriated by women writers and artists as a category that proposes transformation. This argument is made by Mary Russo in her *The Female Grotesque:* "the female body as grotesque ... might be used affirmatively to destabilize the idealizations of female beauty or to realign the mechanisms of desire" (65).[4] It is in this manner that Coutinho employs the grotesque, as a strategy that deconstructs myths of femininity and the ideological repression of female desire.

"Cordélia, a caçadora," which won the 1977 *Revista Status* award for erotic literature, is about a middle-aged, working-class woman, never married, her hair dyed red-brown (19).

Chapter Four

Cordélia is dependent and submissive, and her constant "ar de Vítima" (19; capital letter in the original) or victim's countenance, reveals to men the easy sexual prey she is. Not that she truly enjoys sex; rather, sex is for her a means of obtaining the male companionship that validates her existence. Coutinho explains the character's submissive behavior as a consequence of two factors: the endless "Vocação para a Virtude" (19; *sic*) ["Vocation for Virtue"] and a conservative and repressive upbringing. The author describes Cordélia's situation with irony and in a tone of tragicomedy, while the use of capital letters and hyphenated phrases—two recourses Coutinho employs frequently—emphasizes its banality. In the writer's perspective, it is a situation affecting many women that originates from cultural myths society imposes on them: "Felicidade" ["Happiness"], the "Mulher Livre" ["Free Woman"], the "Mulher Casada" ["Married Woman"], and her "Deveres Conjugais" ["Conjugal Duties"] (19–23).[5] Each one of these myths implies a number of expectations placed on the female subject, and the impossibility of fulfilling them causes a kind of social schizophrenia and a deep sense of failure.

From the outset, Cordélia is presented as a failed individual, not only because she is a middle-aged and single woman or, in other words, a *solteirona* or spinster, but also because of the cultural resonance of the geographical space she occupies. Cordélia lives in a small and modest apartment in the Largo do Machado, a small area adjacent to the Flamengo district in the city of Rio de Janeiro. Since the 1970s, the Largo do Machado has become home largely to a working class and a decadent bourgeoisie that does not have the means to move to better or more influential neighborhoods. This space will contrast with another space to which Cordélia is introduced by a man she meets, Papá, who proposes marriage. Papá takes Cordélia to visit his large oceanfront apartment in Leblon, a beach district in Rio de Janeiro that symbolizes the social status of the upper classes. In addition to his luxurious apartment, Papá has other ways of impressing women: his powerful profession, lawyer, and his manly attire, suit and tie ("Cordélia" 21). All these attributes characterize Papá as powerful and authoritative; indeed, his very name suggests his position as a patriarchal figure. Thus a power relationship is established in which Cordélia submits to him, not only because of his supposed social power and wealth, but mainly because he rescues her from her degrading position as a *solteirona.*

Although the events generally follow a chronological order, "Cordélia" plays also with the subjective time frame of memory. The narrative is structured on three different time levels: the period before the protagonist meets Papá; their first encounter, the courtship, and the married life; and her new life, after Cordélia abandons him. Concomitantly, the protagonist experiences a psychological fragmentation marked by the use of different subject pronouns ("you," "I," and "we") and by the use of different verb tenses (past, present, and future). The second-person pronoun, "you," dominates the narrative, changing occasionally to the first person. This strategy allows the reader to identify the narrator as being Cordélia engaged in a dialogue with herself. It's as if the character were standing in front of a mirror and addressing her reflected image as "you." Therefore, to narrate is not here simply a memoirist activity but, rather, serves to review the past in a methodical and explanatory way. The use of first and second person pronouns also establishes a psychological distance between the character in her present reality and the woman she had been before (a victim, humble, submissive). The last part of the text, however, which narrates the events in Cordélia's life after she has abandoned her married life, suggests a sense of self-integration through the use of "we." In a similar manner, the utilization of the future tense in the last part of the story gives expression to the character's self-affirmation. This happens after she leaves Papá's home and, particularly, after she learns to take pleasure in her own body.

In "Cordélia, a caçadora," Coutinho again depicts marriage as a patriarchal institution in which women are rendered objects of male desire. Nevertheless, humor and mockery are the main strategies the writer employs to deconstruct the patriarchal order Papá embodies. After realizing that the respectful and powerful man is a fake, an old man of unconventional sexual preferences and even given to violence, Cordélia confronts the reality of marriage as a prison within which she must comply with society's demands: to keep the appearance of a normal life.

Cordélia is thus faced with two clear choices: to remain submissive and keep her social status as a married woman or to attempt to regain a sense of integrity but abandon Papá and the

Chapter Four

"Golden Myth" of marriage ("Cordélia" 27). The character opts for her freedom and independence, and from that point on, the narrative describes a process of transformation, as she moves from one social space to another: from Leblon to a solitary room in a boarding house, and from there to a studio in Copacabana. In the anonymity and turbulence of this populous district, where people from different social groups, races, and ages continuously pass each other, Cordélia sets out to construct a new sense of identity. In a dialectical relationship, this new identity is related to the character's renewed enjoyment of her body and sexuality, much like what happens in the story "Uma certa felicidade." If at first sex meant for her a tender moment with a male companion, in the end, Cordélia pursues sex solely for sexual pleasure. She has become Cordélia, the Huntress, actively seeking on the sidewalks of Copacabana young men with perfect bodies who can offer her pleasure.

In Coutinho's fiction, and especially in the stories of *O último verão de Copacabana,* the famous beach district represents a synthesis of the problems of contemporary urban life. Here it is the right background to facilitate the changes Cordélia undergoes. In spite of its decadence since the 1950s, Copacabana still stands for a beach culture centered on the body and physical pleasures. It is therefore an environment where the female character can become reacquainted with her body and her sexuality, while discovering in her sexuality a source of renewed strength and power (27). The transformation in Cordélia's inner self is externally marked by a change in her hair color now dyed "platinum blonde." Her sexual pleasure is anticipated in the self-satisfaction she derives from the smiling image in the mirror: "Olhando-nos ao espelho, veremos um rosto moreno e *voraz* sob os cabelos de palha iluminada, um rosto quase belo, de lábios úmidos, *sem o menor ar de vítima.* Esta noite mesmo, Cordélia, a Caçadora, voltará a excursionar" (27; my emphasis) ["Looking at the mirror we will see a dark and voracious face under the lit-hay-colored hair, an almost beautiful face, wet lips, showing no sign of being a victim. At this very night, Cordélia, the Huntress, will go out again"]. Once more the female subject's sexual liberation takes place only at middle age, after the deconstruction of cultural myths of romantic love, marriage, and women as submissive. At the same time, female eroticism represents not only sexual satisfaction, but also personal realization and a sense of wholeness experienced by the character.

The fact that the character's sexual liberation and personal integration happen at middle age and are marked by a change in her physical appearance is of importance. Moreover, it is very significant that the hair, a cross-cultural symbol of female sexuality, is the physical mark of her transformation. The dyed hair is the most immediate and accessible mask to cover the signs of old age. However, the red-brown tone that Coutinho often describes, represents an attempt to disguise not only the passage of time but also the mask itself. In other words, it is an artifice that tries to hide its artificiality. The "platinum blonde" color, on the other hand, is a mask that reveals itself as such and has the function of *representing* rather than disguising. The "platinum blonde" hair represents, in an extravagant and excessive manner, femaleness.

Cordélia's body/face, framed by hair of ostensibly false color, and parading on the streets of Copacabana, takes to an extreme the theatricality that marks the feminine according to Sontag. The proposition that "Being feminine is a kind of theater" (Sontag 36) complements the idea advanced by Kristeva and other feminist critics that the feminine is a social construct. In "Cordélia, a caçadora," the representation of the female body becomes, in the end, a parody of the consumer society and of the ideology that privileges feminine beauty and youth. In this sense, Cordélia is the carnivalesque body, undermining existing patterns of behavior. As the aging woman *and* the sexual woman, she challenges definitions, resists closure (cf. Armitt 69); she represents the female grotesque as Russo defines it: "the open, protruding, extended, secreting body, the body of becoming, process, and change" (62–63).

Hence Coutinho presents two types of masks. One denies the subject's aging and thus expresses the acceptance of cultural myths of femininity as youth. It implies women's compliance with "the dominant economy of desire in an attempt to remain 'on the market' in spite of everything" (Irigaray 154). The other kind of mask represents resistance and defiance of the dominant patterns of female behavior, since it opens up a space for the aging woman who wants to fully enjoy her sexuality. In other words, the defiant mask creates a social space for the female subject who refuses to act "her age" as determined by the dominant ideology. In this case, if women wish to remain "on the market" of sexual desire they may do so, not as merchandise, but rather as subjects, able to acquire the source of their own satisfaction.

The irony and humor employed in the final characterization of Cordélia are strategies that affirm Cixous's "laugh of the Medusa," and may be found in other stories by Coutinho, such as "Darling, ou do amor em Copacabana" [Darling, or of love in Copacabana] (from *Uma certa felicidade*) and in several stories from *O último verão de Copacabana*. In the latter volume, Coutinho specifically deconstructs the "mythology of mass culture, so typical of city life" (Lobo 168), playing with the image of cinema icons like Lana Turner and Greta Garbo. In deconstructing these myths, the author exposes the dominant ideology that stigmatizes older women, while her female characters search for—and many times find—ways of overcoming such ideology and its concomitant.

In the last two chapters, I have discussed some different strategies of representation employed by Brazilian women writers in depicting the female body, sexuality, and desire, and to problematize women's alienation from their own bodies. Like Luft and Telles, Coutinho utilizes the grotesque, but with different objectives and results. In appropriating the grotesque, the writer is able to create a space wherein the expression of female sexuality, unrestrained by masculinist desire, is possible. In the stories examined here, Coutinho has portrayed female heterosexual desire. In the following chapter, I will discuss how she and other Brazilian women short-story writers represent lesbian desire as a space for the unrestrained expression of female desire and sexuality.

Chapter Five

Contemporary Brazilian Women's Short Stories
Lesbian Desire

The Tradition of Lesbian Writing in Brazil

In his groundbreaking book *Sexual Textualities: Essays on Queer/ing Latin American Literature* (1997), Foster has pointed out that literary critics in Latin America have generally disregarded a tradition of lesbian writings by Latin American women (10). This is certainly true in the case of Brazil. The supposed nonexistence of such a tradition stems from the social and cultural taboos still associated with homosexuality in most segments of Brazilian society. Such taboos have given rise to the censorship and self-censorship that until recently have prevented the open expression of lesbian desire in women's literature. On the one hand, female authors who portray lesbian characters and homosexual desire between women might be identified as lesbians. On the other hand, the explicit representation of lesbian eroticism in fiction or poetry might be quickly labeled pornographic and confined to the literary ghetto of "subliterature."

The lack of recognition of lesbian characters and lesbian desire in works by Brazilian women writers is a result of the ideological "glasses" that make lesbian women invisible to the eyes of society. Sometimes it is the lesbian herself who may prefer to remain invisible rather than face the discrimination against homosexuals still pervasive in Brazil. For example, a lesbian medical doctor in the northern state of Rondônia offers her testimony: "Sometimes, I would ask myself what would happen if the people I was taking care of discovered their medical doctor was a radical and stubborn lesbian. . . . I am sure I would have to live with nasty comments and jokes. . . . there would have been no respect for my right to define my

Chapter Five

own sexuality" (Mendonça 10). Mostly, however, it is society itself that denies the lesbian woman her existence, since lesbians do not fit the acceptable definition of "femininity."

The lesbian subject radically breaks away from the established gendered patterns of behavior because she does not define herself vis-à-vis male desire or vis-à-vis the dominant system of biological reproduction and transmission of economic and ideological values. Therefore, because it is not possible to categorize her according to such cultural patterns, the lesbian woman is reduced to a nonexistence, a nonbeing, that is not named (and if she cannot be named, she does not exist), as Lillian Manzor-Coats states with unequivocal eloquence: "the lesbian exists in a vacuum of unreadability and unnameability both socially and sexually" (xxii). If this situation takes place in society, the recognition of a lesbian tradition in literature requires a certain type of reader, able to recover the lesbian subject and desire from their cultural invisibility. It becomes necessary to have a reader capable of a "queer" reading, as Gloria Anzaldúa suggests when she defends the need for a "lesbian sensibility." She writes: "Queers (including cultural Others) can fill in the gaps in a lesbian text and reconstruct it, where a straight woman might not. I am arguing for a lesbian sensibility, not a lesbian aesthetic" (257). In other words, an ideological openness that allows for a reading between the lines becomes necessary in order to uncover the palimpsest and decode the ambiguity, and at the same time, rescue female homosexuality from the marginalized space of so-called pornographic literature.

However, despite the social and cultural invisibility of the lesbian woman in Brazil, one may find a tradition of female-authored writings about lesbian themes since colonial times and the Holy Inquisition's first visits to Brazilian territory. In the mid-sixteenth century, around the time of the Council of Trent (1545–64) called by Pope Paul III, the Portuguese Inquisition was concerned not only with the persecution of Jews and people accused of witchcraft, but also with cases in which people's sexual behavior was believed to have transgressed religious or civil laws or otherwise accepted social practices. Therefore, adultery, polygamy, any sexual activity by members of the clergy, as well as sodomy—a term used to describe both homosexual acts and anal and oral sex between men and women—were perceived by the Inquisition as "erros de fé, desafios conscientes . . . à doutrina e à moral do catolicismo" (Vainfas, "Homoerotismo" 117) ["errors of faith, conscious acts of defiance . . . against the doctrine and moral of Catholicism"]. From then on, male homosexuality became an act of heresy, and homosexuals suffered the same kind of punishment as those accused of witchcraft, an accusation that led to death at the stake or, for those accused of being Jewish or observing Jewish beliefs and traditions, to death, loss of wealth and property, and disqualification of the accused's descendents (Vainfas, "Homoerotismo" 118, 119).

Unlike male homosexuality, female homosexual relationships were labeled by the Holy Office as "nefarious acts" and were not as strictly regulated. The reason for this relative indulgence was that women, confined to the private space of the home, shared a great degree of proximity and intimacy that was, nonetheless, considered normal. Still, when the Holy Office visited Brazil for the first time, twenty-nine women were called by the inquisitors, accused of "nefarious sins." From these twenty-nine, the Inquisition ultimately prosecuted seven women (Vainfas, *Trópico dos pecados* 24). Some inquisitors eventually proposed that, as long as women did not make use of phallic objects, female homosexual relationships did not constitute matters pertaining to the Holy Office. Such a proposition, that eventually led the Inquisition to concern itself only with male homosexuality, is symptomatic of a masculinist understanding of human sexuality that privileges genital penetration, and that will be pervasive in Brazil and in other Western cultures throughout much of the twentieth century. From the Inquisition's viewpoint, if genital penetration did not take place, there was no sexual act and, therefore, no "nefarious act" with which the Inquisition ought to occupy itself.

The first records of female-authored writings with a lesbian content in Brazil date from the time of the Inquisition's first visit, in the last decade of the sixteenth century. These first writings were the "cartas de requebro," lustful letters Felipa de Souza wrote to Paula de Siqueira expressing her sexual desire for the other woman. In addition to these letters penned by a woman, the testimonies of women forced to confess their "sins" to the inquisitors also recorded lesbian relationships and desire. Their testimonies, however, were transcribed by the confessors, whose male perspective overshadowed that of the confessed. According to Ronaldo Vainfas, the inquisitors could not conceive of the sexual act without the phallus and, therefore, "a sexualidade feminina registrada nos documentos da Inquisição afigura-se imperceptível, quase opaca" (Vainfas, "Homoerotismo" 135) ["female sexuality as recorded in documents of the Inquisition appears imperceptible, practically blurred"]. Ligia Bellini agrees that a heterosexual paradigm informed the interpretation and prosecution of cases of female homosexuality by the Holy Office, since theologians, jurists, and inquisitors adhered to the traditional morphology of the sexual act, central to which was the male body (cf. Bellini 69). And historian Emanuel Araújo adds in his essay "A arte da sedução: Sexualidade feminina na Colônia" [The art of seduction: Female sexuality in the Colony]: "Os homens, decididamente, não entendiam o que se passava sexualmente entre duas mulheres. Na cultura misógina, homem era homem e mulher era mulher: o ato sexual só podia ser compreendido com a presença todo-poderosa do pênis, e portanto as mulheres só encenavam um simulacro do verdadeiro coito" (67) ["Men definitely did not understand what could happen sexually between two women. In a misogynist culture, a man was a man and a woman was a woman: the sexual act could only be conceived in the all-powerful presence of the penis; thus women were just representing a simulacrum of the true coitus"]. For this reason, the Inquisition ultimately categorized female homosexual relationships as acts of "*molície*" (which can be understood as *languor* or *lust*), less serious than "nefarious acts."

Confined to the enclosed space of the household, Brazilian women had their literary activities limited to the private and intimate production of letters and diaries for the next three centuries. With the exception of some isolated names, only in the nineteenth century does Brazil witness an increase and continuity in the literary production of female authors. From the late nineteenth century onward, the number of women who wrote for a public, even if under pseudonyms, kept expanding. This phenomenon has been studied by June Hahner in her work on nineteenth-century women's periodicals in Brazil and, more

Lesbian Desire

recently, by scholars who have been engaged in the critical recovery of female-authored writings and the reevaluation of Brazilian women writers in the early twentieth century and before. An examination of this female-authored literature aimed for the public reveals the expression of lesbian desire since the first decades of the 1900s. However, the kind of "queer" reading suggested by Anzaldúa is necessary in order to determine the existence of an early lesbian tradition in writings by Brazilian women authors. In this manner, it is possible to identify the representation of lesbian desire, for example, in poems by Gilka Machado—as I have discussed in Chapter 2— as well as in works by other writers mentioned here before, such as Nogueira Cobra, Rachel de Queiroz, and Lispector.

Since her first novel, *Perto do coração selvagem,* Lispector has dealt with female desire and sexuality, albeit in a latent or very implicit manner. Generally, that is how the author has addressed female sexuality in her novels and short stories: through a highly lyrical and metaphorical language. In this way, issues concerning sexual relations and sexual satisfaction seem to be all but missing from her fiction, in spite of the central position the female body occupies in her narratives. This centrality is due in part to the predominance of women characters and of a woman's perspective in Lispector's texts; but most importantly, it originates in the corporeality the writer lends her characters' mental and psychological processes. This brings into the text an erotic drive that pervades her discourse, intertwined as it is with the core aspect of Lispector's literature: the search for knowledge and self-knowledge.[1] In Lispector, eroticism is concomitant with a process of self-awareness and sensual awareness of the surrounding environment. Sexual desire —expressed as masturbation, heterosexuality, or homosexuality—is enveloped in a form of elusive language that also describes the character's inner reality and perception of the outside reality. In this way, in Lispector's texts, the "erotic impulse is muted, carefully coded in deeply poetic language" (Fitz 64).

Lispector's "O corpo" (1974; "The Body," 1989), one of her rare texts to focus openly on homosexuality, and which has received considerable critical attention, constituted a major departure from the author's earlier works.[2] In this story about the domestic and sexual relationship among a man, Xavier, and

Chapter Five

his two lovers, Carmem and Beatriz, Lispector is very explicit about the homosexual relationship in which the two women eventually engage. Explicit though it is, this is one of the least erotic of Lispector's texts. The language here employed is stark and colloquial; the sentences are short and provide a minimum of information about the characters and their situation; and the narrative perspective is exterior rather than focusing on the characters' inner, psychological reality. In short, the text lacks the erotic quality characteristic of Lispectorian discourse and, at the same time, the sexual situations involving the three characters do not intend to elicit any erotic pleasure in the readers.

What Lispector does achieve in "O corpo" is to lead her readers into estrangement, and thus into a critical stance regarding the unusual—but socially sanctioned—sexual contract among Xavier, Carmem and Beatriz, the women's reaction to his phallocentric position, their lesbian relationship, and, finally, Xavier's murder. Nelson H. Vieira asserts, "The implications concerning society's reactions in this story . . . translate into Clarice Lispector's strategies for conveying indirect sociological criticism about social repression and the potential rebelliousness in women" (78). Notable in this story is how society, as represented by the police, reacts to Carmem and Beatriz's lesbian identity. As Vieira argues, the two women's ". . . actions and lesbian relationship would corrupt or shatter social and sexual morality," and thus they "are allowed to go free" (78), as long as they move to Montevideo. Lesbianism and the lesbian subject are deemed more dangerous and subversive to the social fabric than male polygamy, or murder, and for this reason the two lesbians are banished from the country or, in other words, made invisible in Brazilian society.

* * *

In his pioneering book *O lesbianismo no Brasil* [Lesbianism in Brazil] (1987), one of the rare studies of this topic, Luís Mott presents detailed research on lesbians in Brazilian literature. His extensive survey goes from fourteenth-century Portuguese literature to the literary production in Brazil in the early 1980s. His criterium for the selection of texts is the presence of lesbian characters or lesbianism as a theme. Mott includes mainly works by male authors, medical manuals or studies of psychology, and even foreign works that were translated and published in Brazil. Few, however, are the works authored by women, which suggests the critical difficulties involving the identification of a female tradition of lesbian literature. Nevertheless, Mott identifies the 1926 novel *Vertigem* [Vertigo] by Laura Villares, a writer all but unknown today, as the first literary work by a Brazilian woman to give expression to lesbian desire. According to the critic, the story line in *Vertigem* recalls the homosexual encounter between Léonie and Pombinha in Azevedo's *O cortiço*. The depiction of lesbianism in *Vertigem*, however, was not as "violent and carnal" as in the naturalist novel, possibly because "being a woman writer, her self-censorship was stronger" than that Azevedo might have experienced (Mott 85).

Mott's assessment of Villares's novel brings up the important issue of how censorship and self-censorship can affect female literary expression. As I have previously discussed in Chapter 2, self-censorship can be responsible for silencing the various forms of expression of female eroticism. But in actuality, self-censorship stems from the social practices that seek to control female sexuality, as well as from the problems a woman writer encounters when searching for a language adequate to the representation of her voice, her body, her sexuality. Therefore, given the urgency to overcome centuries-old social and cultural obstacles, Cixous exhorts us: "Woman must write her self: must write about women and bring women to writing, from which they have been driven away as violently as from their bodies" ("Medusa" 279); and later: "Where is the ebullient, infinite woman who, . . . kept in the dark about herself, . . . hasn't been ashamed of her strength? Who, surprised and horrified by the fantastic tumult of her drives (for she was made to believe that a well-adjusted woman has a . . . divine composure), hasn't accused herself of being a monster?" (Cixous, "Medusa" 280).

Immersed in a culture in which male pornography may be mistaken for eroticism, and eroticism, in turn, considered pornography, a woman's expression of her sexuality and her erotic experience is still quite problematic. More so is the representation of lesbian sexuality, since female homoeroticism radically disrupts the dominant gender relations, given that it excludes the male figure and gives women agency, allowing them to escape the traditionally passive role of objects of male desire. In this way, lesbian desire as represented in works by Brazilian women writers is not only an important dimension of female sexuality, but also serves to expose and question the social control of the female body. Lesbianism opens up a space that allows women's personal and sexual realization; a space wherein the mutual identification between two equal beings makes possible the female subject's sense of integration. Contemporary feminist theorists such as Cixous, Kristeva, and De Lauretis, among others, have located the origins of the physical and psychological identification between women in the Semiotic, a period when the child is in perfect symbiosis with the mother. This first stage of unity will have an influence upon the subject's later relationships and is the origin of women's flowing sexuality (rather than localized on one sexual organ) and openness to bisexuality.[3]

The physical and psychological identification between two women in a lesbian relationship is well characterized in Myriam Campello's lesbian novel, *Sortilegiu* [Sortilege] (1981). In the novel, the protagonist, Ísola, meets and falls in love with Marina, a strange, mysterious Tarot card reader who becomes Ísola's lover. When they first meet, "Ísola sentia a tepidez daquele corpo refletido sobre o seu no espelho, tocando-a, como se a fusão das duas imagens produzisse calor" (*Sortilegiu* 47) ["Ísola could feel the warmth emanating from that body reflected over hers in the mirror, touching her, as if the fusion of those two images produced heat"]. The image of the two bodies juxtaposed in the mirror foreshadows their first sexual encounter. When it takes place, one woman's body functions as a reflection of the other's, and both women experience physical integration and reciprocity in giving and receiving pleasure: "Marina . . . navegava Ísola também multiplicando-se, desdobrada e vária como um prisma sob a luz. Ísola/Marina se desencadeavam prazer como o vento no capim ondulante" (65) ["Marina navigated Ísola, she too multiplying herself, unfolded and various like a prism under light. Ísola/Marina offered each other pleasure like the wind on the wavering grass"].

Married to the king of Joralemon, an imaginary country, Ísola nevertheless finds in the other woman a new kind of nourishment, the full realization of her sexuality, her psychological and emotional satisfaction, as well as a sense of integration Ísola had not found with her husband: "Havia em Marina uma espécie de comida que não encontrava em Leandro" (65) ["There was in Marina a kind of food she did not find in Leandro"]. In this way, her relationship with Marina will nourish and sustain Ísola in her search for a more authentic self-identity. In fact, Ísola's search is announced in the novel's very title, which means in Portuguese *escolha de sortes* or "casting of lots" or, more literally, "choice of destinies." That is what the novel's protagonist is faced with: having to make a choice that will determine her fate and, more importantly, her sense of self.

Sortilegiu is a rather daring novel in its explicit representation of lesbianism. The story focuses on the sexual relationship between the two female characters but succeeds also in portraying them in all their human complexity, particularly the protagonist. Making the female erotic experience central to the narrative, the author is able to represent lesbian eroticism in an unveiled manner through the use of a very lyrical language that is, nonetheless, not abstract, ambiguous, or vague in any way. The explicit quality of Campello's lesbian novel is noteworthy if we consider the strong censorship still prevalent through the end of the previous decade, when the novel was written. In this regard, however, the narrative temporal and spatial frame has an important function. The novel is set in an old, medieval-like time, and the setting is that of castles and knights; thus the author creates an atmosphere of legend, magic, and mystery, elements suggested in the title of the novel. In fact, it should be noted that the spelling *sortilegiu*, with a final *u,* is not Portuguese but rather Medieval Latin.

Most of the narrative events take place against this background, with the protagonist briefly going into the "modern section of Joralemon" (55). Here elements of the North-American culture are abundant: "Haagen-Dazs," the subway, "structures of glass and steel," as well as references to Penn Station, the Brooklyn Bridge, and the streets of New York. In her

Chapter Five

construction of the narrative setting—both the anachronistic space of castles and knights and the foreign space of the United States—the author makes use of a strategy that provides for herself and for her readers a distance from the protagonist's life experiences. It may be inferred that this strategy is a way of avoiding censorship, from publishers, literary critics, or the public. In any case, the importance of Campello's lesbian novel lies in its open representation of the erotic relationship between two women, described in an often-poetic language, yet without subterfuges. In this way, Campello depicts lesbianism as a sexual, psychological, and emotional space wherein women's self-realization becomes possible.

Annis Pratt, in *Archetypal Patterns in Women's Fiction* (1981), affirms that "Through the experience of Eros with other women, . . . women experience themselves for the first time not as others but as essences, reaching that place in their consciousness where they can tap the sources of their own libidinal energy" (112). Thirteen years later, in *The Practice of Love,* Teresa De Lauretis comes to a similar conclusion, stating that lesbian desire "affirms and enhances the female-sexed subject and represents her possibility of access to a sexuality autonomous from the male" (xvii). The concept of an autonomous female sexuality stands in opposition to a sociocultural discourse that privileges male over female desire, while defining women's bodies exclusively within the established gender hierarchy. Therefore, lesbian sexuality and desire can be understood as a rejection of the dominant system or, in other words, as the "act of resistance" proposed by Adrienne Rich in her well-known essay "Compulsory Heterosexuality and Lesbian Existence" (1980).

De Lauretis sees "the figure of the lesbian in contemporary feminist discourse [as representing] the possibility of female subject *and* desire: she can seduce and be seduced, but without losing her status as subject . . ." (156; author's emphasis). De Lauretis refers to the theoretical place lesbianism can occupy in feminist criticism and, I would add, in literary discourse: "a place from where female homosexuality figures, for women, the *possibility* of subject and desire" (De Lauretis 156; author's emphasis). She continues:

> To the extent that all women have access to that place, female homosexuality . . . guarantees women the status of sexed and desiring subjects, wherever their desire may be directed. . . . the desire expressed in the figure, in the trope, of female homosexuality may be predicated unconditionally of the female subject; it becomes one of her properties or constitutive traits. . . . [and] it need not be confined in the patriarchal frame of a "heterosexual love story." (156–57)

De Lauretis's theoretical proposition offers a useful approach to understanding and situating lesbian desire and the lesbian subject in the short stories I discuss later in this chapter. In Van Steen's "Intimidade," Coutinho's "Fátima e Jamila," Campello's "A mulher de ouro," Telles's "A escolha," and Denser's "Tigresa," the representation of lesbian desire and sexuality privileges women's agency and, at the same time, stages a critique of the dominant gender system.[4] While "A escolha" tells of a lesbian relationship that took place in the recent past, outside the narrative frame, the other texts are erotic short stories that defy the kind of masculinist sexual fiction in which female homosexuality serves as a locus of pleasure for the male voyeur. Therefore, lesbian desire constitutes a rupture with the socio-sexual context defined by patriarchy and a disruption of gender relations framed by the "heterosexual love story." The expression borrowed from De Lauretis points to the ideology that binds women to certain social and narrative roles (e.g., the virgin woman awaiting marriage, the "easy" woman, or the prostitute). This explains why the very word *love* is at times rejected in the lesbian narrative economy: it is ideologically charged with connotations of romantic love, hierarchical relationships, power, and submission.

Lesbian Desire in Late-Twentieth-Century Brazilian Short Stories

The stories I chose to discuss in this chapter are representative of a lesbian tradition within Brazilian women's literature. However, one should not overlook the fact that characterizing them as lesbian fiction can be problematic, not only because of the issues concerning censorship and self-censorship discussed before, but also because of the complex critical discussion on the definition of "lesbian literature." Critics such as Bonnie Zimmerman, Barbara Smith, Lillian Faderman, and Marilyn R. Farwell defend different and sometimes contradictory explanations of what constitutes "lesbian literature." Zimmerman categorically affirms that "the nature of lesbian fiction makes it impossible to separate the text from the imagination that engenders it" (15). Thus the categorization of the lesbian text depends upon the author's intentionality or, perhaps, upon whether or not the author is a homosexual. For Smith, the defining element of lesbian literature is the textual critique of heterosexual institutions (188). On the other hand, both Faderman and Farwell point to the difficulties and complexity of the issue and see the reader as the "locus of the lesbian in the lesbian text" (Farwell, *Heterosexual Plots* 7). In other words, the reader (or critic) is the agent who can recognize the identifying elements of a lesbian narrative or poem.

In this way, both Faderman and Farwell reiterate the need for a kind of reading that will name—and consequently confer existence to—lesbian desire and the lesbian subject, even if the text itself does not explicitly do so. This is what Anzaldúa identifies as a "queer" reading, and which I accomplish in my analyses of these short stories. It is my intention, particularly in regards to Van Steen's, Telles's, and Coutinho's stories, that my reading will make obvious evidence that lies in the subtexts, therefore foregrounding the lesbian subject and lesbian desire in these narratives.

A "queer" reading as described above is particularly valuable in the Brazilian context, considering the ambiguity and contradictions involving sexual relations, sexual behavior, and sexual identity in the country. Brazilians have tended to reject strict terms of (self-)definition, and this rejection concerns not only race and ethnicity, but also sexual preference. In spite of Brazil's *machismo*—or perhaps in part because of it—there is today a considerable segment of society that experiences homosexuality and bisexuality without finding it necessary to categorically define its identity. The rejection of a rigid and exclusive identity can be understood as part of the process of sexual liberation that has taken place in Brazil since the late

1960s. For Richard Parker (95–97), the refutation of rigid sexual categories is linked to the emergence of a new discourse he identifies with an intellectual elite in Brazil, but that in fact can be found, albeit inconsistently, throughout different social groups.

The above considerations are pertinent for the analysis that follows. For example, not all the characters in these short stories would identify themselves as lesbians. In Van Steen's "Intimidade" and Coutinho's "Fátima e Jamila," the main characters are married women who experience a moment of sexual desire for each other. These two stories represent examples of what George E. Haggerty and Zimmerman, in the introduction to *Professions of Desire* (1995), identify as "the historical phenomenon of 'romantic friendship' among married women" (3). Pratt makes a similar observation, noting the existence of a long tradition in women's literature of "a strong, if muted, bonding among women. . . . For all its ambivalence women's fiction has not always muted the depth of women's feelings for each other" (96). In Van Steen's and in Coutinho's stories, both authors make use of ambiguity and suggestion—and in Coutinho's specific case, of strong imagery—in order to create texts with a clear erotic overtone; thus it is possible to read them as an expression of lesbian desire. In a discussion of Anglo-American literature from the 1800s, Vinetta Colby makes a pertinent comment, stating that passion between women in female-authored fiction often "is sublimated in relationships that modern readers would immediately designate as lesbian" (qtd. in Pratt 96).

"Intimidade" and "Fátima e Jamila" present similar narrative situations: each depicts two women characters talking to each other within the intimate space of the home. However, each story contains a fundamentally *carnal* eroticism that allows the reader to pinpoint the homosexual desire that flows throughout the text. The element of "carnality" distinguishes the situation lived by the characters from a simple friendship between women. For Catherine Stimpson, in fact, this element identifies the lesbian as "a woman who finds other women erotically attractive and gratifying." She adds: "Of course, a lesbian is more than her body, . . . but lesbianism partakes of the body. . . . That carnality distinguishes it from gestures of political sympathy with homosexuals and from affectionate friendships in which women enjoy each other, support each other" (301). While I maintain the inappropriateness of rigid sexual categories when applied to the Brazilian context, I agree with Stimpson in her assessment of the centrality of the body and of the erotic experience in the understanding of lesbianism and of the lesbian subject. In other words, what I consider valid in Stimpson's position is that it excludes any simple demonstration of friendship or political support among women, and proposes, on the contrary, the homosexual erotic expression as a distinctive element.

Other issues concerning lesbian desire are raised in Telles's "A escolha" and in Campello's "A mulher de ouro." Both stories, albeit with different approaches and styles, problematize gender relations in Brazilian society and, at the same time, raise the issue of the lesbian's social invisibility and "unnameability." While Telles employs with her usual mastery the ambiguity that characterizes her fiction, Campello weaves in her text a strong tone of defiance. In "A mulher de ouro," she makes use of humor and sarcasm as forceful narrative strategies in order to open a space for the representation of lesbian desire. In spite of the differences between them, the reader finds in both stories a textual *excess*—the ambiguity not easily clarified, the narrative voice's defiant sarcasm—originating precisely in the excess that culturally marks the lesbian body and desire. In many Western cultures, the female body is commonly associated with a notion of excess because of its capacity to *ex-cede,* expel, overflow (vaginal secretions, menstruation, giving birth, etc.). Female sexuality is thus excessive, and the dominant discourse tries to control this excess through various social and cultural mechanisms (Foucault, *History of Sexuality. An Introduction* 104 ff.). The lesbian body, in turn, can be considered twice as excessive because it "exceeds [the gender] system by being what the system constructs as the ultimate threat: a female body, a woman's sexuality, independent of the male" (Farwell, "Lesbian Narrative" 161). Therefore, the lesbian body constitutes the "monster" par excellence, in opposition to the phallic discourse that aims at subjecting chaos and excess to the phallocentric order (see Harris 6).

This excess is "shamelessly" proclaimed by Campello's protagonist-narrator, while in Telles's story, it lies within the reticence, the ambiguity, within that which is not named but whose presence is very palpable. These two stories, as well as Denser's "Tigresa," necessitate a kind of reading that acknowledges the text's economy and how it disrupts traditional narrative as well as gender categories (Farwell, *Heterosexual Plots* 8–9). The lesbian text, says Farwell, presents "a disruptive female body that reorders the traditional narrative structure" ("Lesbian Narrative" 165). Diana Marini, the protagonist in "Tigresa," embodies this disruptive and excessive female presence, from whose central position the text is woven as a transgressive and somewhat chaotic discourse, critical of sociosexual relations within the Brazilian bourgeoisie.

"Intimidade" and "Fátima e Jamila": Lesbian Desire and the "Heterosexual" Woman

In 1977, Van Steen, along with Coutinho, won the *Revista Status* award for erotic literature. Van Steen's fiction often focuses on issues concerning the characters' sexual identity and tends to disrupt gender categories. Her female protagonists are frequently depicted in a search for personal and sexual realization, striving to achieve a sense of identity. Within the context of Brazilian patriarchal society, it is not uncommon for these women to fail in their search, which may lead them to create alternative spaces wherein the female subject's personal and sexual realization becomes possible. In "Intimidade," the homosexual desire shared by the two characters, Ema and Bárbara, represents such an alternative space.

"Intimidade" constitutes a snapshot of the two women's everyday life. The story will reveal, however, another level of reality, deeper and more intimate, beyond the routine events. From this newly unveiled reality, the intimacy of the title acquires a new dimension. Ema and Bárbara are inseparable friends who look alike; their husbands work together, and the two women got pregnant and had children at about the same time. In this way, everything works to reinforce the idea of identity between the two women. The narrative depicts them talking to each other, alone, late at night, while the children sleep and the husbands have gone out. Thus the two women are able to enjoy one of their "raros instantes de intimidade . . . tão bons" (68; "moments of intimacy . . . so rare and so pleasant"; 50).[5] This break in their routine contrasts with their everyday lives centered on the system of a "compulsory heterosexuality." In the story, the two husbands represent patriarchal culture, and the male presence implies the nullification and silencing of the woman: "Se o marido estivesse em casa a obrigaria a assistir à televisão, porque ele mal chegava, ia ligando o aparelho, ainda que soubesse que ela destestava sentar que nem múmia diante do espelho" (66; "If her husband were around he'd make her watch television, because the second he got home he turned on the set, though he knew she hated sitting like a mummy in front of the TV"; 48). Contrary to this quotidian scene revolving around male desire, the female friend's presence generates for each woman an atmosphere of intimacy, identity, and unity, allowing them to act spontaneously, to be themselves, without feeling repressed in any way: "Um sentimento de liberdade interior brotava naquele silencio" (68; "A feeling of inner freedom bloomed in that silence"; 51).

Having a rather banal situation as a background, in which sexual desire seems to be buried by domesticity, the narrative begins to provide isolated signs of the women's corporeality, of the physical dimension each one acquires in the other's imagination. Watching Bárbara, Ema sees "uma linha de luz dourada [que] valorizava o perfil privilegiado" (65; "a golden shaft of light [that] accentuated her attractive profile"; 48); Bárbara, in turn, "looked admiringly" at Ema, her "cabelos soltos, caídos no rosto, [que] escondiam os olhos cinzas, azuis ou verdes, conforme o reflexo da roupa" (66; "loose strands of hair [that] hid her eyes, gray, blue or green, reflecting whatever color she wore"; 48). And later: "Cintura fina, pele sedosa, busto rosado e um dorso infantil. . . . Louras e esguias, seriam modelos fotográficos, o que entendessem, em se tratando de usar o corpo" (67; "Narrow waist, satin skin, pink breasts, her back sleek as a child's. . . . Thin and blond, they could be photographers' models, or anything else they wanted if they were to make use of their bodies"; 50). Fragmentary at first, these textual marks situate the female body at the center of the narrative economy. In addition, they hint at the homosexual desire the two women experience when they go into Ema's room and take their clothes off in order to compare the size of their breasts, touching and caressing each other. Noteworthy too is the enunciation and displacement of objects normally eroticized in a male discourse, such as the bra, the bedroom, and the new sheets on Ema's bed. Shown here as part of the everyday domestic life, such objects seem to lose their erotic quality. However, they in fact work together to construct a new kind of eroticism that originates exclusively in the female body and desire. At the end of the narrative, after they live a moment of desire and pleasure, the characters experience conflicting feelings. Thinking of their domestic lives brings a "tristeza delicada, de quem está de luto" (68; "delicate sadness, like someone in mourning"; 50), but at the same time, they feel a "sentimento místico, meio alvoroçado, de alguém que, de repente, descobriu que sabe voar" (68; "mystical feeling, almost elation, like someone who has suddenly discovered she can fly"; 51). Thus lesbian desire constitutes a rupture in the quotidian existence and is represented in the text as a space of self-liberation and personal and sexual satisfaction for the female subject.

* * *

In Coutinho's "Fátima e Jamila" too, lesbian desire constitutes an alternative space that isolates and joins the two women characters in the story, insulating them from the larger outside space of male power and desire. The latter is clearly described at the beginning of the narrative:

> Sentado à cabeceira da mesa comprida armada na varanda dos fundos, benevolente e soberano como um chefe patriarcal, o Marido presidira o encontro de Homens em Trajes Escuros e as mulheres de cabelos em penteados altos, roupas volumosas enfeitadas com rendas e jóias em demasia: dignos representantes da Nobreza Colonial Extinta, exibindo um antigo luxo trazido em caravelas de Portugal. ("Fátima e Jamila" 132 [27])

Chapter Five

The capital letters are a strategy commonly employed by Coutinho in her fiction. Here they are used to present the dominant social order through critical lenses, characterizing it as an anachronistic colonial ideology. This larger reality serves as a backdrop to the intimate space that is established between the two female characters. In terms of narrative structure, it functions like a first "establishing shot" taken by a movie camera. Thus the "camera" first presents the social context of the narrative action, and then begins to close the shot until it focuses exclusively on the two women. However, the narrative action itself is practically nonexistent. In this respect, Coutinho's story is less explicit than Van Steen's is in its representation of lesbian desire. For example, the text contains no references to caresses or any physical contact as in "Intimidade." Nevertheless, the narrative displays a strong erotic quality constructed by the choice of words and in the words themselves. More than anything, the erotic resides in the text itself, in the words impregnated with and emanating smells, tastes, an excess of life, that connote lust and sensuality. For example:

> A brisa vinda do mar, lá longe, espalha pela sala o aroma pesado das frutas empilhadas nas cestas . . . : umbus cuja acidez termina em doçura final dissolvendo-se na boca, bananas pontudas e recurvas como adagas, mangas rosadas cabendo na mão feito um seio ovalado e cujo grosso caldo amarelo escorre pelo queixo, cajus quase púrpura, o travo das pitangas. (131–32 [28])

The narrative appeals to all the senses, including hearing. For example, Coutinho uses words evocative of exotic places, or that convey sensuality, as they unfold phonetically in alliterations and proparoxytones: "a requintada *pourriture* do Tokay"; "sabores aveludados e sápidos"; "As sombras já se alongam entre os troncos dos *flamboyants* e das acácias," etc. ("Fátima e Jamila" 133) ["the Tokay's sophisticated *pourriture*"; "velvety and sapid flavors"; "the shadows elongated among the acacia and the flamboyant trees"]. Sylvia Molloy's commentary about eroticism in literature by Latin American women writers is pertinent here:

> Women's eroticism appears to express itself in forms more diverse . . . than the primarily sexual. . . . What one often

> finds in women writers, in terms of erotic desire, is a slippage from sex to text: the text itself is an erotic encounter in which the poet [or the writer] makes love to her words. . . . Not limited to the physical body, and certainly not repressing it, desire in these cases extends to the body of writing. (120)

Coutinho employs language in order to construct a highly sensual narrative. In addition to using the sound of words to achieve a sensual effect, she makes use also of images and metaphors such as an orchid Fátima picks up from the table. The orchid is a cross-cultural symbol of female sexuality, but here it is described in detail by Fátima, who states that flowers are hermaphrodite (133). This statement highlights the presence of various sexual symbols, both masculine and feminine, in the preceding paragraph and in other passages of the story.

The text continues to emphasize the excessive quality of the elements that form the narrative setting: the heat, the stifling air, the different smells, and the exuberant vegetation. These elements reflect the culturally perceived excess of female sexuality, conveyed also in the way Fátima is described: "o ardor maduro do corpo de Fátima era o do excesso de sumo que precede a decomposição" (135) ["the mature ardor of Fátima's body was that of the fruit's excessive juice that precedes its decomposition"]. In order to achieve the overall effect of sensuality, they are woven together with the few physical descriptions of Fátima (Jamila remains "hidden" from the reader, who sees only her back), her few, yet mysterious gestures, and with the stories of love and seduction she tells her friend. The conversation, apparently purposeless, eventually takes the reader to an important scene of seduction: "Quem você vai enfeitiçar, desta vez?" (134) ["Whom are you going to bewitch now?"], asks Jamila. The answer lies not in the events, actions, or plot, but rather at a textual level, in the words themselves. In this way, lesbian desire is condensed in a series of images metonymically linked:

> Como se repentino o cantor de flamenco rompesse, no grito pungente da saeta, o silêncio branco/negro de casas caiadas sob o sol vertical do meio-dia—com estranha inquietação, . . . um arrepio de presságio descendo-lhe pelos rins, quem sabe a Compreensão, Fátima se voltou e viu o rosto de Jamila. (135 [29])

Chapter Five

Fátima and Jamila thus face each other in the ambiguous game of seduction, in which each one plays the role of seducer and seduced. Lesbian desire places both women in a position of agency, a position frequently forbidden women within the dominant gender system, as Coutinho reminds us here and in other stories.

Márcia Denser's Transgressive Discourse

Diana Marini, a writer, the paradigmatic protagonist and cynical narrator in Denser's short stories, constantly transgresses the established patterns of feminine behavior by playing the role normally attributed to men within gender relations. Diana is the huntress who actively looks for pleasure for the sake of pleasure.[6] Diana is not a passive woman who awaits the masculine initiative in matters of sex, nor is she the prostitute willing to satisfy male desire. Diana looks for the satisfaction of her own sexuality and for that she makes use of "a própria arma do dominador" ["the [male] conqueror's very weapon"], in other words, the erotic seduction. For this reason, "o homem, acostumado a 'controlar' vê-se ineficiente diante dela" (Franconi, "Eroticism" 57) ["the man, used to 'controlling,' finds himself inefficient before her"]. Playing the active role in the game of seduction, Diana subverts gender relations without, however, actually rupturing them: ". . . in the regime of compulsory heterosexuality, women's power of seduction . . . is the flip side of their powerlessness as objects of seduction" (De Lauretis 155).

Diana hunts her sexual (male) prey, but the traps she uses are the so-called feminine artifices, apparently submitting to the men with whom she has sex. Nevertheless, she is very aware and very critical of her position as a woman vis-à-vis male desire. Diana's sexual behavior is subversive of gender roles because she rejects the social mechanisms of control of the female body and declines to take part in the system of procreation and transmission of economic and ideological values. Still, it is Diana's cynicism as narrator, as much as Denser's own narrative style, that destabilizes the dominant gender system. Diana's cynical meditations on the sexual act and on the nature of relations between men and women critically expose the hypocrisies permeating Brazilian society, particularly its large middle class. Denser's style underscores the character's meditations, through the use of stream of consciousness and a rapid, almost chaotic rhythm that conveys to the reader a sense of urgency, frustration, and even despair. In this way, the author makes clear how men and women's mechanical behavior toward sex, excessive self-indulgence, and desire for power make it impossible to achieve the authentic expression of Eros.

Denser utilizes eroticism in order to examine power relations not only between men and women, but also between individuals from different social classes and racial groups. In fact, Diana Marini, in spite of inverting the gender hierarchy and displaying types of behavior generally unacceptable for women, shares much of the ideological prejudices of the Brazilian bourgeoisie, especially regarding social classes but also in relation to homosexuality. The short story "Tigresa" exemplifies well these two types of ideological prejudice, of race and of sexual orientation. In the story, the protagonist does not hide her disdain for members of the lower classes: "Olhei-o dum jeito de estremecer até os bagos do seu tataravô, se é que essa gente tem raça. Brotam da lixeiras" (123–24) ["I looked at him in such a way as to make even his great-great-grandfather's balls tremble, if these people have any ancestry at all. They sprout from the trash"]. Nor does she try to disguise her discomfort when faced with another woman's desire for her: "Aquele olhar untuoso e apaixonado de odalisca me incomodava" (132) ["That impassioned and syrupy stare, like an odalisque's bothered me"].

"Tigresa" is an excellent example of Denser's transgressive narrative: it is fragmented, fast, and chaotic, with interrupted dialogues and the protagonist's stream of consciousness, as she is engaged in her hurried evaluation and judgment of the other characters. In the story, which at times resembles a kind of comedy of errors, Diana is unexpectedly invited to a party by an unknown but enthusiastic female admirer. The young woman, Lila, calls Diana *tigresa,* and the protagonist immediately responds by playing up the role of the writer as a superior or special entity and, at the same time, as an irresistible and seductive woman. The invitation made over the phone begins the game of seduction that will continue at the party, in an

Chapter Five

upper-middle-class apartment that belongs to Lila's parents. Encouraged by her own vanity and then by the alcohol she copiously consumes, Diana goes to the party convinced of her power to seduce. However, all too soon she finds out that someone else has already planned a game of seduction, laid out the rules, and determined the roles each guest is to play. Hence the *tigresa* is Lila: she seduces Diana (or tries to), exchanges heated kisses with another woman causing a scandal among some of the guests, and in a sense seduces or fascinates everyone present. Nevertheless, Lila's homosexual behavior does not express her desire for Diana or for the other woman. In reality, it is an expression of Lila's hope to "*épater les bourgeois*" (cf. Faderman 50). Therefore, by inviting Diana to the party, Lila wants more than anything to establish her *difference* from both her conservative family and her bourgeois friends.

In the last part of the story, an exchange of roles takes place again, and Diana is once more the seducer rather than the seduced she had been during the party:

> ... Lila segurou-me pelos ombros e debaixo do meu sono e cansaço percebi outra vez o olhar gorduroso do desejo. Está bem, pensei, eu me rendo, doce Lila, mas costumo terminar o que começo. Vamos ver até onde você vai.
> ... Lila encostou-se melosamente na parede, com infinitos dengos de sedução. ... Então, calmamente mandei:
> —Tira a roupa....
> —Tira tudo. Se você quer é pra valer, meu bem. Lila engoliu o riso. (135–36 [30])

Diana uses Lila's own weapon, achieving the same effect the young woman had intended. Lila wanted to live a homosexual experience in order to "*épater les bourgeois*" and thus create her own space set off by her difference. However, as a true bourgeois herself, she is the one stunned and even humiliated by the experience. The protagonist, in turn, feels not like the seductive tigress, but rather like the tiger who, feeling threatened, is capable of wounding: "não sei porque, lembrei aquela frase do Ernest Hemingway em *As neves do Kilimanjaro* a respeito de um tigre que foi encontrado morto, enregelado entre os cumes cobertos pela neve e que ninguém, ninguém jamais soube explicar como e por que ele chegou até lá" (136) ["I don't know why, I remembered that sentence in Ernest Hemingway's 'The Snows of Kilimanjaro' about a tiger found dead, frozen amidst the snow-covered peaks, and that nobody could ever explain how and why it got up there"]. In this way, it is Diana and not Lila who sets her difference, her marginal space, and her loneliness within the larger space of Brazilian bourgeois society.

Lygia Fagundes Telles and Myriam Campello: To Name or Not To Name, That Is the Question

By 1985, when "A escolha" was first published, lesbianism was not a new literary theme for Telles. The author had already addressed it openly in her first novel, *Ciranda de pedra*, which I have mentioned in Chapter 3, although reflecting the social prejudices dominant then. In the novel, Letícia, a woman in her early twenties, after living through a frustrated heterosexual love, begins to seduce younger women and eventually falls in love with the protagonist, Virgínia. In one passage, the two women kiss, and Letícia proposes that Virgínia move in with her. Despite being quite progressive for the time it was published (1954), the novel represents Letícia's homosexuality as an "evil" she is doing to herself and to the young women she seduces. Her homosexual identity is said to have resulted from a disillusion she had with a man. In addition, Letícia herself plays a masculinist role in relation to her female lovers, who submit to her socio-economic power and authority. Almost twenty years later, in *As meninas* (1973), Telles presents a less prejudiced view of lesbianism, depicting it in a straightforward manner. Nevertheless, the homosexual experience is practically an accident in the character's life. Lião, one of the three protagonists, has her first sexual experience with another young woman, and this initiation is characterized as a stage in her process of growing up. In other words, it is a "passing phenomenon" in a process of development that eventually will take her to heterosexual "normalcy," in a representation of lesbianism not at all uncommon. In fact, both Pratt (97) and Foster (*Sexual Textualities* 2) comment on literary works in which lesbianism

Chapter Five

is represented as a passing experience in the female characters' sexual development. For these women, "normalcy" or "maturity" would eventually be reached once they engaged in a heterosexual relation and through procreation.

While in the works mentioned above, Telles openly depicts lesbianism, in short stories such as "Tigrela" [Tigress] (1977) and "A escolha," lesbianism truthfully represents the narrative's central theme, even determining how the text is structured.[7] In "A escolha" the author problematizes the textual and social representation of the lesbian subject and lesbian desire. Thus Telles accomplishes here what Foster has characterized as a strategy of "[textualizing] . . . the problems of writing about a subject that cannot be satisfactorily accommodated within the dominant discourse" (*Gay and Lesbian* 141). Telles's solution for this problem of representation highlights the lesbian woman's "invisible" position in Brazilian society. In the Brazilian social context, a lesbian's existence for the most part is either acknowledged with irony and not named, and thus she is kept socially "invisible," or is rejected with violence, and she is reduced to prostitution and promiscuity (Míccolis, "Prazer" 89–90).

In order to expose these two social models of representation, Telles reproduces them in her narrative through the use of certain textual strategies. For example, the image of red roses stands for the love between two women, Gina and Oriana, who remain silent and their desire invisible. In actuality, the two are absent from the text: Gina has died and Oriana has been robbed of her voice, and their presence is affirmed through the red roses Oriana—silently but persistently—lays on Gina's tomb. The story is narrated by another woman, Gina's mother, whose white roses contrast and compete with the red ones, just as she continues to fight with Gina's lover for her daughter's affection, even after her death. The unreliable narrator and the non-enunciation of Gina and Oriana's homosexuality serve to structure in the text the ambiguity that characterizes much of Telles's fiction.

Gina and Oriana's relationship is presented through the jealous and hostile voice of the mother and is forced into hiding, situated as it is in the obscured space of closed doors and muffled voices. The narrator's perspective depicts the daughter in an ambiguous manner, at the same time "dissimulada" ["dissimulating"] and "inocente" ["innocent"] (Telles, "A escolha" 131), while Oriana is vile, "suja" ["dirty"] (129). The same excess that socially marks lesbian sexuality characterizes the women's love, symbolized in the image of red roses. The roses Oriana leaves on her lover's tomb are "vermelhonas, completamente desabrochadas. . . . deslavadas ao sol, quase obscenas de tão abertas" (129) ["deep red, completely full-blown. . . . naked under the sun, so completely open that they looked almost obscene"]. In contrast with the excess of the roses' "vermelhonegro," or deep, almost black, red tone (129), the white color of the roses the mother leaves on Gina's tomb represents what is discreet, controlled, and socially acceptable.

Split between her mother and her lover, Gina is violently forced to make a choice and, in a sense, to define herself. The confrontation she has with her mother reproduces the violence with which society often treats the lesbian woman: ". . . de repente comecei a gritar, batendo com os punhos nos joelhos" (131) ["suddenly I began to scream, hitting my fists on my knees"], says the narrator; and then: "Faça o que quiser, vá-se embora com Oriana ou fique comigo, a decisão é sua, tem todo o direito de escolher" (133) ["Do whatever you want, go away with Oriana or stay with me, it's your decision, you have the right to decide"]. The mother voices the dominant ideology in her attempt to control her daughter's sexuality. Gina, however, does not choose either one of the options society, represented by the mother, imposes on her. She neither opts for the social marginality of the lesbian, nor does she renounce her love for another woman. Her final decision comes as a surprise to the reader as well as to the narrator: "Me lembrei de tanta coisa, tanta mas em nenhum instante me ocorreu que além das opções que lhe ofereci havia uma terceira. Que ela escolheu em surdina, fechada lá no seu mundo secreto" (133) ["I thought of so many possibilities, so many, but never did it occur to me that there was a third possibility besides the options I gave her. That she chose quietly, locked in her secret world"]. In this way, suicide seems to be the only possible resolution to the conflict in which she is placed by a homophobic society. Nevertheless, this resolution is also ambiguous. On the one hand, it gives expression to the lesbian woman's agency and authority

Chapter Five

over her own body; on the other hand, it reflects her silence, as a mute act that takes her back to the invisibility to which society reduces the lesbian subject.

* * *

Like the story discussed above, Campello's "A mulher de ouro" addresses the lesbian subject's (in)visibility, the silencing of lesbian desire in Brazilian society, and the problem of how to name them within an inadequate socio-linguistic system. However, the narrative strategies employed by Campello are different from those Telles utilizes. Telles makes use of the very social code that discriminates against lesbians and chooses not to name lesbian desire as a means of highlighting how society makes it invisible. Campello, to the contrary, defiantly enunciates female homosexual desire and thus opens a space for the lesbian subject. In doing so, the author announces the possibility of a new social order wherein homosexuality will have its legitimate place:

> Aqui uma nota: Proust esperou até que a mãe morresse para poder dizer as coisas. Mas a minha está viva e terá que agüentar. Paciência, mamãe. Sei que tem vizinhos, parentes e amigos, mas a verdade queima, louca para sair. Além disso é bom ir se acostumando, gente fresca o lobo vai comer e lamber os beiços nesta década, para mim está claro como água. ("A mulher de ouro" 59 [31])

Here the maternal figure represents again the dominant ideology against which the homosexual woman has to rebel in order to affirm the right to define her sexuality, to define herself and thus reject the proposed pact of silence. By brazenly stating her sexual desire for another woman, Campello's protagonist-narrator anticipates with sarcasm society's disapproval: "Oh, Senhor, o que fazer desse desejo? E, oh, Senhor, uma mulher!" (61) ["Oh, Lord, what to do with my desire? And, oh, Lord, for a woman!"]. Her sarcastic comment not only makes clear that lesbianism does not have a place within this social context, but also that female desire is something to be controlled or hidden. The unequivocal enunciation of lesbian sexuality and the use of humor and sarcasm are the narrative strategies Campello utilizes in order to create a lesbian space.

In "A mulher de ouro," the protagonist recounts how, after her latest marriage fell apart (60), she met the "golden" woman in a dance hall. Nonetheless, lesbian desire is not characterized here as consolation for a frustrated heterosexual love. In fact, Campello creates a protagonist who is aware of her own sexuality, a woman who had previously lived homosexual as well as heterosexual experiences, and thus illustrates the idea of a "sexual continuum" found in Freud (De Lauretis xiii, 41), Foucault, and Rich. The "sexual continuum" explains both homosexuality and heterosexuality as possible forms of expression of human sexuality. However, "A mulher de ouro" clearly privileges lesbian desire, while at the same time it critiques the dominant gender relations and marriage as defined according to "séculos de herança medieval, amor eterno, babaquices lançadas sobre [a mulher] . . ." ("A mulher de ouro" 60) ["centuries of a medieval heritage, eternal love, bullshit imposed on a woman"] since she is born.

The protagonist is a woman who looks for a kind of relationship that would not represent a form of imprisonment. She has discarded the false promises implied in romantic (heterosexual) love and searches now for a nonhierarchical relationship wherein both subjects are equal, finding the possibility of its realization in lesbian desire. With the "golden woman," she lives an idyllic relationship, in which the two women fully express their sexuality and are free of societal ties. The protagonist states: "Não lhe perguntava nada. Mal sabia seu nome, evitando por minha vez lhe dar informações que penderiam incômodas" (63) ["I didn't ask her anything. I barely knew her name, and avoided giving her any information that could cause uneasiness"]. The idyll, however, is over when the woman utters the forbidden word: "num momento de selvagem doçura a mulher de ouro . . . me olhando nos olhos disse que me amava. . . . Foi nossa última noite. Não quis mais vê-la" (63) ["in a moment of wild tenderness, looking in my eyes, the golden woman said she loved me. . . . It was our last night. I didn't want to see her again"]. For the protagonist, the love declaration connotes a power struggle, possession and submission,

Chapter Five

and hierarchies common in heterosexual love, and she opts for breaking up, although the text suggests that she has chosen that option in spite of her love for the other woman.

In the end, "A mulher de ouro" is a lesbian love story, as romantic as any heterosexual love story can be. Nevertheless, it should be stressed that it represents female homosexual love as possible and natural, and the lesbian subject as any woman from any social group: "Ela era diferente de mim. Simples, tímida, trabalhava em qualquer repartição do governo" (59) ["She was different from me. Simple, shy, she worked in any government office"]. In addition to the sarcasm Campello boldly employs in order to rescue the lesbian woman from her invisibility and silence, the author also displays a concern with creating a language adequate to reproduce, in the most authentic way possible, the experience of a homosexual woman. In this regard, the author is particularly concerned with adequately representing her sexual and erotic experiences:

> ... uma febre oceânica me devorou, uma tempestade me comeu, toda a mitologia hindu visitava meus desvãos solitários enquanto Brahma, Vishnu e Siva corriam pelos nervos de raiz à mostra, o que era, Senhor, esse olho de tufão me empurrando pra fronteiras tão longínquas que eu nem sabia existirem. ... e não eram só os orgasmos tremulando por meu corpo como carrilhões de catedral que me conduziam a essa perplexidade de prazer, era o espaço perfeito deixado por seu rastro na minha alma, uma anulação tão grande na plenitude que me vi à beira do êxtase religioso. (61–62 [32])

Campello's story alternates erotic passages such as the one quoted above with humorous segments that anticipate any negative reaction to lesbian eroticism: "imagino que deva haver alguém na distinta platéia que se questione aflito, mas o que podem fazer duas mulheres juntas? Respostas para o Ministério da Educação" (62) ["I suppose there must be someone in the audience wondering upset, what can two women do together? Answers to the Ministry of Education"]. The blending of these two linguistic levels, the erotic and the humorous, serves to underscore the author's accomplishments in this text as well as in *Sortilegiu* and in other works in which she addresses homosexuality.[8] Campello is able to create a narrative space wherein the affirmation of lesbian identity and desire is possible. In addition, she creates a female erotic discourse independent of male desire, and simultaneously lends a didactic function to her narrative, offering a new perspective on the issue of lesbian desire and preparing her readers for the new social order she has announced.

* * *

In the short stories I have examined here, lesbian desire is central to the narrative and even determines the story's formal construction. Although the narrative strategies, style, and tone differ, in all of them, lesbian desire is a locus that allows a woman the exercise of her subjectivity, a space wherein she abandons the passive role to which she has been confined by the dominant gender system. In this way, lesbianism not only opens a channel for the more authentic expression of female eroticism, but also effects a critique of hierarchical heterosexual relationships.

Van Steen, Coutinho, Denser, Telles, and Campello make use of a wide range of strategies, from suggestion and ambiguity to humor and the clear enunciation of the lesbian body and desire. The narratives are not always explicit and often require a "queer" reading to affirm what is present but not named: female homosexual desire. Telles's story best textualizes this problem, working with a cultural code that makes the lesbian woman socially invisible. Similarly, Van Steen's and Coutinho's texts are structured over such a paradox, representing lesbian eroticism without naming it. As a matter of fact, Coutinho writes passages of deep eroticism and sensuality in "Fátima e Jamila," wherein the erotic expression goes beyond what is sexual in the plot to eroticize the words themselves. Campello also creates a language adequate to the representation of the lesbian woman's life experiences—sexual and nonsexual. Denser's story, in turn, is characterized by a transgressive discourse that subverts and disrupts the dominant gender system. Through the protagonist's viewpoint, Denser exposes the discursive practices that marginalize female homosexuality; at the

Chapter Five

same time, she points to the appropriation of lesbianism by Brazilian bourgeois classes, which makes of lesbian desire, more than a mark of difference, a symbol of status.

In spite of the differences I have discussed here, these stories exemplify the construction of a literary space that offers a place for lesbian subjectivity, a space where the lesbian character as well as other female characters can fully live their sexuality and desire (Farwell, "Lesbian Narrative" 157). Therefore, it is the creation of such space and the centrality of lesbian desire in these works that make them part of a lesbian tradition in female-authored Brazilian literature.

Chapter Six

The Works of Márcia Denser and Marina Colasanti

Female Agency and Heterosexuality

In the previous chapter I have focused on late-twentieth-century short stories in which lesbian desire is central to the narrative. It is important to highlight the existence of a lesbian tradition in literature by Brazilian women writers, in an effort to lift the silence usually surrounding the lesbian woman and lesbian sexuality in Brazil. As an expression of human sexuality and, in an ample sense, of human experience, lesbianism has been recurrently present in writings by twentieth-century Brazilian women. And as the end of the 1900s approached, these writers have depicted lesbianism more explicitly and with fewer veils, while the social stigmas that either mark or render invisible the lesbian woman have been slowly but firmly challenged.

As I noted in Chapter 5, the inscription of lesbian desire in literature creates a space not only for the validation of female homosexuality, but also for the liberating affirmation of female sexuality in general. Lesbianism becomes a liberating space for women because in it lies implicit a challenge to the dominant gender system, i.e., to compulsory patriarchal heterosexuality. While lesbian feminists may disagree with my assertions here, I side with Ruth Salvaggio (1999), who states: ". . . placing oneself as a lesbian in writing hardly means ascribing to some fixed message or even to a defined sexuality. Far from that, identity becomes process. . ." (85). In this way, Salvaggio underscores the existence of a common ground for lesbian and queer theories. I propose that, similarly, there is a commonality between lesbian desire and a queer stance toward one's self-identity and toward the social group: both afford the female subject the rejection of fixed categories of gender.

Therefore, lesbian desire effects queer identities, if we understand queer as "anything that challenges or subverts the straight, the compulsory heterosexual, through either an ironizing of its limited view of human potential or through the *overt defiance of its conventions*" (Foster, *Sexual Textualities* 71; my emphasis).

Women who engage in heterosexual relationships may also assume a queer stance if they continually reject fixed categories of identity and the ideology of dominance that is part of patriarchal heterosexuality. As I discussed in Chapter 4, some of Coutinho's protagonists do just this: as in the case of Cordélia, from "Cordélia, a caçadora," they overtly defy the conventions of compulsory patriarchal heterosexuality while not repressing their heterosexual desire. In that particular story, the female grotesque allows the protagonist a strategy for living her identity as a process, as movement and change—and challenge—consequently undermining the dominant gender system. Coutinho thus has been successful in depicting women as they move on in their struggle for self-affirmation and for freely living their desire and sexuality, be it in heterosexual or in lesbian relationships. The author's female protagonists herald Brazilian women in the new millennium, and the possibility of new forms of gender relations.

Denser, whose short story "Tigresa" I analyzed in Chapter 5, is another writer whose work in the last decades of the twentieth century was instrumental in the examination and undermining of the dominant gender system, and the emergence of a new female voice in Brazilian literature. Through her paradigmatic protagonist, Diana Marini, Denser radically challenges the conventions of patriarchal heterosexuality, not only in the few stories in which she depicts female homosexual desire, but also—and especially—in those in which Diana Marini, Diana the Huntress, hunts down her male partners and engages in heterosexual acts. Diana not only takes the initiative in the game of seduction and sex, but also is only interested in her sexual pleasure, a behavior that has bothered some readers, who have accused the character of "acting like a man." In fact, Diana is the aggressor, the conqueror; she *uses* the men with whom she sleeps, much as some men act toward women.

Denser's subversion of the dominant gender system is achieved precisely in this way: by placing Diana in a role traditionally exclusive to the male, the author claims for women the ability and the right to freely seek sexual satisfaction. In addition, Denser exposes the system of power and domination inherent in patriarchal heterosexuality, by inverting the usual positions men and women occupy in heterosexual relationships.

This most important aspect of Denser's fiction has been well analyzed by both Quinlan and Franconi. Quinlan, for example, examines the inversion of traditional gender roles in Denser's short stories, and states that "Exposing the problems inherent in male-female relationships through inversion is one way to draw attention to the need for a collective solution" (Quinlan, "*O animal dos motéis*" 134). Denser herself does not offer solutions or alternatives for a binary gender system in which one subject dominates and uses the other as an object. Instead, she makes her readers face the problem through estrangement: in place of the culturally accepted subjugation of women by men, Denser depicts a situation that is not the norm, and therefore leads to discomfort. Diana is shown as calculating, cynical, and critically aware of her position vis-à-vis the men with whom she goes to bed: she seeks sexual satisfaction; they do too, as they do a prize, a trophy, and a conquest. According to Diana, her partners see her as a "mulher culta + bonita + avançada = satisfação garantida, a render juros, livre de impostos" ("Welcome to Diana" 17) ["learned woman + beautiful + liberated = guaranteed satisfaction, generating interest, and tax-free"]. There are no obligations, no commitments, for her relationships are devoid of emotion, love, or any other personal attachment between the partners.

Through Diana's cynical perspective, the heterosexual act is represented in its animal dimension, in scenes that often approximate the grotesque. For example:

> Ele diz: esse motel já foi bom, e eu olho o banheiro, . . . os lençóis castanhos com ramagens duvidosas entre encardido e vestígios de cor, os três espelhos redondos montados em curvim (um em frente do outro, no meio a cama, o terceiro no teto, sobre a cama), claro que para nos transformar numa espécie de confuso coquetel de siris assados: pernas, braços,

Chapter Six

> carnes vivas, canteiro de patas, antenas, pêlos moventes, espiando de esguelha uma outra hidra em perspectiva no espelho da frente, de trás, de cima, debaixo, devassados, misturados, confundidos, a 850,00 a diária, porque (e então eu sei porque) todos os motéis é sempre o mesmo motel.
> . . . (Denser, "O animal dos motéis" 47–48 [33])

And once the sexual act is over: "Lá em cima, no espelho, duas, quatro, seis, oito larvas rotas, libertas do emaranhado" (52) ["Up above, in the mirror, two, four, six, eight broken larvae, free from the tangle"]. Denser's discourse recalls Aluísio Azevedo's Naturalism, with its emphasis on, and exaggeration of, men and women's negative, pathological, or animal-like characteristics. In fact, her fiction has been labeled an expression of Neo-Naturalism, alongside that of Dalton Trevisan (1925) and Rubem Fonseca (1925).

Denser's work has been closely associated with the emergence in Brazil of a female erotic discourse, not only because of the two important collections of female erotica she edited in the 1980s, but also because of the main themes she addresses in her own fiction: female desire and sexuality. Without a doubt, Denser's short stories are examples of what Charney characterizes as "sexual fiction." However, the label "erotic" is more problematic when applied to them. Denser's fiction clearly displays her aesthetic preoccupations and her skill as a crafter of the word. Often employing stream of consciousness, and through skillful word choice, Denser weaves a narrative that is fast and apparently chaotic, and that is also poignant and poetic. Therefore, her narrative displays the intrinsic tie between eroticism and the poetic word, although hers is the poetry of the postmodern cosmopolis—fast, sarcastic, and crude.

Another element in Denser's stories that would help characterize them as examples of erotic literature is the consensual nature of Diana Marini's sexual encounters, as each partner seeks her or his own sexual pleasure. Nevertheless, her fiction in fact calls into question the concept of erotic, as it lacks a fundamental element of erotic discourse, i.e., the celebration of the human body. Instead, male and female bodies appear fragmented and faceless, and are described in their animal appearance or as machines for pleasure and self-pleasure:

Female Agency and Heterosexuality

> Estava deitada, fumando, quando sua massa rija desabou sobre mim. Procurei seus lábios mas ele disse não, estou resfriado. Então esperei. Você gosta assim? perguntou, ajeitando-me de bruços. Abraçava-me com palmas e dedos gelados, comprimindo minhas costelas, machucando-as, em vez de acariciá-las. A coisa funciona só da cintura para baixo, como um vibrador elétrico, mas é bom, pensei, deixando-me penetrar rijamente pelas costas, usando, por assim dizer, só uma parte do meu corpo, como se o resto estivesse paralisado, ou morto, como se ninguém suportasse um dramático relacionamento frontal, com beijos, . . . com um rosto, um nome, uma biografia. ("Hell's Angels" 76 [34])

So is Denser's fiction erotic? Or is it pornographic? "Sexual fiction" is certainly an appropriate label and even a compromise, for her stories challenge conventional notions of eroticism and pornography. On one hand, Diana and her partners engage in consensual sex; on the other hand, however, there is a mutual exploitation between them, since both render the other an object, a faceless body, or simply a sexual organ. In this way, if we consider pornography as the sexual exploitation of one individual by another, or even the crude representation of men and women's genitalia, Denser's fiction fits the category. However, the sexual act is not depicted here with the intent of sexually arousing the reader, an intention that generally characterizes pornography. Rather, the stories serve other objectives. First, they give expression to female heterosexual desire during a historical period following the sexual and cultural revolutions of the 1960s, a period in which the liberation of customs coexisted with the marks left by the political repression of the Brazilian military dictatorship. And second, seen through the cold and analytical lens of Diana Marini's mind, heterosexual relationships serve the author as tools to dissect gender relations in Brazilian society, and to denounce cultural-sexual conventions intrinsic to phallocentric or masculinist eroticism.

In a rather ironic way, then, Denser's female protagonist finds agency while living up her heterosexuality. Diana Marini's agency, however, does not lead her to reject phallocentric heterosexuality, nor does it allow her self-realization. Instead, Diana plays and acts—hunts her male prey, satisfies

Chapter Six

her sexual appetite—within the frame of conventional gender relations, which demand that the woman submit, at least apparently, to male desire, to his authority as well as his vanity. Diana's great advantage over her partners is her deep understanding of the power struggle inherent therein, as well as the cynical awareness of the choices she has and makes.

With the stories in *Diana Caçadora* (1986) and others, Denser goes a step further than other Brazilian women writers of the late 1970s and 1980s. Like Cunha and Felinto, whose novels I examined in Chapter 2, Denser creates a female character aware of her own body, sexuality, and desire. And while the author still depicts female heterosexuality within the frame of phallocentrism, she does so concomitantly to a critique of the dominant gender relations, thus inviting the reader to engage in a rethinking of heterosexuality in order to disassociate heterosexual desire from a patriarchal ideology of power and domination. This disassociation is portrayed in Brazilian women's literature of the last decade of the twentieth century, when some writers create female poetic voices or fictional characters who are very comfortable with their bodies and sexuality, engaging in consensual heterosexual relationships devoid of sexual hierarchies and power struggles.

* * *

One such writer is Colasanti, whose first book of poetry, *Rota de colisão* [Collision route], was published in 1993. By that time Colasanti had already been a familiar name within Brazilian literature for almost a quarter of a century, having published her first book, *Eu sozinha* [Me on my own], in 1968. Since then she has become widely known in Brazil thanks to her work as a journalist, and to the *crônicas* she wrote for the women's magazine *NOVA,* beginning in 1977, and to other magazines like *Ele e ela* [He and she], and *Cláudia.* In these periodicals, but also in books such as *A nova mulher* [The new woman] (1980), Colasanti has written extensively on gender relations and on women's issues, like divorce, careers, sexuality, and motherhood. In *A nova mulher* and in other nonfictional writings, the author inaugurates a new vein in the Brazilian essay, one that combines autobiographical elements and an intimate narrative tone with the objective examination of social topics relating to women.

Peggy Sharpe comments that "Ao explorar a relação entre identidade cultural e de gênero, as crônicas e ensaios pessoais de Marina Colasanti se ajustam com exatidão à tradição de mulheres escritoras que empregam o autobiográfico e o subjetivo como significantes de uma nova linguagem" (47) ["Exploring the relationship between cultural and gender identities, Marina Colasanti's *crônicas* and personal essays fit exactly within the tradition of women writers who employ autobiographical and subjective elements as signifiers of a new language"].

In her poetry, Colasanti continues to rely on her personal experiences as a woman, creating, however, a female poetic voice that is universal, for her personal experience is also a collective female experience that can transcend barriers of class and race.

Rota de colisão was very well received by critics and public alike, and was awarded the *Jabuti* Prize in 1994.[1] The poems in this collection have in common the exquisite quality of their visual and aural imagery, and the striking plasticity of the language employed; "Verão em Campo Grande" [Summer in Campo Grande] is a good example:

> É o tempo em que as mangueiras
> se vestem de vermelho.
> Folhas de fulva seda
> cintilar de cetim.
> Redondas como seios
> ou ventres
> as copas brotam
> cor de carne nova.
> E nos troncos,
> espesso como sangue,
> escorre
> o cantar das cigarras. [35]

The visual dimension the words acquire in Colasanti's poems may very well have originated in the poet's training as an artist, for she studied in the National School of Fine Arts in

Chapter Six

Rio de Janeiro, and continues to paint and draw. Her interest in painting and other visual arts is conveyed in the many poems she has written on art museums, famous painters, and paintings, such as "Vincent," about Vincent Van Gogh, or "Em Tóquio, no museu" [In Tokyo, at the museum], below:

> Sobre o pano de seda
> deitada e curvilínea
> como uma mulher nua
> a lâmina da espada. [36]

Colasanti's attention to the form, shape, and color of objects translates into the refinement and craft with which she works the poetic image, and into the resultant sensuality found in so many of her poems; this sensuality then becomes a characteristic that permeates all her poetry, as the poems quoted above well illustrate.

The delicate and exquisite qualities of Colasanti's poetry should not be mistakenly understood as elements of a sappy poetics, and not even for any kind of Platonism, for the sensuality of her poems achieves an eroticism that is in fact very corporeal. Rather, these qualities reflect the poet's attention to detail: she derives meaning from the word as if from a minute jewel, resulting in the aesthetic effects she carefully weaves in the message of her poems. This attention to details, a mark of the feminine according to Naomi Schor (1987), is even more striking when coupled with the explicit tone assumed by the poetic voice in her erotic poems, or with the gloomy reality the poet describes in others.

When *Rota de colisão* was published, erotic literature by Brazilian women was nothing new. Nevertheless, a more explicit eroticism tended to be more easily found in poets considered "alternative" or "minor" names in the Brazilian literary scene, and thus generally ignored by the critics. As I state in Chapter 2, the silence on the part of mainstream critics over the erotic production by Brazilian women poets still has been the norm in the last decades of the twentieth century. At the same time, a kind of "lyric" or "romantic" eroticism by women poets has been more easily accepted, while a more explicit eroticism or explicit references to the female body and sexual-

Female Agency and Heterosexuality

ity have remained associated with "poesia marginal." Says poet Claudia Roquette-Pinto:

> Existe um acordo tácito entre os poetas, certas palavras que não devem ser usadas "porque não são táticas," certos temas que são considerados de mau gosto. Menstruação, gravidez, parto, maternidade, a própria sexualidade feminina—tudo isso deve ser tratado de uma forma, digamos, elegante (esfriada ou cerebral), sob o risco de ser dispensado como "coisa de mulher." Independente da qualidade do poema. Ou seja, está tudo bem, contanto que você escreva "de fora," como homem. (Qtd. in "Vinte e duas poetas hoje" 210 [37])

As will become clear from the examples below, Colasanti's poetry violates this tacit code Roquette-Pinto mentions. Colasanti's is an eroticism "of the body"; it challenges the accepted defining principles of eroticism and of pornography, employing terms and expressions that still today are deemed by some to be vulgar and not "proper" for a woman.

Colasanti's poetry gives voice to the heterosexual desire of a woman who celebrates her own body, represented not as the present-day aesthetic ideal of a young and thin (or in other words, childlike) female body, but rather as a womanly body, full, excessive, secreting fluids and blood. An example is the following fragment of "Eu sou uma mulher" [I am a woman]:

> Eu sou uma mulher
> que sempre achou bonito
> menstruar.
>
> Os homens vertem sangue
> por doença
> sangria
> ou por punhal cravado,
> . . . .
>
> Em nós
> o sangue aflora
> como fonte
> no côncavo do corpo
> olho-d'água escarlate
> encharcado cetim

Chapter Six

> que escorre
> em fio. [38]

The same poetic voice is engaged in consensual heterosexual relationships, at ease with her body and sexuality, and thoroughly enjoys the sexual act with her male partner:

> Teu sexo
>
> Teu sexo em minha boca
> me preenche
> como se pela boca
> penetrasse a vagina.
> Teu sexo em minha boca
> me engravida
> me põe túrgida
> prenhe
> mel coando dos peitos
> sobre a cama. [39]

In this representation of oral sex, the poet does not allude directly to the *active* role the woman plays when giving pleasure to her partner, but rather describes the pleasure that she herself derives from the penis. The short verses and the use of enjambment lend the poem a very sensual rhythm suggestive of the female subject's sexual enjoyment.

In other poems, the characteristic delicate imagery of Colasanti's poetry is woven together with vulgar words, as for example, "pau" ("dick") and "pentelho" ("pubic hair"). She thus appropriates a form of expression typically associated with mass-consumption pornography, in which the aesthetic construction of the text is usually not a concern, and which depicts the human body in a crude or even debasing manner. Conversely, Colasanti's eroticism celebrates both the female and male bodies, and the heterosexual acts represented in her poems are often forms of encounter between the female poetic voice and her partner. Therefore, heterosexuality becomes in Colasanti's poetry a form of wholeness that is very physical as well as metaphysical for, through the sexual act, female and male achieve the connection and unity Bataille has described as a basic human yearning. This sense of unity is present in the poem below:

Female Agency and Heterosexuality

Corpo adentro

Teu corpo é canoa
em que desço
vida abaixo
morte acima
procurando o naufrágio
me entregando à deriva.

Teu corpo é casulo
de infinitas sedas
onde fio
me afio e enfio
invasor recebido
com licores.

Teu corpo é pele exata para o meu
pena de garça
brilho de romã
aurora boreal
do longo inverno. [40]

Giving voice to the female subject to speak of her own desire, Colasanti inverts the roles usually assigned the partners in a heterosexual relationship. Here the woman is the one who journeys, while her partner's body is the vessel that takes her to ecstasy. His body is also the protective cocoon, as well as the skin that envelops her, two bodies thus becoming one.

In this way, Colasanti is able to construct in her poems a female subject who exercises her agency in heterosexual relationships. Her poetic voice takes pleasure in her own sexuality as well as in her male companion's body. In addition, in her poetry, female heterosexuality does not privilege penetration, nor is the penis necessarily a site of phallocentric desire. Nevertheless, the agency of the heterosexual female voice, and the absence of relationships of power and domination in a woman's sexual life, does not result in her exclusion from what Butler has called "the matrix of power" (30). Colasanti is aware of women's position, as social entities, within the larger institution of heterosexuality, or "compulsory heterosexuality," as Rich has termed it.

Heterosexuality as an institution rigidly conceives human beings in either side of the binary *masculine* versus *feminine*,

Chapter Six

and "entails women's subordination to men" (S. Jackson 175). Colasanti has written extensively about this issue; in *Rota de colisão* she raises the problem in poems such as "Hematoma da infidelidade" [Hematoma of infidelity]:

> Pertenço à eterna estirpe
> das traídas
> mulher que tece e fia
> enquanto o macho
> entre as coxas de outra
> afia mentira e gozo. (Fragment [41])

Just as a hematoma is blood below the skin surface, the pain caused by the male's deceit remains covered, yet hurting, in these women:

> É sempre o mesmo macho
> sempre o mesmo percurso.
> Nenhum me foi fiel
> a mim a minha mãe
> minhas irmãs.
> E nenhuma de nós
> soube achar o caminho
> que sem sair do amor
> conduz à indiferença. [42]

Obviously the problem of infidelity is not exclusive to heterosexual relationships; however, the social double standard that characterizes the male as "naturally" permissive, while it deems feminine "nature" to be sexually (and emotionally) monogamous, is a cultural myth endorsed by compulsory heterosexuality, and supported by dubious notions of biological evolution.[2] This double standard is a manifestation of the culturally sanctioned subordination of women by men, which has wide repercussions socially for all human beings.

The theme of male infidelity in "Hematoma da infidelidade" underscores the poetic voice's belonging to a female lineage. Through the female body and through common female experiences—specifically female heterosexuality, autoeroticism, and women's position within gender relations—Colasanti constructs a "sorority," expressing a solidarity that brings together women from different backgrounds, classes, and races. The pain the poetic voice expresses in "Hematoma da infidelidade," as well as the pleasure expressed in other poems, are millenary; in a sense, the poetic subject is *every woman*. There exists, then, an intent of immediate communication and identification with other women, other Marinas, an intent the author had previously expressed in other writings:

> Comecei a falar para mulheres quase paralelamente ao início da minha atividade jornalística, e na verdade não lembro períodos . . . em que não estivesse de forma mais direta ligada ao público feminino. Falar *para* elas logo transformou-se em falar *delas* e *com* elas.
> . . . Descobri, no infinito reflexo de tantas e tantas mulheres, meu eu mulher. E floresci comovida um sentimento de irmandade que me liga indissoluvelmente às do meu sexo. (*A nova mulher* 9 [43]; author's emphasis)

Consequently, the desire for connection with the other does not manifest itself only in poems that give expression to a woman's sexuality. It is also expressed in poems that speak of—and to—other women. Such poems may speak of the poetic voice's understanding of her social Other, women of other social groups as, for example, in "Rumo à caixa" [Toward the cashier]:

> Na fila do mercado
> à minha frente
> empunha a cesta
> e espera pela vez.
>
> Mulher magra
> sem peitos
> quase seca.
> Pele escura
> sem viço
> quase negra.
> Pés cascudos.
>
> Escrita na blusa
> em letras bordadas
> uma só palavra
>   LUXÚRIA [44]

Chapter Six

In this poem, Colasanti depicts a woman from the lower classes, maybe someone else's maid, a woman who struggles in life without *luxo* ("luxury"), but with *luxúria*. The poet does not attempt to speak for this other woman, though. Rather, the woman expresses herself out loud through her choice of attire, even if an elitist class society tries to render her voiceless: she too is a sexual being.

The possibility of identification among women from different social groups lies in the feminine as a mark of difference, which Colasanti has never rejected. Indeed, it is a difference that the writer has always embraced, and recognizes at the very source of her writing: "... tudo que escrevo vem do meu olhar de mulher, vem dos meus hormônios, vem do meu ciclo e da minha relação com a lua" (Colasanti, "Caçadora" 9) ["everything I write comes from my female way of seeing things, comes from my hormones, from my cycle and from my relation to the moon"]. Colasanti thus posits herself against the notion of gender "neutrality," particularly as it refers to women's literary and artistic production. In this manner, she represents a minority view among Brazilian women writers who, still today, prefer to defend the idea that literature is "genderless."[3]

Her position does not mean, however, that she believes in some form of essentialism, even though she sings in her poetry the natural phenomena of a woman's body. Colasanti understands a woman's experience as culturally marked by her social environment, by her class, her race, her economic status. Yet, all these categories lie framed by the institution of compulsory heterosexuality or, in other words, are primarily impacted by it. In this regard, says Heleieth Saffioti:

> ... relações de poder exprimem-se *primordialmente* através das relações de gênero. Tal fato é .... primevo, porquanto antecedeu, e de muito, a emergência das sociedades centradas na propriedade privada dos meios de produção.... É primordial, ainda, pelo fato de permear absolutamente todas as relações sociais, sejam elas de classe social ou étnicas. (197 [45])

Colasanti concurs with Saffioti's analysis. At the same time that heterosexuality is in her poems a valid expression of a woman's desire, she does not lose sight of the phallocentric society that lies beyond, and that regulates the lives of women—and men. The poem "Sexta-feira à noite" [Friday night], below, illustrates this point:

> Sexta-feira à noite
> > os homens acariciam os clitóris das esposas
> > com dedos molhados de saliva.
> > O mesmo gesto com que todos os dias
> > contam dinheiro papéis documentos
> > e folheiam nas revistas
> > a vida dos seus ídolos
>
> Sexta-feira à noite
> > os homens penetram suas esposas
> > com tédio e pênis.
> > O mesmo tédio com que todos os dias
> > enfiam o carro na garagem
> > o dedo no nariz
> > e metem a mão no bolso
> > para coçar o saco.
>
> Sexta-feira à noite
> > os homens ressonam de borco
> > enquanto as mulheres no escuro
> > encaram seu destino
> > e sonham com o príncipe encantado. [46]

* * *

In examining in this chapter Denser's short stories and Colasanti's erotic poetry, I have addressed a question raised earlier in this volume: Can female desire be rendered in a way other than submissive to male desire, and to what extent can the dialectics of *domination* versus *subordination* be left out of the erotic exchange? The two writers here discussed offer different responses. Both Denser and Colasanti give expression to a woman's heterosexual desire and eroticism. Both also recognize the existence of a dominant masculinist ideology that privileges male desire, and necessarily impacts gender relations in Brazilian society. This fact is very clearly represented in Denser's stories through the critical perspective of Diana Marini. Usually characterized as female eroticism, however,

Chapter Six

Denser's writings may be more correctly identified as a kind of anti-erotic sexual literature, for the heterosexual act here does not bring to the partners any sense of wholeness or unity, nor does the female protagonist seem to find sexual satisfaction. Nonetheless, through the portrayal of female heterosexuality, Denser realizes an excellent critique of the dominant phallocentric ideology.

In turn, in her poetry Colasanti succeeds in creating an erotic discourse in which female heterosexual desire finds fulfillment and satisfaction, while the woman is given agency in the sexual act and in her relationship with her partner. The fact that Colasanti's poems were published some ten years after Denser's stories should not be overlooked, as it may indicate some changes Brazilian women have achieved regarding their bodies, their sexuality, and their identities, vis-à-vis a still patriarchal, phallocentric society.

Conclusion
Brazilian Women Writers in the New Millennium

Since the beginning of the twentieth century, Brazilian women writers have come a long way in their representation of female desire, eroticism, and sexuality. From the first decades of the century with Gilka Machado's daring poetry, through the pioneering fiction of Rachel de Queiroz, Clarice Lispector, and Lygia Fagundes Telles in the 1930s and 1940s, to the work of Leila Míccolis, Márcia Denser, Sonia Coutinho, Marina Colasanti, and others in the latter part of the twentieth century, Brazilian women have written and rewritten the female body and identity, and have deconstructed masculinist cultural myths of femininity. By the end of the first millennium, these writers have reinscribed women in Brazilian history and culture, giving their female characters agency and letting them find their own voices.

In order to achieve this, Brazilian women writers strived to create a new discourse, each poet or fictionist searching for her own language, a language that could give authentic expression to a woman's life, especially her erotic experiences, for sexuality stands at the very core of a person's sense of self-identity. For Brazilian women, the universal impulse toward self-knowledge has been coupled with the urge to reject images of the female body and sexuality originated in male desire. In Brazil, still a male-centered society in spite of women's many social advances, female sexuality has been described and prescribed by a masculinist culture. Women characters have "desired" forms of male desire, have "been" insatiable *femmes fatales* or dangerous Medusas, or have "spoken" as dummies through the voice of a ventriloquist.

Hence finding their voices has meant for Brazilian women writers letting their female protagonists explore their sexuality

Conclusion

and erotic drives, while they too have explored the erotic in language. In this way, one of the main focuses of this book has been the creation of a female erotic discourse, the obstacles and problems Brazilian women writers have encountered in doing so, as well as the poetic and narrative strategies they have employed in the depiction of female eroticism. As I began my analysis of the poems and narratives here discussed, two important questions emerged that guided the writing of these chapters. One question was, "What is an appropriate definition of the erotic?" and the second, "Can female desire be rendered in a way other than submissive to male desire?" Or, in other words, "Can the dialectic *subordination* versus *submission* be left out of the erotic exchange?"

In Chapter 1, I pointed out that this dialectic was in fact at the core of gender relations as depicted in canonical, male-authored, Brazilian nineteenth-century novels. It was as well at the basis of the creation of female protagonists such as Vidinha, Luisinha, Iracema, Rita Baiana, and other characters, who came to represent, since the second-half of the 1800s and throughout much of the 1900s, rigid myths of the feminine ideal in the Brazilian imaginary.

In Chapter 2, I focused on the creation of an erotic discourse by different women poets and fiction writers, and thus addressed the issue of an appropriate definition of the erotic. I was able to find satisfying working definitions of what is a "pornographic" discourse and what is an "erotic" one. Based on the theoretical works of Susan Griffin, Audre Lorde, Rosalind Coward, and others, I have considered the erotic discourse as an aesthetic endeavor that privileges a mutually consensual exchange between equals, while the pornographic discourse seeks to depict the domination of one subject by another. In fact, the pornographic text can be understood as a kind of "poetics" of the Other's oppression. However, given the many different sexual preferences that human beings display at different times of their lives, these are meant to be strictly working definitions for the purpose of the analyses I have effected in this book. Although many in Brazil generally accept the distinction I have made here between pornography and eroticism, it would be wise to accept Maurice Charney's term "sexual fiction" (or sexual literature), for Brazilian women writers have often challenged or problematized the distinction between the two categories.

In the 1970s and 1980s, Brazilian women poets and fiction writers spoke with progressively greater openness of the female body and sexuality, often challenging or deconstructing traditional myths of femininity. Each one of them sought to find new forms of linguistic expression, in an effort to let the female voice speak in a most authentic way. In this regard, both Helena Parente Cunha and Marilene Felinto stood out for their formally innovative novels *Mulher no espelho* and *As mulheres de Tijucopapo*. While different in the formal solutions they achieve, Cunha and Felinto have in common the depiction of an unequivocally daring female voice that speaks up for herself in each of these two novels. In addition, Cunha creates some of the most beautiful erotic passages in Brazilian fiction when portraying her protagonist engaging in forms of self-pleasure. Felinto too presents a compelling female erotic discourse in *Tijucopapo*. In the end, however, neither author is fully able to think female eroticism outside of hierarchical heterosexual relationships that privilege the phallus, penetration, and female passivity.

Cunha's and Felinto's novels exemplify the kind of obstacles twentieth-century Brazilian female authors were trying to overcome in their works. Some of the problems these writers faced emerged from the fact that they too are cultural beings living and writing within a specific dominant ideology. While challenging, questioning, and deconstructing this ideology and the cultural myths that have supported its existence, they often had to revisit their own beliefs as they invited their readers to do the same. In the 1970s and 1980s, many Brazilian women poets and fiction writers expressed an ambiguity and discomfort concerning the female body and female identity that reflected well the reality lived by many middle-class women in Brazil at the time. As Brazilian women were being confronted with new possibilities of self-realization and self-pleasure, on the one hand, and traditional female roles on the other hand, writers like Lya Luft and Telles, whose novels I discuss in Chapter 3, employed strategies such as elements of the fantastic and the grotesque to represent a deeply fragmented female subject and her conflicts.

Conclusion

In Chapter 4, again I examine the use of the grotesque by another Brazilian woman fictionist, Coutinho. However, rather than using the grotesque to express the disruption between the female character and her body or her society, as seen in the previous chapter, Coutinho appropriates it as a strategy to represent—even *parade*—the aging sexual female body. By bringing together two categories that are culturally perceived as mutually exclusive, the aging body, and the sexual and sensual body, Coutinho deconstructs old myths of femininity that relate a woman's sexual desire and prowess with youth, and her desirability with traditional standards of beauty. The female grotesque thus offers the female subject a cultural-literary space wherein she is able to find agency and give expression to her sexuality and desire outside of the parameters set out by the dominant masculinist culture.

Likewise, as I discuss in Chapter 5, lesbian desire and sexuality open up a space for female subjectivity and agency. There exists in Brazil a long-standing tradition of lesbian literature that includes such mainstream authors as Telles and, more recently, Denser and Myriam Campello, among others. However, the recognition of such a tradition often requires a "queer" reading that will foreground the lesbian subject, much as one hundred years ago readers needed to look for the palimpsest in a woman's text in order to find there the authentic female voice.

In Chapter 6, I focus once more on female heterosexual desire as represented in Denser's short stories and in the erotic poems of Colasanti. Whereas both writers are successful in the representation of female sexuality, Denser's fiction problematizes the expression of female eroticism within a gender system still centered on masculinist desire. Colasanti, in turn, is successful in creating an erotic discourse that gives agency to the female subject; while in other poems she depicts and critiques the dominant ideology that frames men and women's relationships.

As we move along through the twentieth-first century, Brazilian female authors will continue to deconstruct any rigid cultural myths that posit women in reductive ways, in a process of continual critical revisionism. As they question, subvert, and re-create masculinist myths of femininity, perhaps women writ-

Conclusion

ers will also engage in a process of mythmaking. Nevertheless, these female-authored "myths," especially since the last quarter of the twentieth century, are not to be read as static or prescriptive forms of female behavior. Rather, they recurrently offer dynamic, plural representations of an evolving female subject. In the new millennium, then, the Brazilian "New Woman" will have, in fact, many faces, many voices, and will be ever more self-assertive, comfortable with her body and sexuality, *senhora* of her desire.

Appendix
English Translations

The following are English translations for the longer Portuguese quotations. They are keyed to the text by the number in brackets. All translations are mine unless a published translation/translator is given as a source.

Chapter One
Female Body, Male Desire

1 Vidinha was a mulatto girl some eighteen or twenty years old, of average height, with broad shoulders, salient breasts, a slim waist, and tiny feet. She had very black, dancing eyes, thick, moist lips, and extremely white teeth. Her speech was a bit slow but sweet and melodic. Every sentence she uttered was punctuated with a long, sonorous giggle and a certain backward toss of her head.... (Almeida, *Memoirs* 110)

2 ... the blazing light of midday; the fierce heat of the farm where he had toiled; the pungent scent of clover and vanilla that had made his head spin in the jungle; the palm tree, proud and virginal, unbending before its fellow plants. She was poison and sugar. She was the sapotilla fruit, sweeter than honey, and sumac, whose fiery juice burned through his skin. She was a green snake, a slithering lizard, a mosquito that for years had buzzed around his body, stirring his desires, ... piercing his veins to rouse his blood with a spark of southern love.... (Azevedo, *The Slum* 61)

3 As the one who presides over the home and is its guardian, the woman will always be able to instill in the man the solid principles that are so dear and essential to our [the nation's] character.
   A woman's influence upon the shaping of our qualities, and all the *Brasileira* can contribute to the organization of national character....

English Translations to Pages 31–43

> Maternal qualities will influence considerably the constitution of the moral profile of men, who need women in order to solidly build our national actions. (Austregésilo v–vi)

4 They held some kind of mysterious, active fluid, a force that dragged one in, like the undertow of a wave retreating from the shore on stormy days. So as not to be dragged in, I held on to anything around them . . . ; but as soon as I returned to the pupils of her eyes again, the wave emerging from them grew towards me, deep and dark, threatening to envelop me, draw me in and swallow me up. (Machado de Assis, *Dom Casmurro,* trans. Gledson 63)

Chapter Two
Brazilian Women Writers: The Search for an Erotic Discourse

5 Sensual

> When, far from you, alone, I reflect
> on this pagan affection that, ashamed, I hide
> comes to my nostrils the exquisite perfume
> that your body emanates and your very countenance holds.
>
> The fervent confession of this infinite affection
> for a long time, afraid, I have buried in my lips,
> for your lascivious stare fixed on me, firmly,
> is like an insult to my chastity.
>
> If by chance you are far away, the colossal barrier
> of reproaches that formerly I made to myself
> from proud virtue, rises up haughtily.
>
> But, if you are at my side, the barrier falls,
> and I feel the thick and cold slug of voluptuousness
> pollute my flesh with repugnant drool.
>   (G. Machado, "Sensual," *Cristais partidos*)

6 Voluptuousness

> I have you, stretched out in the veins of my blood
> at your sensation I detach myself from my surroundings;
> my verses are completely filled
> with your strong poison, invincible and flowing.
>
> Because I bring you within me, I've acquired, taken,
> your subtle manner, your indolent gesture.

English Translations to Pages 44–46

Because I bring you within me I adapted to your sinuous movements,
my intimate, nervous and ruby serpent.

Your lethal poison makes my eyes dull,
and my pure soul that repudiates you,
in vain yearns to escape your ties.

Your lethal poison makes my body languid,
in a long, slow, smooth flow,
up and down, in the current of my blood.
    (G. Machado, "Volúpia," *Estados de alma*)

7 An Evocation to Sleep

Sleep! from your bronze and cold cup
give me so that I can exhaust the ether, the anesthesia . . .
Here I am: body and soul—whole,
for your orgy.
I seek to forget my hypochondria
in your drunkenness.
I want to feel your soft faint
take hold of my being
and drifting off,
wavering,
slowly go, slipping down,
through the infinity of pleasure.

. . . .
Come! —already a sensual shiver takes hold of me,
my whole being lies in total abandonment . . .
Give me your cold kiss,
Sleep!
Let me stretch my slim body
over your body that is, like soft feathers, smooth.
. . . .
Here I am, languid and naked,
for your lust.
. . . .
Make your caress,
like an oil, run down my skin;
your caress, moist and emollient
that gives my body movements like a serpent
and indolence like a worm.
(G. Machado, "Invocação ao sono," fragments, *Cristais partidos*)

8 You dance . . . your gestures are gentle strokes
  your dance is a vague caress

English Translations to Page 48

    it is touch itself tickling
    the melodies of tenderness . . .

    You dance, and I become, at times,
    overwhelmed with singular joy;
    and I dream that you caress me,
    and I feel over all my body your gesture pass.
        (G. Machado, "Impressões do gesto," fragment, *Mulher nua*)

9 You dance, your limbs you agitate again,
    all your being seems to be taken
    by convulsions of infinite pain. . .
    and from that tragic crescendo
    of gestures filling the silence with moans
    you slow down,
    descending,
    as if from a spell,
    captive of a mystical curse . . .
    you dance and I imagine I see myself in you.

    Your movements
    are
    full
    of my desires;
    your dance is the expression
    of all that I feel:
    my imagination
    and my instinct
    move in your dance alternately;
    my lust, I see it twirl, in the air,
    when your body, languid, indolent,
    personifies the quiet in the ambient;
    rising, diminishing
    in the slithering of a serpent
    . . . .
    . . . in your light limbs, almost ethereal,
    I contemplate my inner gestures,
    my pleasures, my tedium, my pains!

    Your dance is everlasting,
    I see myself in it, I hold it within me,
    constantly thus!
        (G. Machado, "Impressões do gesto," stanzas 11–13, *Mulher nua*)

10 In the highest joy, in the deepest sorrow,
     may I be active, even if I am languid,

English Translations to Pages 51–65

>   I hold you in the madness of my blood
>   for Good, for Evil, dancing, dancing! . . .
>   (G. Machado, "Impressões do gesto," stanza 14, *Mulher nua*)

11 The Phallus is a symbol of the patriarchal, capitalist power, insatiable in its desire for expansion and control over human beings, who are given certain characteristics within pornographic fantasy as a reflection of social relationships in reality; [these relationships are] seen only from the viewpoint of sexuality and sexual arousal: continuity of male domination of women . . . , enforcement of racism . . . , affirmation of unequal social relations. . . . (Winckler 81)

12 I'm not well-behaved.
   A whore and a lesbian
   and whatever else comes to my mind,
   I'm like a crazy bird
   looking for scarecrows and traps,
   looking to expand like sleep
   over tired eyelids,
   to explode with violence
   within the conformists' silence.
   A whore and a lesbian
   and whatever else comes to my mind
   I'm the sequence
   unfolding from that first gesture.
   (Míccolis, "Na vida," fragment, *Mulheres da vida* 44)

13 My mother used to repeat certain phrases. Rules for living. In the first place, her husband, second, her husband, third, her husband. After that, the children. Yes, she was quite happy. Sweet-smelling, she waited for my father to come home from work. She used to wait for him. Perfumes, silences, whisperings. (Cunha, *Woman between Mirrors* 12)

14 At the times when I am really home alone, I lock myself in my room, turn on the record player and start dancing. Sound pulsing through. I leap to the other shore, free of the knots and the rules. Moving with the heavy beat, my whole body comes together in a rhythm that goes in deep. I like to put on my forbidden dresses. . . . I smile, I'm in on this with myself. . . . Who is that sultry provocative woman in the mirror? (Cunha, *Woman between Mirrors* 25)

15 My hands stroke my body, from top to bottom. They stop at my neck and fluff out my hair to make it fall free, on my shoulders.

English Translations to Pages 73–84

My hands, circling around my breasts, gently reach the erect tips, they've only known the fat sweaty hands of one man. I can feel the pleasure awaiting my lonely breasts. My hands run on down to my waist, to my buttocks, sink into my sex, ripe humid flesh cradled away from soarings and divings. . . .
. . .
I step out of the mirrors looking for the fur rug. I lie down on the floor and my pores come to know the bristly softness of the hairs. The wind from off the sea brings me the smell of ripe mangoes. I curl up, I stretch out, I roll. (Cunha, *Woman between Mirrors* 81–82)

16 . . . the sounds that came together in an aria that was ours, of him a man and me a woman traversing a night of rare honeyed moon. The man and I alighted in the mares' stable and went in. The man and I lay down on the hay where the mares lie down. It was on that hay that I loved a man under that rare night of honeyed moonlight. I felt that, with that man, I was sleeping with all the other acts I had slept with before with other men. I had come with all the acts and I felt that this act of mine would be almost perfect. (Felinto, *Women of Tijucopapo* 96)

17 The man touched me as if no part of my body were left untouched, I was entirely the man's, . . . I was being voided and invaded as only the salt water of the sea can sweep through me and invade me and exhaust me. I was being deep-plumbed and saturated. The man pressed me against the walls of the mares' stable and penetrated me with his member, . . . invading me, spraying me with spittle, submerging me and saturating me until I cried out in exhaustion and he cried out in exhaustion and we fell onto the edge of a sea of hay. (Felinto, *Women of Tijucopapo* 96)

Chapter Three
Representation of the Female Body and Desire:
The Gothic, the Fantastic, and the Grotesque

18 Mounting the demon, the smell of his own semen mixed with that of sweat and animal gases, he howled with pleasure and fear, hatred and victory. He expelled feces and urine, and finally fell into the embrace where he would be only Camilo, dissolved in beauty, liberated in a water without banks. . . . (Luft, *Island of the Dead* 92–93)

19 Maybe Clara knew about their invasions of Ella's room, but Renata lacked the courage to ask her. Her sister-in-law would look

English Translations to Pages 88–101

at her, smiling, saying: what harm was there in it? It was only an invalid's room. Ella was not an animal. Or was she? Clara would ask with her eyes wide open, like a child, like an insane person, like a savant. (Luft, *Island of the Dead* 66)

20 ... I didn't attain the fame of the poultice, I wasn't a minister, I wasn't a caliph, I didn't get to know marriage. The truth is that alongside these lacks the good fortune of not having to earn my bread by the sweat of my brow did befall me. ... on arriving at this other side of the mystery I found myself with a small balance, which is the final negative in this chapter of negatives—I had no children, I haven't transmitted the legacy of our misery to any creature. (Machado de Assis, *Brás Cubas,* trans. Rabassa 203)

21 The only advantage an animal has over men is the unawareness of death, and of death I am very aware. It remains for me as consolation to know that I will die but will carry no luggage, I leave behind only a flea collar. Two bowls and a pillow. (Telles, *As horas nuas* 114)

22 Ananta heard the circular steps following their fatal round, still in awe. Still in calculated self-control, he awaited in preparation. When his breathing accelerated, there began the spasms, his body growing intensely with the music ... exploding in snout, hooves, mane. ... Breathing wet and furious through his teeth, swollen veins, his eyes. The throbbing intensifying, as flesh and skin struggled to settle and fit. ... (Telles, *As horas nuas* 70)

Chapter Four
Sonia Coutinho's Short Fiction: Aging and the Female Body

23 Stopping at the corner of Bolívar Street, waiting for the traffic light to change, she noticed that the young man driving the big red car, stopped at the corner, was looking right at the blond young woman at her left side, and not at her. That's when, like a slap on her face, she realized that her golden dreams, the deep sorrows, and the great projects were all things from the past. (Coutinho, "Uma mulher" 121)

24 she had no lesson to teach, unlike what was believed, in the past, that the elders would be able to do. In the past, ah, in the past it was believed that the elders were sources of infinite knowledge and of magic powers. Now, everything changed too fast, Copacabana was like a whirlwind where today she felt like a precious,

useless and pathetic *avis rara*, . . . oh, God, she was getting old and didn't know anything. (Coutinho, "Uma mulher"125–26)

25 Naked before the mirror, brushing my hair, I observe—my soft, decaying flesh, like flesh that time has molded. I am not so young any longer, but this realization tastes like honey and red wine, on a warm morning in May, in Rio de Janeiro.
. . .
Tanned and fresh body burning inside, laughing at the mirror, sharp little teeth—a vampire. . . . I look at myself in the mirror and decide: you bitch, for that's what you are. (Coutinho, "Uma mulher" 55–56)

26 the man's leg naked over the woman's naked leg, she saying you are like a black panther, a big and calm panther licking the big, black paws, the man turning to get a cigarette, a man's naked back is very beautiful, his buttocks, solid, hard flesh, strong and curvilinear at the same time, an ugly man with a feline's face . . . (Coutinho, "Uma mulher" 42)

Chapter Five
Contemporary Brazilian Women's Short Stories: Lesbian Desire

27 Seated at the head of the long table set up in the verandah at the rear of the house, looking benevolent and sovereign like a patriarch, the Husband presided over the meeting of Men in Dark Suits and women with styled hair and voluminous clothes embellished with too much lace and jewelry: dignified representatives of the Extinct Colonial Nobility, displaying an old luxury brought in the Portuguese caravels. (Coutinho, "Fátima e Jamila" 132)

28 The breeze coming from the sea, far away, spreads around the room the heavy scent of the fruit piled in baskets . . . : *umbus* with an acidity that ends in sweetness as it dissolves in the mouth, pointy and bowed bananas like daggers, rosy mangoes that fit in a hand as an oval breast, their thick, yellow juice running down the chin, cashew fruit almost purple, and the sourness of the cherry *pitangas*. (Coutinho, "Fátima e Jamila" 131–32)

29 As if suddenly the *flamenco* singer broke, in the arrow's poignant scream, the white/black silence of the bleached houses under the vertical midday sun—with a strange uneasiness, . . . the shivering of a presage going down her guts, perhaps the Understanding,

English Translations to Pages 134–46

Fátima turned and saw Jamila's face. (Coutinho, "Fátima e Jamila" 135)

30 Lila held me by my shoulders, and under my sleepiness and tiredness I noticed again that greasy stare of desire. Ok, I thought, I succumb, sweet Lila, but I'm used to finishing off what I begin. Let's see how far you'll go.
    Lila, with affectation, leaned against the wall, making endless seductive gestures. . . . Then, calmly, I ordered her:
    —Take your clothes off . . .
    —Take it all off. If you want it, it'll be for real, dear. Lila stopped smiling. (Denser, "Tigresa" 135–36)

31 A parenthesis: Proust waited for his mother to die before he could say some things. But mine is alive and she'll have to put up with it. Be patient, Mom. I know you have neighbors, relatives and friends, but the truth is burning inside, it must be let out. Besides, it's good to get used to it, during this decade the wolf will eat all prudes and it'll lick its mouth, for me it's clear as water. (Campello, "A mulher de ouro" 59)

32 an oceanic fever devoured me, a storm swallowed me, all the Hindu mythology visited my solitary, innermost recesses, while Brahma, Vishnu and Shiva ran through my exposed nerves, what was that, Lord, the eye of a storm pushing me to limits so distant I didn't even know of their existence. . . . and it was not only the orgasms, ruffling through my body like a cathedral's carillon, that led me to such a perplexity of pleasure, it was the perfect space her trail imprinted on my soul, an abnegation so great in plenitude that I saw myself at the edge of religious ecstasy. (Campello, "A mulher de ouro" 61–62)

Chapter Six
The Works of Márcia Denser and Marina Colasanti: Female Agency and Heterosexuality

33 He says: this motel used to be good, and I look at the bathroom, . . . the brown sheets with suspicious bouquets, somewhere between stains and traces of color, the three round mirrors framed in fake leather (one before the other, the bed in the middle, the third one on the ceiling above the bed), obviously so as to transform us into some kind of a crazy cocktail of baked crabs: legs, arms, raw flesh, flower bed of paws, antennae, moving hairs, peeking at another hydra in the mirror in front, behind, above, below,

we wide open, mixed, confounded, at $25 a night, because (and then I know why) all motels are always the same motel. (Denser, "O animal dos motéis" 47–48)

34 I was lying down, smoking, when his hard mass fell on me. I sought his lips, but he said no, I've got a cold. So, I waited. Do you like it this way? he asked, turning me over. He embraced me with freezing fingers and hands, pressing my rib bones, hurting instead of caressing them. It works only from the waist down, like an electric vibrator, but it's good, I thought, letting myself be rigidly penetrated from behind, using, so to speak, only one part of my body, as if the rest were paralyzed, or dead, as if no one could bear a dramatic frontal relation, with kisses, ... with a face, a name, a biography. (Denser, "Hell's Angels" 76)

35 This is the season when the mango trees
dress in red.
Leaves of tawny silk
shiny satin.
Round like breasts
or abdomens
color of new flesh.
And on the trunks,
dense as blood,
trickles down
the cicadas' song.
        (Colasanti, "Verão em Campo Grande," *Rota de colisão*)

36 Over the silk fabric
lying and curvilinear
like a naked woman
the blade of the sword.
        (Colasanti, "Em Tóquio, no museu," *Rota de colisão*)

37 There is a tacit agreement among poets, certain words that should not be used "because they are not tacit," certain themes that are considered to be in bad taste. Menstruation, pregnancy, giving birth, motherhood, female sexuality itself—all of this should be addressed, let's say, in an elegant (cold or cerebral) way, or it risks being dismissed as "a woman's thing." Independently from the poem's quality. In other words, everything is OK, as long as you write "from the outside," like a man. (Roquette-Pinto, qtd. in "Vinte e duas poetas hoje" 210)

38 I am a woman
who always thought it beautiful
to menstruate.

English Translations to Pages 152–53

Men pour out blood
for illness
bleeding
or a nailed dagger
. . . .

In us
blood flows
like a fountain
in the concave body
scarlet spring
soaked satin
dripping
in a thread.
             (Colasanti, "Eu sou uma mulher," *Rota de colisão*)

39 Your sex

Your sex in my mouth
fills me
as if through my mouth
it penetrated my vagina.
Your sex in my mouth
impregnates me
makes me turgid
pregnant
honey sieved from my breasts
on the bed.
             (Colasanti, "Teu sexo," *Rota de colisão*)

40 Into the body

Your body is a canoe
in which I descend
down life
up death
looking to sink
letting the current take me.

Your body is a cocoon
of infinite silks
where I spin
sharpen myself and enter
an invader welcomed
with liqueurs.

Your body is an exact skin for mine
a herring's feather
a pomegranate's shine

English Translations to Pages 154–55

    aurora borealis
    of a long winter.
               (Colasanti, "Corpo adentro," *Rota de colisão*)

41 I belong to the eternal lineage
     of betrayed women
     female who weaves and spins
     while the male
     between another woman's thighs
     sharpens deceit and pleasure.
               (Colasanti, "Hematoma da infidelidade," fragment,
                                    Rota de colisão)

42 It's always the same male
     always the same path.
     No one was faithful to me
     to me, to my mother
     my sisters.
     And none of us
     could find the way
     that, staying in love
     leads to indifference.
               (Colasanti, "Hematoma da infidelidade," fragment,
                                    Rota de colisão)

43 I began to talk to women almost simultaneously to the beginning of my journalistic career, and in fact I don't recall any period . . . during which I was not connected in the most direct way with the female public. Talking *to* them soon became talking *about them* and *with* them.
     . . . I found out, in the infinite reflection of so very many women, my female I. And so, moved, I have blossomed a feeling of sisterhood that forever binds me to those of my own sex. (Colasanti, *A nova mulher* 9; emphasis in original)

44 In line at the market
     ahead of me
     she holds the basket
     and waits her turn.

     Skinny woman
     no breasts
     almost flat.
     Dark skin
     no shine

almost black.
Hoof-like feet.

Written on the blouse
in embroidered letters
a single word
    LUST
        (Colasanti, "Rumo à caixa," *Rota de colisão*)

45 power relations manifest themselves primordially through gender relations. Such fact is . . . primeval, since it preceded, by much, the emergence of societies centered on the private ownership of means of production. . . . It is primordial, also, because it totally permeates all social relations, be they class or ethnic relations. (Saffioti, "Rearticulando" 197)

46 Friday night
    men caress their wives' clitoris
    with fingers wet from saliva.
    The same gesture with which everyday
    they count money papers documents
    and skim through in magazines
    their idols' lives

Friday night
    men penetrate their wives
    with tediousness and penis.
    The same tediousness with which everyday
    they put the car in the garage
    the finger in their nose
    and dig into their pockets
    to scratch their balls.

Friday night
    men snore on their bellies
    while women in the dark
    face their destiny
    and dream of Prince Charming.
        (Colasanti, "Sexta-feira à noite," *Rota de colisão*)

Notes

Introduction

1. For example, many articles and editorials published in *A mensageira* identify their authors only by their initials: "M. P. C. D.," "V. M. de Barros," "L. F." The most famous case of a woman using pen names is that of Emília Moncorvo Bandeira de Melo (1852–1910), who signed her writings at different times as Carmen Dolores, Júlia de Castro, and Leonel Sampaio.

2. Argentine critic Cecilia Luque de Penazzi, in "La recurrencia de imágenes de mujer y familia como criterio de periodización histórica de la literatura brasilera" agrees: "En obras como *Diana Caçadora* . . . (Márcia Denser, 1986) y *O beijo no asfalto* . . . (Nelson Rodrigues, 1961) se puede ver la persistencia de los valores de las instituciones patriarcales en la estructura familiar y social moderna, a pesar de que el patriarcalismo señorial, como sistema económico-social, ya ha desaparecido" (74) ["In works such as Márcia Denser's *Diana Caçadora* and Nelson Rodrigues's *O beijo no asfalto,* one can see the persistence of patriarchal values in the modern social and family structure, even though patriarchy as a socio-economic system has already disappeared"].

3. In addition to George's "Women Writers and the Quest for Identity: From Fiction into Playwriting" (*Flash & Crash Days* 57–118), see also Elza Cunha de Vincenzo, *Um teatro da mulher: dramaturgia feminina no palco brasileiro contemporâneo* [Women's theater: Female dramaturgy on the contemporary Brazilian stage].

Chapter One
Female Body, Male Desire

1. See also Sommer's *Foundational Fictions: The National Romances of Latin America,* in which the critic dedicates a whole chapter to the discussion of José de Alencar's Indianist novels *O Guarani* and *Iracema.* It should be noted here that I differ slightly from Sommer, who characterizes these two novels as "Indigenist," alongside Clorinda Matto de Turner's *Aves sin nido* (1889) and other later Spanish American novels.

2. I quote here from the 2000 English translation of Alencar's *Iracema* by Clifford E. Landers.

3. See, for example, Sommer's *Foundational Fictions* 169. Duarte finds that the characterization of Iracema as a seductive Eve stems from the narrative itself. The critic states: "O maniqueísmo do discurso falocêntrico debita à mulher e à sua magia telúrica todo o poder de sedução, fazendo do homem uma vítima" (199) ["The Manicheism of phallocentric discourse charges the woman and her telluric magic with all the power of seduction, while making a victim of the man"].

4. The letter from Pero Vaz de Caminha, the scribe in Pedro Álvares Cabral's crew, to the Portuguese king describes with awe the beauty, and

also the innocence, of the Indians. Several decades later, however, these same innocent Indians were described by many Europeans as lascivious animals indulging freely in their lust. Paulo Prado, in his seminal *Retrato do Brasil: Ensaio sobre a tristeza brasileira* [Portrait of Brazil: Essay on the Brazilian sadness], offers an invaluable account of how lust and sensuality came to characterize Brazil as seen from an Eurocentric perspective.

    5. All English-language quotes are from Ronald W. Sousa's translation, *Memoirs of a Militia Sergeant.*

    6. I quote from the most recent English translation of *O cortiço, The Slum,* by David H. Rosenthal.

    7. See, for example, Ingrid Stein, *Figuras femininas em Machado de Assis;* Therezinha Mucci Xavier, *A personagem feminina no romance de Machado de Assis;* Pedro Maligo, "O desejo em Machado de Assis: um estudo sobre Helena, Virgilia e Sofia."

    8. On Machado de Assis's ambiguity in *Dom Casmurro,* see: Keith Ellis, "Technique and Ambiguity in 'Dom Casmurro'"; Silviano Santiago, "Retórica da verossimilhança"; John Gledson, *The Deceptive Realism of Machado de Assis: A Dissenting Interpretation of "Dom Casmurro";* Paul Dixon, "A auto-referência e o paradoxo em *Dom Casmurro.*"

    9. In "Manhas e artimanhas de um narrador alucinado," Mindlin enumerates many critics who have taken a stand against or for Capitu.

    10. I quote here from John Gledson's 1997 translation of Machado de Assis's *Dom Casmurro.*

    11. The fact that these household notebooks existed, and often hid their female owners' secret diaries, is presented by Lygia Fagundes Telles in her 1980 book *A disciplina do amor* [The discipline of love]. Telles sees them as one of Brazilian women's initial attempts at writing, at a time when it was deemed an exclusively male activity, and refers specifically to her own grandmother, in the last part of the twentieth century. Like other married women of the period, Telles's grandmother wrote her thoughts, feelings, secrets, and some poetry in her household notebook, hidden among recipes, domestic expenses, and other notes (*Disciplina* 16–17).

    12. The song was the theme song for the *samba* school Portela in the Carnival of 1966, and was recorded for the first time in 1971 by the famous *sambista* Martinho da Vila.

Chapter Two
Brazilian Women Writers: The Search for an Erotic Discourse

    1. See Ferreira-Pinto, "La mujer y el canon poético en Brasil a principios del siglo XX: hacia una reevaluación de la poesía de Gilka

Machado." It should be noted that the term "Pre-Modernist" has been used by many critics of Brazilian literature to describe the literary production in Brazil between 1900 and 1922. The year 1922 marks the beginning of the Modernist movement in Brazil, an avant-garde movement in literature, music, and visual arts that was influenced by various European movements, such as Surrealism and Futurism.

2. All translations of Gilka Machado's poetry are my own.

3. Colasanti made these comments in a personal conversation in October 1998.

4. All English-language quotes are from *Woman between Mirrors*, by Cunha, trans. Ellison and Lindstrom.

5. All English-language quotes are from *The Women of Tijucopapo*, by Felinto, trans. Matthews.

6. Lampião is the nickname of Virgulino Ferreira da Silva (1897–1938).

Chapter Three
Representation of the Female Body and Desire: The Gothic, the Fantastic, and the Grotesque

1. English-language quotes from Luft's *O quarto fechado* are from McClendon and Craige's translation, *The Island of the Dead*.

2. Telles's novels are: *Ciranda de pedra* (1954; *The Marble Dance*, 1986), *Verão no aquário* [Summer in the aquarium] (1963), *As meninas* (1973; *The Girl in the Photograph*, 1982), and *As horas nuas*.

3. Brás Cubas is the dead protagonist-narrator in Machado de Assis's *Memórias póstumas de Brás Cubas*. In this chapter, the English-language quotes are from the 1997 translation by Gregory Rabassa, *The Posthumous Memoirs of Brás Cubas;* the translations of excerpts from Telles's *As horas nuas* are my own.

Chapter Four
Sonia Coutinho's Short Fiction: Aging and the Female Body

1. In her *The Female Voice in Contemporary Brazilian Narrative*, Quinlan discusses the androgynous protagonist in *Ifá* (Quinlan 150–51), and androgyny as a textual strategy (169–71, 173–74).

2. See, for example, the kinds of ads that appear in magazines such as *Veja* and *Isto é*.

3. Erik Erikson (*Insight and Responsibility*) discusses the conflict between integration and despair or non-integration that characterizes the aging process.

4. Russo's essay was first published in 1986, and later included in her 1995 book *The Female Grotesque: Risk, Excess and Modernity*.

5. All these quotes are from Coutinho's "Cordélia"; my translations.

Chapter Five
Contemporary Brazilian Women's Short Stories: Lesbian Desire

1. On the erotic drive in Lispector's fiction, see Earl E. Fitz's *Sexuality and Being in the Poststructuralist Universe of Clarice Lispector,* particularly ch. 3, "The Erotics of Being: Self, Other, and Language," and pages 169–75 of ch. 6, "Psychoanalysis and the Poststructural Anxieties of the Lispectorian Universe."

2. On "O corpo" and the other stories from Lispector's *A via crucis do corpo* (*Soulstorm: The Stations of the Body,* 1989), see: Earl E. Fitz, "A Writer in Transition: Clarice Lispector and *A via crucis do corpo*"; Nelson H. Vieira, "The Stations of the Body, Clarice Lispector's *Abertura* and Renewal"; and Maria José Somerlate Barbosa, *Clarice Lispector: Spinning the Webs of Passion,* especially p. 28.

3. There is an extensive bibliography about the topic; see, among others, "The Laugh of the Medusa" (1975) and other essays by Cixous; Luce Irigaray's *Ce sexe qui n'en est pas un* (1977; *This Sex Which Is Not One,* 1981); Kristeva's "Stabat Mater" (1986); and De Lauretis's *The Practice of Love* (1994).

4. A new and revised version of "A escolha" appears in Telles's *A noite escura e mais eu* [The dark night and me] (1992) with the title "Uma branca sombra pálida" [A pale white shadow]. Likewise, "A mulher de ouro" appears, with few changes, in Campello's volume of short stories *Sons e outros frutos* [Sounds and other fruit] (1998). I chose to use the original versions of the two stories for my analysis, a choice particularly relevant in the case of Telles, whose original story is much more ambiguous than the second version.

5. I quote from the English translation by David George ("Intimacy," *A Bag of Stories,* by Edla Van Steen).

6. The meaning of the character's name is made clear in the title of the book where it first appeared, *Diana Caçadora* [Diana, the Huntress] (1986), and has been discussed by critics such as Rodolfo Franconi, "Eroticism" (1987; *Erotismo,* 1997), and Quinlan, "*Animal dos motéis*" (1991).

7. Eva Paulino Bueno presents an excellent analysis of Telles's "Tigrela" as a lesbian narrative in *Latin American Writers on Gay and Lesbian Themes.*

8. See also Campello's *São Sebastião Blues* (1993).

Chapter Six
The Works of Márcia Denser and Marina Colasanti: Female Agency and Heterosexuality

1. Colasanti, whose works have been translated into English, Spanish, Italian, French and German, is also the critically acclaimed author

of short stories, children's books, and fairy tales. She has been awarded some important literary prizes at home and abroad. Among her books of narrative prose are: *Zooilógico* [Zooillogical] (1975), *A morada do ser* [The being's dwelling] (1978), *Contos de amor rasgado* [Stories of torn love] (1986), *Eu sei mas não devia* [I know, but I shouldn't] (1996), and *Longe como o meu querer* [Far away as my love] (1997), which won the prestigious Latin American prize "Norma-Fundalectura" in 1996. As of this writing, Colasanti has published another book of poetry: *Gargantas abertas* [Open throats] (1998).

2. See Angier's *Woman: An Intimate Geography* for an interesting discussion and debunking of such notions.

3. See "Vinte e duas poetas hoje" [Twenty-two women poets today], a round-table discussion led by Lúcia Helena with contemporary Brazilian women poets, among them Adélia Prado, Hilda Hilst, Olga Savary, and Leila Míccolis (Colasanti was not one of the twenty-two poets). In her introduction to the discussion, Helena summarizes the poets' opinions over the question of whether poetry is gender marked: "Em sua maioria, relutam em acreditar que a poesia tenha sexo" (Helena, "Corpo de escrita" 205) ["In their majority, they hesitate to believe that poetry has sex"]. While Hilst and Savary radically reject the idea, and Míccolis, on the other hand, defends it, most of the poets agree that a woman's poetry reflects her life experiences and perspective, and that these are different from a man's. However, most reject the label of "*poesia feminina*" ("feminine poetry"). Others still defend the idea of poetry—perhaps literature in general—as an androgynous manifestation.

Bibliography

Albuquerque, Severino João. *Violent Acts: A Study of Contemporary Latin American Theatre.* Detroit: Wayne State UP, 1991.

Alencar, José Martiniano de. *Iracema.* 1865. 21st ed. São Paulo: Melhoramentos, 1969.

———. *Iracema.* Trans. Clifford E. Landers. New York: Oxford UP, 2000.

Almeida, Manuel Antônio de. *Memórias de um sargento de milícias.* 1853. São Paulo: Círculo do Livro, n.d. [199?].

———. *Memoirs of a Militia Sergeant.* Trans. Ronald W. Sousa. New York: Oxford UP, 1999.

Althusser, Louis. "Ideología y humanismo marxista." *Ideología y aparatos ideológicos de estado.* Spec. issue of *Cuadernos de educación* [Caracas, Venezuela] 9–10 (Nov.–Dec. 1973): 13–20.

Alvarez, Sonia E. *Engendering Democracy in Brazil: Women's Movements in Transition Politics.* Princeton: Princeton UP, 1990.

Amado, Jorge. *Dona Flor e seus dois maridos.* São Paulo: Martins, 1966.

———. *Gabriela, cravo e canela.* São Paulo: Martins, 1958.

Angier, Natalie. *Woman: An Intimate Geography.* Boston and New York: Houghton, 1999.

Anzaldúa, Gloria. "To(o) Queer the Writer—Loca, escritora y chicana." *InVersions: Writings by Dykes, Queers and Lesbians.* Ed. Betsy Warland. Vancouver: Press Gang, 1991. 249–63.

Araújo, Emanuel. "A arte da sedução: Sexualidade feminina na colônia." *História das mulheres no Brasil.* Ed. Mary Del Priore. São Paulo: Contexto, 1997. 45–77.

Armitt, Lucie. *Theorising the Fantastic.* London: Arnold, 1996.

Armstrong, Nancy. *Desire and Domestic Fiction: A Political History of the Novel.* New York: Oxford UP, 1987.

Austregésilo, Antonio. *Perfil da mulher brasileira (Esboço acerca do feminismo no Brasil).* 1922. 2nd ed. Rio de Janeiro: Guanabara, 1938.

Azevedo, Aluísio. *O cortiço.* 1890. 27th ed. São Paulo: Ática, 1995.

———. *The Slum.* Trans. David H. Rosenthal. New York: Oxford UP, 2000.

Barbosa, Maria José Somerlate. *Clarice Lispector: Spinning the Webs of Passion.* New Orleans: UP of the South, 1997.

Bibliography

Barbosa, Maria José Somerlate. "*Espaçamento* como registro cultural na obra de Helena Parente Cunha." *Entre resistir e identificarse: Para uma teoria da prática narrativa brasileira de autoria feminina.* Ed. Peggy Sharpe. Florianópolis: Mulheres; Goiânia: UFG, 1997. 139–52.

Bataille, Georges. *Erotism: Death and Sensuality.* San Francisco: City Lights, 1986.

Beard, Laura. "La sujetividad femenina en la metaficción feminista latinoamericana." *Revista Iberoamericana* 64.182–83 (Jan.–June 1998): 299–311.

Bellini, Ligia. *A coisa obscura: Mulher, sodomia e Inquisição no Brasil colonial.* São Paulo: Brasiliense, 1987.

Benstock, Shari. "The Female Self Engendered: Autobiographical Writing and Theories of Selfhood." *Women and Autobiography.* Ed. Martine Watson Brownley and Allison B. Kimmich. Wilmington, DE: Scholarly Resources, 1999. 3–13.

Berkin, Carol. "'Dangerous Courtesies' Assault Women's History." *Chronicle of Higher Education,* 11 Dec. 1991: 44.

Bernardet, Jean Claude. "Pornografia, o sexo dos outros." *Sexo e poder.* Ed. Guido Mantega. São Paulo: Brasiliense, 1979. 103–08.

Bonassi, Fernando. "Autobiografia de leitura." *Revista Sem Terra* 8 (Aug.–Sept. 1999): 72–73.

Brandão, Ruth Silviano. "A fascinante (in)quietude do feminino." *A mulher escrita.* By Lúcia Castello Branco and Brandão. Rio de Janeiro: Casa Maria, Livros Técnicos e Científicos, 1989. 25–35.

Bueno, Eva Paulino. "Lygia Fagundes Telles." *Latin American Writers on Gay and Lesbian Themes: A Bio-Critical Sourcebook.* Ed. David William Foster. Westport, CT, and London: Greenwood, 1994. 424–27.

Butler, Judith. *Gender Trouble: Feminism and the Subversion of Identity.* New York: Routledge, 1990.

Caldwell, Helen. *The Brazilian Othello of Machado de Assis: A Study of "Dom Casmurro."* Berkeley: U of California P, 1960.

Campello, Myriam. "A mulher de ouro." Denser, *O prazer é todo meu* 59–63.

———. *São Sebastião Blues.* São Paulo: Brasiliense, 1993.

———. *Sons e outros frutos.* Rio de Janeiro: Record, 1998.

———. *Sortilegiu.* Rio de Janeiro: Civilização Brasileira, INL, 1981.

Candido, Antonio. "Dialética da malandragem (Caracterização das *Memórias de um sargento de milícias*)." 1970. *Memórias de um sargento de milícias.* By Manuel Antônio de Almeida. São Paulo: Círculo do Livro, n.d. [199?]. 187–217.

———. "Literature and the Rise of Brazilian National Identity." Trans. Richard Graham. *Luso-Brazilian Review* 5.1 (June 1968): 27–43.

Carlson-Leavitt, Joyce Anne. "Gilka Machado and Adélia Prado: Two Brazilian Women Poets' Vision of the Female Experience." Diss. U of New Mexico, 1989.

Castello Branco, Lúcia. "As incuráveis feridas da natureza feminina." *A mulher escrita.* By Castello Branco and Ruth Silviano Brandão. Rio de Janeiro: Casa Maria, Livros Técnicos e Científicos, 1989. 87–109.

Cavalccante, Joyce. *O discurso da mulher absurda.* São Paulo: Global, 1985.

Charney, Maurice. *Sexual Fiction.* London and New York: Methuen, 1981.

Chaui, Marilena. Preface. Felinto, *As mulheres de Tijucopapo* 9–12.

Cixous, Hélène. "Coming to Writing." 1977. *"Coming to Writing" and Other Essays.* Ed. Deborah Jenson. Cambridge, MA, and London: Harvard UP, 1991. 1–58.

———. "The Laugh of the Medusa." 1975. Trans. Keith Cohen and Paula Cohen. *The Signs Reader: Women, Gender and Scholarship.* Ed. Elizabeth Abel and Emily K. Abel. Chicago: U of Chicago P, 1983. 279–97.

Coelho, Nelly Novaes. "À guisa de posfácio." *O conto da mulher brasileira.* Ed. Edla Van Steen. São Paulo: Vertente, 1978. 241–52.

———. "Eros e Tanatos: A poesia feminina na primeira metade do século XX." *Mulher e literatura: Anais do Quinto Seminário Nacional Mulher e Literatura.* 1–3 Sept. 1993. Natal: Universidade Federal do Rio Grande do Norte, Editora Universitária, 1995. 50–62.

———. "A presença da mulher na literatura brasileira contemporânea." 1991. *A literatura feminina no Brasil contemporâneo.* São Paulo: Siciliano, 1993. 11–26.

Colasanti, Marina. "Uma caçadora de metáforas na floresta do inconsciente." Interview with Márcio Vassallo. *Lector* 22 (1997): 8–9.

———. *A nova mulher.* 7th ed. Rio de Janeiro: Nórdica, 1980.

———. *Rota de colisão.* Rio de Janeiro: Rocco, 1993.

Bibliography

Costa, Jurandir Freire. *Ordem médica e norma familiar.* Rio de Janeiro: Graal, 1979.

Coutinho, Sonia. *Uma certa felicidade.* 1976. Rio de Janeiro: Rocco, 1994.

———. "Uma certa felicidade." Coutinho, *Uma certa felicidade* 9–57.

———. "Cordélia, a caçadora." *Os venenos de Lucrécia.* São Paulo: Ática, 1978. 19–27.

———. "Darling, ou do amor em Copacabana." Coutinho, *Uma certa felicidade* 59–64.

———. "O dia em que Mary Batson fez 40 anos." Coutinho, *O último verão* 67–71.

———. "Fátima e Jamila." Coutinho, *Uma certa felicidade* 131–35.

———. *O jogo de Ifá.* São Paulo: Ática, 1980.

———. "Josete se matou." Coutinho, *O último verão* 13–18.

———. "Uma mulher sem nenhuma importância." Coutinho, *Uma certa felicidade* 121–29.

———. *Nascimento de uma mulher.* Rio de Janeiro: Civilização Brasileira, 1970.

———. *Os seios de Pandora—uma aventura de Dora Diamante.* Rio de Janeiro: Rocco, 1998.

———. "Sobre a escrita feminina." Conference. University of Texas at Austin. Apr. 1997.

———. *O último verão de Copacabana.* Rio de Janeiro: José Olympio, 1985.

Coward, Rosalind. "Female Desire and Sexual Identity." *Women, Feminist Identity and Society in the 1980's: Selected Papers.* Ed. Myriam Díaz-Dicaretz and Iris Zavala. Amsterdam and Philadelphia: Benjamins, 1985. 25–36.

Cranny-Francis, Anne. *Feminist Fiction: Feminist Uses of Generic Fiction.* New York: St. Martin's, 1990.

Cunha, Helena Parente. "O desafio da fala feminina ao falo falocêntrico." *Literatura e feminismo: Propostas teóricas e reflexões críticas.* Ed. Christina Ramalho. Rio de Janeiro: Elo, 1999. 151–71.

———. *Mulher no espelho.* 1983. São Paulo: Art, 1985.

———. *Woman between mirrors.* Trans. Fred P. Ellison and Naomi Lindstrom. Austin: U of Texas P, 1989.

De Lauretis, Teresa. *The Practice of Love: Lesbian Sexuality and Perverse Desire.* Bloomington: Indiana UP, 1994.

Denser, Márcia. "O animal dos motéis." Denser, *Diana* 46–52.

———. *Diana Caçadora*. São Paulo: Global, 1986.

———. "Hell's Angels." Denser, *Diana* 67–77.

———, ed. *Muito prazer*. Rio de Janeiro: Record, 1980.

———, ed. *O prazer é todo meu: Contos eróticos femininos*. Rio de Janeiro: Record, 1984.

———. "Tigresa." Denser, *Diana* 119–36.

———. "O vampiro da Alameda Casabranca." Denser, *Muito prazer* 37–48.

———. "The Vampire of Whitehouse Lane." Trans. Darlene J. Sadlier. *One Hundred Years after Tomorrow: Brazilian Women's Fiction in the Twentieth Century*. Ed. and introd. Sadlier. Bloomington: Indiana UP, 1992. 205–14.

———. "Welcome to Diana." Denser, *Diana* 11–44.

Dixon, Paul B. "A auto-referência e o paradoxo em *Dom Casmurro*." *Brasil/Brazil* 1.1 (1988): 30–40.

———. *Reversible Readings: Ambiguity in Four Modern Latin American Novels*. University: U of Alabama P, 1985.

Duarte, Eduardo de Assis. "*Iracema*: A expansão portuguesa sob o signo de Eva." *Literatura e feminismo: Propostas teóricas e reflexões críticas*. Ed. Christina Ramalho. Rio de Janeiro: Elo, 1999. 195–202.

Durigan, Jesus Antônio. *Erotismo e literatura*. São Paulo: Ática, 1985.

Eagleton, Terry. *Ideology: An Introduction*. London and New York: Verso, 1991.

Ellis, Kate Ferguson. *The Contested Castle: Gothic Novels and the Subversion of Domestic Ideology*. Urbana: U of Illinois P, 1989.

Ellis, Keith. "Technique and Ambiguity in *Dom Casmurro*." *Hispania* 45 (1965): 436–40.

Erikson. Erik. *Insight and Responsibility*. New York: Norton, 1964.

Faderman, Lillian. "What Is Lesbian Literature? Forming a Historical Canon." Haggerty and Zimmerman 49–59.

Farwell, Marilyn R. *Heterosexual Plots and Lesbian Narratives*. New York and London: New York UP, 1996.

———. "The Lesbian Narrative: 'The Pursuit of the Inedible by the Unspeakable.'" Haggerty and Zimmerman 156–68.

Felinto, Marilene. *As mulheres de Tijucopapo*. Rio de Janeiro: Paz e Terra, 1982.

Bibliography

Felinto, Marilene. *The Women of Tijucopapo.* Trans. Irene Matthews. Lincoln and London: U of Nebraska P, 1994.

Ferreira-Pinto, Cristina. "La mujer y el canon poético en Brasil a principios del siglo XX: hacia una reevaluación de la poesía de Gilka Machado." *La Torre* 34 (Apr.–June 1995): 221–41.

Fitz, Earl E. *Sexuality and Being in the Poststructuralist Universe of Clarice Lispector: The "Différance" of Desire.* Austin: U of Texas P, 2001.

———. "A Writer in Transition: Clarice Lispector and *A via crucis do corpo.*" *Latin American Literary Review* 32 (1988): 41–52.

Foster, David William. *Gay and Lesbian Themes in Latin American Writing.* Austin: U of Texas P, 1991.

———. *Sexual Textualities: Essays on Queer/ing Latin American Writing.* Austin: U of Texas P, 1997.

Foucault, Michel. *The History of Sexuality.* Vol. 1: *An Introduction.* 1976. Trans. Robert Hurley. New York: Vintage, 1990.

———. *The History of Sexuality.* Vol. 2: *The Use of Pleasure.* 1984. Trans. Robert Hurley. New York: Vintage, 1990.

———. "What Is an Author?" 1969. *The Foucault Reader.* Ed. Paul Rabinow. New York: Pantheon, 1984. 101–20.

Franconi, Rodolfo Alberto. "Eroticism and Power in the Brazilian Fiction of the '80s" (text in Portuguese). Diss. Vanderbilt U, 1987.

———. *Erotismo e poder na ficção brasileira contemporânea.* São Paulo: Annablume, 1997.

Frazer, James George. *The Golden Bough.* 1890. New York: Avenel, 1981.

George, David S. *Flash & Crash Days: Brazilian Theater in the Postdictatorship Period.* New York and London: Garland, 2000.

Gledson, John. *The Deceptive Realism of Machado de Assis: A Dissenting Interpretation of "Dom Casmurro."* Liverpool: Francis Cairns, 1984.

Gotlib, Nádia Battella. "Com Dona Gilka Machado, Eros pede a palavra (Poesia erótica feminina brasileira nos inícios do século XX)." *Polímia* 4 (1982): 23–47.

Griffin, Susan. *Pornography and Silence: Culture's Revenge against Women.* London: Women's, 1981.

Guerra-Cunningham, Lucía. "Estética fantástica y mensaje metafísico en 'Lo secreto' de María Luisa Bombal." *María Luisa Bombal: apreciaciones críticas.* Ed. Marjorie Agosín, Elena Gascón, and Joy Renjilian-Burgy. Tempe, AZ: Bilingual/Bilingüe, 1987. 82–87.

Haberly, David T. *Three Sad Races: Racial Identity and National Consciousness in Brazilian Literature.* New York: Cambridge UP, 1983.

Haggerty, George E., and Bonnie Zimmerman, eds. *Professions of Desire: Lesbian and Gay Studies in Literature.* New York: MLA, 1995.

Hahner, June. *Emancipating the Female Sex: The Struggle for Women's Rights in Brazil: 1890–1940.* Durham: Duke UP, 1990.

Harpham, Geoffrey Galt. *On the Grotesque: Strategies of Contradiction in Art and Literature.* Princeton: Princeton UP, 1982.

Harris, Bertha. "What We Mean to Say: Notes toward Defining the Nature of Lesbian Literature." *Heresies: A Feminist Publication on Arts and Politics* (Fall 1977): 5–8.

Helena, Lúcia. "Corpo de escrita: Poesia tem gênero?" Introduction. "Vinte e duas poetas hoje." *Poesia sempre* 10 (Feb. 1999): 203–08.

———. "Perfis da mulher na ficção brasileira dos anos 80." *A mulher na literatura.* Ed. Ana Lúcia Almeida Gazolla. Belo Horizonte: Imprensa da Universidade Federal de Minas Gerais, 1990. 86–96.

Hendricks, Jon, and Cynthia A. Leedham. "Making Sense: Interpreting Historical and Cross-Cultural Literature on Aging." *Perceptions of Aging in Literature: A Cross-Cultural Study.* Ed. Prisca von Dorotka Bagnell and Patricia Spencer Soper. Westport, CT: Greenwood, 1989. 1–16.

Hilst, Hilda. *O caderno rosa de Lori Lamby.* São Paulo: Massao Ohno, 1990.

———. *Cartas de um sedutor.* São Paulo: Paulicéia, 1991.

———. *Contos d'escárnio: Textos grotescos.* São Paulo: Siciliano, 1990.

Hunt, Lynn. Introduction. *Eroticism and the Body Politic.* Ed. Hunt. Baltimore: Johns Hopkins UP, 1991. 1–13.

Irigaray, Luce. 1977. *This Sex Which Is Not One.* Trans. Catherine Porter. Ithaca: Cornell UP, 1985.

Jackson, Rosemary. *Fantasy: The Literature of Subversion.* 1981. London and New York: Routledge, 1988.

Jackson, Stevi. "Heterosexuality, Power and Pleasure." *Feminism and Sexuality: A Reader.* Ed. S. Jackson and Sue Scott. New York: Columbia UP, 1996. 175–79.

Bibliography

Jameson, Fredric. "Nostalgia for the Present." *South Atlantic Quarterly* 88.2 (1989): 517–37.

Kristeva, Julia. *Proust and the Sense of Time.* Trans. and introd. Stephen Bann. London: Faber and Faber, 1993.

———. "Stabat Mater." *The Female Body in Western Culture: Contemporary Perspectives.* Ed. Susan Rubin Suleiman. Cambridge, MA: Harvard UP, 1986. 99–118.

La Belle, Jenijoy. *Herself Beheld: The Literature of the Looking Glass.* Ithaca: Cornell UP, 1988.

Leite, Dante Moreira. *O amor romântico e outros temas.* São Paulo: Cia. Editora Nacional, 1979.

Lemaire, Ria. "Re-Reading *Iracema:* The Problem of the Representation of Women in the Construction of a National Brazilian Identity." *Luso-Brazilian Review* 26.2 (Winter 1989): 59–73.

Lesnoff-Caravaglia, Gary. "Double Stigmata: Female and Old." *The World of the Older Woman: Conflicts and Resolutions.* Ed. Lesnoff-Caravaglia. New York: Human Sciences, 1984. 11–20.

Lispector, Clarice. "O corpo." *A via crucis do corpo.* Rio de Janeiro: Artenova, 1974. 27–37.

———. *Perto do coração selvagem.* 1944. 7th ed. Rio de Janeiro: Nova Fronteira, 1980.

———. *Soulstorm: Stations of the Body.* New York: New Directions, 1989.

Lobo, Luiza. "Sonia Coutinho Revisits the City." *Latin American Women's Writing: Feminist Readings in Theory and Crisis.* Ed. Anny Brooksbank Jones and Catherine Davies. New York: Oxford UP, 1996. 163–78.

López, Kimberle S., and Alice A. Brittin. "Marginality in the Contemporary Female Brazilian Bildungsroman." Unpubl. ms., 1990.

Lorde, Audre. "Uses of the Erotic: The Erotic as Power." 1978. *Modern Feminisms: Political, Literary, Cultural.* Ed. Maggie Humm. New York: Columbia UP, 1992. 285–86.

Lucas, Fábio. "Lygia Fagundes Telles." *Dictionary of Literary Biography: Modern Latin-American Fiction Writers.* Vol. 113. Detroit: Bruccoli Clark Layman, 1992. 287–92.

Luft, Lya. "Fiction and the Possible Selves." Interview with Judith A. Payne. *Brasil/Brazil* 5 (1991): 104–14.

———. *As parceiras.* 1980. 5th ed. Rio de Janeiro: Guanabara, 1986.

———. *O quarto fechado.* 1984. 3rd ed. Rio de Janeiro: Guanabara, 1986.

---. *The Island of the Dead.* Trans. Carmen Chaves McClendon and Betty Jean Craige. Athens: U of Georgia P, 1986.

Luque de Penazzi, Cecilia. "La recurrencia de imágenes de mujer y familia como criterio de periodización histórica de la literatura brasilera." *Chasqui: Revista de Literatura Latinoamericana* 26.1 (May 1996): 72–95.

Machado, Ana Maria. *A audácia dessa mulher.* Rio de Janeiro: Nova Fronteira, 1999.

Machado, Gilka. *Cristais partidos.* 1915. G. Machado, *Poesias completas* 17–108.

---. *Estados de alma.* 1917. G. Machado, *Poesias completas* 109–97.

---. *Mulher nua.* 1922. G. Machado, *Poesias completas* 199–262.

---. *Poesias completas.* Rio de Janeiro: Cátedra; Brasília: INL, 1978.

Machado de Assis, Joaquim Maria. *Dom Casmurro.* 1899. 12th ed. São Paulo: Ática, 1981.

---. *Dom Casmurro.* Trans. John Gledson. New York: Oxford UP, 1997.

---. *Memórias póstumas de Brás Cubas.* 1881. 6th ed. São Paulo: Ática, 1977.

---. *Posthumous Memoirs of Brás Cubas.* Trans. Gregory Rabassa. New York: Oxford UP, 1997.

Maligo, Pedro. "O desejo em Machado de Assis: Um estudo sobre Helena, Virgilia e Sofia." *Espelho: Revista Machadiana* 3 (1997): 67–88.

Manzor-Coats, Lillian. Introduction. *Latin American Writers on Gay and Lesbian Themes: A Bio-Critical Sourcebook.* Ed. David William Foster. Westport, CT; London: Greenwood, 1994. xv–xxxvi.

Matthews, Irene. Afterword. Felinto, *The Women of Tijucopapo* 123–32.

Mayrink, Geraldo. "Dona da palavra." *Veja* 21 May 1997: 138–39.

McClendon, Carmen Chaves. "Theoretical Dialogue in *O quarto fechado.*" *Chasqui: Revista de Literatura Latinoamericana* 17.2 (1988): 23–26.

McClendon, Carmen Chaves, and Betty Jean Craige. Translators' Preface. *The Island of the Dead.* By Lya Luft. Athens: U of Georgia P, 1986. ix–xii.

McGann, Jerome J. *The Romantic Ideology: A Critical Investigation.* Chicago: U of Chicago P, 1983.

Bibliography

Melamed, Elissa. *Mirror Mirror: The Terror of Not Being Young.* New York: Simon 1983.

Mendonça, Nana. "International Lesbianism: Brazil." *Feminist Review* 34 (Spring 1990): 8–11.

A Mensageira: Revista literaria dedicada à mulher brazileira. 1897. Facsimile ed. Vol. 1. São Paulo: Imprensa Oficial do Estado, Secretaria de Estado da Cultura,1987.

Míccolis, Leila, ed. *Mulheres da vida.* São Paulo: Vertente, 1978.

———. "Prazer, gênero de primeira necessidade." *Jacarés e lobisomens: Dois ensaios sobre a homossexualidade.* Míccolis and Herbert Daniel. Rio de Janeiro: Achiamé, SOCII-Pesquisadores Associados em Ciências Sociais, 1983. 69–119.

Mindlin, Dulce Maria Viana. "Manhas e artimanhas de um narrador alucinado (Uma leitura de *Dom Casmurro*)." *Espelho: Revista Machadiana* 1 (1995): 72–73.

Molloy, Sylvia. "Female Textual Identities: The Strategies of Self-Figuration." *Women's Writing in Latin America: An Anthology.* Ed. Sara Castro-Klarén, Molloy, and Beatriz Sarlo. Boulder, CO: Westview, 1991. 107–24.

Mora, Gabriela. "Escritura erótica: Cristina Peri Rossi y Tununa Mercado." *Carnal Knowledge: Essays on the Flesh, Sex and Sexuality in Hispanic Letters and Film.* Ed. Pamela Bacarisse. Pittsburgh: Tres Ríos, 1991. 129–40.

Mott, Luís. *O lesbianismo no Brasil.* Porto Alegre: Mercardo Aberto, 1987.

Muzart, Zahidé Lupinacci, ed. *Escritoras brasileiras do século XIX: Uma antologia.* Florianópolis: Mulheres; Santa Cruz do Sul, RS: EDUNISC, 1999.

Paixão, Sylvia Perlingeiro. "À sombra de eros." *Anais do Quarto Seminário Nacional "Mulher e Literatura."* Ed. Lúcia Helena Vianna. Niterói: Coordenação de Pós-Graduação em Letras da Universidade Federal Fluminense, Abralic, 1992. 115–28.

———. "A fala-a-menos: A repressão do desejo na poesia feminina do final do século XIX e início do século XX, no Brasil." *A mulher na literatura.* Vol. 3. Ed. Nádia Batella Gotlib. Belo Horizonte: Imprensa da Universidade Federal de Minas Gerais, 1990. 136–42.

Parker, Richard G. *Bodies, Pleasures and Passions: Sexual Culture in Contemporary Brazil.* Boston: Beacon, 1991.

Peixoto, Afrânio. *Noções de história da literatura brasileira.* Rio de Janeiro: Francisco Alves, 1931.

Penna, João Camillo. "Marilene Felinto e a diferença." *Revista de Crítica Literaria Latinoamericana* 41 (1995): 213–53.

Pescatello, Ann. "The Brazileira, Images and Realities in Writings by Machado de Assis and Jorge Amado." LASA Conference. Austin, TX. 1971.

Piñon, Nélida. *A casa da paixão.* 1972. 5th ed. Rio de Janeiro: Francisco Alves, 1988.

Pleasure in the Word: Erotic Writing by Latin American Women. Ed. Margarite Fernández Olmos and Lizabeth Paravisini-Gebert. New York: Plume, 1994.

Prado, Paulo. *Retrato do Brasil: Ensaio sobre a tristeza brasileira.* 1928. 2nd ed. São Paulo: IBRASA; Brasília: INL, 1981.

Pratt, Annis, with Barbara White, Andrea Loewenstein, and Mary Wyer. *Archetypal Patterns in Women's Fiction.* Bloomington: Indiana UP, 1981.

Py, Fernando. Prefácio. *Poesias completas.* By Gilka Machado. Rio de Janeiro: Cátedra; Brasília: INL, 1978. xix–xxviii.

Queiroz, Cristina de. "A chave na fechadura." Denser, *Muito prazer* 9–16.

Queiroz, Rachel de. *As três Marias.* 1939. Rio de Janeiro: José Olympio, 1960.

———. *The Three Marias.* Trans. Fred P. Ellison. Austin: U of Texas P, 1963.

Quinlan, Susan C. "*O animal dos motéis: Novela em episódios:* I Write to Describe All Sides of Myself." Quinlan, *Female Voice* 103–37.

———. *The Female Voice in Contemporary Brazilian Narrative.* New York: Peter Lang, 1990.

Ramalho, Christina. *Um espelho para Narcisa: Reflexos de uma voz romântica.* Rio de Janeiro: Elo, 1999.

Reis, Roberto. "Representations of Family and Sexuality in Brazilian Cultural Discourse." *Bodies and Biases: Sexualities in Hispanic Cultures and Literature.* Ed. David William Foster and Reis. Minneapolis: U of Minnesota P, 1996. 79–114.

Resende, Otto Lara. *As pompas do mundo.* Rio de Janeiro: Rocco, 1975.

Rich, Adrienne. "Compulsory Heterosexuality and Lesbian Existence." 1980. *The Signs Reader: Women, Gender and Scholarship.* Ed. Elizabeth Abel and Emily K. Abel. Chicago: U of Chicago P, 1983. 139–68.

Russo, Mary. *The Female Grotesque: Risk, Excess, and Modernity.* New York: Routledge, 1995.

Saffioti, Heleieth I. B. "Rearticulando gênero e classe social." *Uma questão de Gênero.* Ed. Albertina de Oliveira Costa and Cristina Bruschini. Rio de Janeiro: Rosa dos Tempos; São Paulo: Fundação Carlos Chagas, 1992. 183–215.

Salvaggio, Ruth. *The Sounds of Feminist Theory.* Albany: State U of New York P, 1999.

Sant'Anna, Affonso Romano de. *O canibalismo amoroso: O desejo e a interdição em nossa cultura através da poesia.* São Paulo: Brasiliense, 1984.

———. *Música popular e moderna poesia brasileira.* Petrópolis: Vozes, 1978.

Santiago, Silviano. "Retórica da verossimilhança." *Uma literatura nos trópicos.* São Paulo: Perspectiva, 1978. 29–48.

Savary, Olga, ed. *Carne viva.* Rio de Janeiro: Anima, 1984.

Schor, Naomi. *Reading in Detail: Aesthetics and the Feminine.* 1987. New York: Routledge, 1989.

Schumaher, Schuma, and Érico Vital Brazil, eds. *Dicionário mulheres do Brasil: De 1500 até a atualidade biográfico e ilustrado.* Rio de Janeiro: Jorge Zahar, 2000.

Schwarz, Roberto. *Duas meninas.* São Paulo: Companhia das Letras, 1997.

Sharpe, Peggy. "Imagens e poder: Construindo a obra de Marina Colasanti." *Entre resistir e identificar-se: Para uma teoria da prática da narrativa brasileira de autoria feminina.* Ed. Sharpe. Florianópolis: Mulheres; Goiânia: UFG, 1997. 43–55.

Silva, Vera Maria Tietzmann. *A metamorfose nos contos de Lygia Fagundes Telles.* Rio de Janeiro: Presença, 1985.

Silveira, Homero. "Mulheres romancistas." *Aspectos do romance brasileiro contemporâneo.* São Paulo: Convívio; Brasília: INL-MEC, 1977. 88–98.

Smith, Barbara. "Toward a Black Feminist Criticism." *Women's Studies International Quarterly* 2.2 (1979): 183–94.

Sommer, Doris. *Foundational Fictions: The National Romances of Latin America.* Berkeley and Los Angeles: U of California P, 1991.

———. "Not Just Any Narrative: How Romance Can Love Us to Death." *The Historical Novel in Latin America: A Symposium.* Ed. Daniel Balderston. 1986. Gaithersburg, MD: Hispamérica, 1986. 47–73.

Sontag, Susan. "The Double Standard of Aging." *No Longer Young: The Older Woman in America.* Occasional Papers in Gerontology

11. Ann Arbor: Institute of Gerontology, U of Michigan; Detroit: Wayne State U, 1975. 31–39.

Spivak, Gayatri Chakravorty. "Can the Subaltern Speak?" *Marxism and the Interpretation of Culture.* Ed. Cary Nelson and Lawrence Grossberg. Urbana and Chicago: U of Illinois P, 1988. 271–313.

Stein, Ingrid. *Figuras femininas em Machado de Assis.* Rio de Janeiro: Paz e Terra, 1984.

Stimpson, Catherine. "Zero Degree Deviancy: The Lesbian Novel in English." *Criticial Inquiry* 8.2 (1981): 363–79.

Suleiman, Susan Rubin. *Subversive Intent: Gender, Politics, and the Avant-Garde.* Cambridge, MA: Harvard UP, 1990.

Telles, Lygia Fagundes. "The Baroness of Tatuí." Interview with Edla Van Steen. *Review: Latin American Literature and Arts* 36 (1986): 30–33.

———. "Uma branca sombra pálida." *A noite escura e mais eu.* Rio de Janeiro: Nova Fronteira, 1992. 159–82.

———. *Ciranda de pedra.* 1954. 20th ed. Rio de Janeiro: Nova Fronteira, 1984.

———. *A disciplina do amor.* 6th ed. Rio de Janeiro: Nova Fronteira, 1980.

———. "A escolha." *Histórias de amor infeliz.* Ed. Esdras do Nascimento. Rio de Janeiro: Nórdica, 1985. 129–33.

———. *As horas nuas.* Rio de Janeiro: Nova Fronteira, 1989.

———. *As meninas.* 1973. 4th ed. Rio de Janeiro: José Olympio, 1974.

———. "Tigrela." 1977. *Mistérios: ficções.* 3rd ed. Rio de Janeiro: Nova Fronteira, 1981. 91–99.

———. *Verão no aquário.* 1963. 8th ed. Rio de Janeiro: Nova Fronteira, 1984.

Todorov, Tzvetan. *The Fantastic: A Structural Approach to a Literary Genre.* Trans. Richard Howard. Cleveland: Case Western Reserve UP, 1973.

Vainfas, Ronaldo. "Homoerotismo feminino e o Santo Ofício." *História das mulheres no Brasil.* Ed. Mary del Priore. São Paulo: Contexto, 1997. 115–40.

———. *Trópico dos pecados: Moral, sexualidade e Inquisição no Brasil colonial.* Rio de Janeiro: Campus, 1989.

Van Steen, Edla. "Intimidade." *Antes do amanhecer.* São Paulo: Moderna, 1977. 65–68.

Bibliography

Van Steen, Edla. "Intimacy." *A Bag of Stories.* Trans. and introd. David George. Pittsburgh: Latin American Review Press, 1991. 47–51.

Vieira, Nelson H. "The Stations of the Body, Clarice Lispector's *Abertura* and Renewal." *Remate de males* 9 (1989): 71–84.

Villares, Laura. *Vertigem.* São Paulo: Antonio Tisi, 1926.

Vincenzo, Elza Cunha de. *Um teatro da mulher: Dramaturgia feminina no palco brasileiro contemporâneo.* São Paulo: Perspectiva, EDUSP, 1992.

"Vinte e duas poetas hoje." Interview with Lúcia Helena. *Poesia sempre* 10 (Feb. 1999): 203–53.

Walker, Nancy A. *Feminist Alternatives: Irony and Fantasy in the Contemporary Novel by Women.* Jackson: U of Mississippi P, 1990.

Williams, Linda. *Hard Core: Power, Pleasure, and the Frenzy of the Visible.* Berkeley and Los Angeles: U of California P, 1989.

Winckler, Carlos Roberto. *Pornografia e sexualidade no Brasil.* Porto Alegre: Mercado Aberto, 1983.

Woodward, Kathleen. "The Mirror Stage of Old Age." *Memory and Desire: Aging—Literature—Psychoanalysis.* Ed. Woodward and Murray M. Schwartz. Bloomington: Indiana UP, 1986. 97–113.

Xavier, Therezinha Mucci. *A personagem feminina no romance de Machado de Assis.* Rio de Janeiro: Presença, 1986.

Zimmerman, Bonnie. *The Safe Sea of Women: Lesbian Fiction, 1969–1989.* Boston: Beacon, 1990.

Index

adultery, 20, 23, 30, 33, 53, 70, 71, 114
African heritage, 11, 95
Afro-Brazilian culture, 66. *See also* Candomblé
agency, female, 120, 123, 132, 137, 159
   and female grotesque, 162
   and heterosexuality, 73, 74, 153, 158
aging, 4, 6, 86, 91, 95, 107, 111, 162
Alencar, José Martiniano de, 4, 8, 10, 11, 12, 14, 15, 24, 36
   Iracema, 4, 8, 9, 12–14, 24, 32, 36, 59, 160, 179Ch1nn1–3
Almeida, Júlia Lopes de, *xi*, 38–39
Almeida, Manuel Antônio de, 4, 15, 19, 36
   Memórias de um sargento de milícias, 4, 15–18, 19, 35, 180n5
Amado, Jorge, 8, 18, 19, 52
   Dona Flor e seus dois maridos, 18
   Gabriela, cravo e canela, 8, 19, 52
Amai e . . . não vos multipliqueis (Maria Lacerda de Moura), *xi*
Amália [de Campos], Narcisa, 41
Amaral, Maria Adelaide do, 3
androgyny, 83, 85
   in writing, 94, 181Ch4n1
Anzaldúa, Gloria, 114, 117, 124
Assunção, Leilah, *xii*, 3
   Fala baixo senão eu grito, *xii*
audácia dessa mulher, A (Ana Maria Machado), 34–35
autoeroticism, 5, 44, 45, 46, 64, 65, 154, 161. *See also* eroticism
Azevedo, Aluísio, 4, 8, 19, 36
   O cortiço, 4, 8, 18, 19–24, 36, 180n6

Bataille, Georges, 45, 83, 152
Bengell, Norma, 54, 55
"branca sombra pálida, Uma" (Lygia Fagundes Telles), 182n4
Butler, Judith, 105, 153

caderno rosa de Lori Lamby, O (Hilda Hilst), 52
Campello, Myriam, 7, 120, 123, 126, 127, 135, 162, 182n4 and n8
   "A mulher de ouro," 7, 123, 126, 138–41
   Sortilegiu, 120–23, 140
Candomblé, 66
Carne viva (Olga Savary), 57
Cartas de um sedutor (Hilda Hilst), 52
casa da paixão, A (Nélida Piñon), 54
casa dos Budas ditosos, A (João Ubaldo Ribeiro), 53
Castro, Consuelo de, 3
Catholicism, 42, 69, 115
Cavalcante, Joyce, *O discurso da mulher absurda*, 58
Cem mentiras de verdade (Helena Parente Cunha), 60
censorship
   during Brazil's military dictatorship, 57–58
   and lesbianism, 113, 119
   and self-censorship, 39, 49, 76, 119, 121, 122, 123
"certa felicidade, Uma." *See under* Coutinho, Sonia
Christianity
   Christian ideology and women, 13–14, 32
   and pornography, 51

Index

Church, and social regulation, 33, 42
Ciranda de pedra. See under Telles, Lygia Fagundes
Cixous, Hélène, 46, 69, 91, 92, 93, 112, 119, 120, 182n3
Cobra, Ercília Nogueira, 5
Colasanti, Marina, 3, 7, 52, 143, 149, 157, 158, 162, 181Ch2n3, 182Ch6n1, 183n3
   A nova mulher, 148, 155
   Rota de colisão, 148, 149, 150–59
Contos d'escárnio: Textos grotescos (Hilda Hilst), 52
"Cordélia, a caçadora" (Sonia Coutinho), 107–12
"corpo, O" (Clarice Lispector), 117–18
cortiço, O. See under Azevedo, Aluísio
Coutinho, Sonia, 3, 6, 34, 55, 92, 93, 94, 95–96, 98, 124, 125, 127, 141, 144, 159, 162
   and aging in fiction, 99–107
   "Uma certa felicidade," 97, 103–05, 106
   "Fátima e Jamila," 7, 123, 129–32
   and the female grotesque ("Cordélia, a caçadora"), 107–12
   O jogo de Ifá, 76, 94
   "Uma mulher sem nenhuma importância," 100–03, 105
   Os seios de Pandora, 96
   O último verão de Copacabana, 106, 110, 112
Cristais partidos. See under Machado, Gilka
Cunha, Helena Parente, 6, 34, 59, 60, 67, 74, 75, 148, 161, 181Ch2n4
   Cem mentiras de verdade, 60
   As doze cores do vermelho, 61

Mulher no espelho, 6, 59, 60–67, 161

De Lauretis, Teresa, 47, 120, 122, 123, 182n3
Denser, Márcia, 3, 132–33, 141, 143, 144–48, 157, 158, 159, 162, 179Intro n2, 182n6
   Muito prazer, xiii, 56, 57
   A ponte das estrelas, 76
   O prazer é todo meu, xiii, 56, 57
   "Tigresa," 7, 123, 127, 133–35, 144
   "O vampiro da alameda Casabranca," 57
discurso da mulher absurda, O (Joyce Cavalccante), 58
Dolores, Carmen [*pseud.*]. See Melo, Emília Moncorvo Bandeira de
Dom Casmurro. See under Machado de Assis, Joaquim Maria
Dona Flor e seus dois maridos (Jorge Amado), 18
doze cores do vermelho, As (Helena Parente Cunha), 61

education, *x, xi,* 27, 28–29, 33
eroticism, 56, 180Ch2n1. See also autoeroticism
   definitions, 50, 146–47
   erotic drive in Clarice Lispector, 117, 182Ch5n1
   erotic literature by women, *xiii,* 40–41, 53–58
   erotic poetry in Gilka Machado, 5, 42–48
   and female identity (Helena Parente Cunha), 59–67
   and female identity (Marilene Felinto), 67–74
   female in literature, 4, 6–7, 159–60
   and/in language, 129, 130, 141, 160

Index

lesbian, 113, 121, 122, 140
versus pornography, 49–53, 151, 152. *See also* pornography
and self-empowerment, 54
and social censorship, 39, 49, 52–53, 119
and social power, 133, 157
"escolha, A." *See under* Telles, Lygia Fagundes
Estados de alma. See under Machado, Gilka

Fala baixo senão eu grito (Leilah Assunçao), *xii*
"Fátima e Jamila." *See under* Coutinho, Sonia
Felinto, Marilene, 6, 59, 67, 161, 181Ch2n5
  As mulheres de Tijucopapo, 6, 59–60, 67–74, 75, 161
female grotesque, 107, 111, 144, 162. *See also* grotesque
Floresta [Brasileira Augusta], Nísia, *x*
Foucault, Michel, 15, 18, 20, 35, 43, 76, 139

Gabriela, cravo e canela. See under Amado, Jorge
Galvão, Patrícia [*pseud.:* Pagu], 5, 53
  Parque industrial, 5
gender, 56, 57
  discrimination, 69
  disruption of gender categories, 127
  hierarchy, 7, 122, 133
  of literature, 183n3
  and race, 59
  roles, 53
gender relations, 39, 56, 57, 74, 94, 105, 120, 123, 139, 154, 157, 160
  critique of, 75, 148

grotesque, 145, 161. *See also* female grotesque
  in Brazilian fiction by women, 76
  and the female body, 92, 94, 107, 112, 162
  in Lya Luft (*O quarto fechado*), 81–85
  in Lygia Fagundes Telles, 87, 90
  in women's literature, 77–79

Helena. See under Machado de Assis, Joaquim Maria
heterosexuality, 74, 123, 139, 140
  compulsory, 47, 122, 128, 132, 153, 154, 156
  critique of, 124, 141, 143
  and power in Márcia Denser, 145
  as social norm, 4, 15, 116
heterosexuality, female, 7, 161, 162
  in Helena Parente Cunha (*Mulher no espelho*), 65, 66
  in Márcia Denser, 144–48
  in Marilene Felinto (*As mulheres de Tijucopapo*), 73
  in Marina Colasanti, 151–54, 156–57, 158
  in Sonia Coutinho, 112
Hilst, Hilda, 3, 52–53, 183n3
  O caderno rosa de Lori Lamby, 52
  Cartas de um sedutor, 52
  Contos d'escárnio: Textos grotescos, 52
homosexuality, female. *See* lesbianism
hora da estrela, A (Clarice Lispector), 69
horas nuas, As. See under Telles, Lygia Fagundes

Iaiá Garcia (Machado de Assis), 25
incest, 83

201

Index

Inquisition, 1, 42
  and female homosexuality, 114–16
"Intimidade." *See under* Van Steen, Edla
Iracema. See under Alencar, José Martiniano de
Irigaray, Luce, 46, 47, 111, 182n3

jogo de Ifá, O. See under Coutinho, Sonia
Júlia, Francisca, 38–39

Kristeva, Julia, 97, 111, 120, 182n3

lesbian desire
  in Brazilian women's fiction, *xiii*, 53, 112, 123–27
  in Clarice Lispector ("O corpo"), 117–18
  in Gilka Machado, 5, 47
  in Lygia Fagundes Telles ("A escolha"), 135–38
  in Sonia Coutinho ("Fátima e Jamila"), 129–32
lesbianism
  and the Inquisition in Brazil, 115–16
  in Myriam Campello ("A mulher de ouro"), 138–41
  in Myriam Campello (*Sortilegiu*), 120–22
  as "perverse," 20, 23, 137
  as "resistance," 122, 123, 143, 144
  and social invisibility, 113–14, 138
lesbian literature
  definition, 124
  tradition in Brazil, 7, 113, 118–19, 142, 162
Lispector, Clarice, *xii*, 1, 3, 53, 117, 118, 159, 182Ch5nn1–2
  "O corpo," 117–18
  A hora da estrela, 69

Perto do coração selvagem, xii, 53, 117
Luft, Lya, 6, 76, 79, 91–92, 112, 161
As parceiras, 80
O quarto fechado, 76, 80–85, 91, 181Ch3n1

Machado, Ana Maria, *A audácia dessa mulher,* 34–35
Machado, Gilka, 4, 5, 34, 38, 40–41, 46, 117, 181Ch2n2
  Cristais partidos, 5, 40, 42, 44, 46
  Estados de alma, 40, 42, 43
  Mulher nua, 46
  transgression in, 48–49
Machado de Assis, Joaquim Maria, 4, 25, 36, 87, 180n7
  Dom Casmurro, 4, 8, 25, 26, 27, 30–35, 59, 166, 180n8 and n9
  Helena, 25, 180n7
  Iaiá Garcia, 25
  Memórias póstumas de Brás Cubas, 26, 88, 181Ch3n3
  Ressurreição, 25
Margarida La Roque: A ilha dos demônios (Dinah Silveira de Queiroz), 76
marriage
  and Brazilian women's civil rights, *xiii*, 30
  and female sexuality in Aluísio Azevedo (*O cortiço*), 23
  and lesbian desire, 125
  and myths of femininity, 17
  in Sonia Coutinho ("Cordélia, a caçadora"), 105, 106, 109–10
  and women's social roles, 15, 33, 99
masturbation, 53, 117. *See also* autoeroticism

Index

Melo, Emília Moncorvo Bandeira de, 179Intro n1
Memórias de um sargento de milícias. See under Almeida, Manuel Antônio de
Memórias póstumas de Brás Cubas. See under Machado de Assis, Joaquim Maria
meninas, As. See under Telles, Lygia Fagundes
Míccolis, Leila, 54, 136, 159, 183n3
Mulheres da vida, 54–56
Modernism, Brazilian, 5, 181Ch2n1
mother, 62, 64, 72, 81, 120, 136, 137
  and Christian ideology, 32
  in Lygia Fagundes Telles ("A escolha"), 136, 137
  in Marilene Felinto (*As mulheres de Tijucopapo*), 67, 68, 71, 72
  "phallic mother," 31
  and the Semiotic, 120
mother-daughter relationship, 69–70
mothering, 73
  and women's education, 29
Moura, Maria Lacerda de, *xi*
  Amai e . . . não vos multipliqueis, *xi*
  A mulher é uma degenerada?, *xi*
Muito prazer. See under Denser, Márcia
"mulher de ouro, A." *See under* Campello, Myriam
Mulheres da vida (Leila Míccolis), 54–56
mulheres de Tijucopapo, As. See under Felinto, Marilene
mulher é uma degenerada?, A (Maria Lacerda de Moura), *xi*
Mulher no espelho. See under Cunha, Helena Parente
Mulher nua (Gilka Machado), 46
"mulher sem nenhuma impotância, Uma." *See under* Coutinho, Sonia
myth, 9
  cultural, 7, 9, 10, 154
  of femininity, 2, 95
  foundational, 12
  racial, 14, 18
  of *vagina dentata*, 31
mythmaker, 71

Naturalism, 20, 146
Neo-Naturalism, 146
Néri, Adalgisa, 41
nova mulher, A. See under Colasanti, Marina

Oliveira, Rosiska Darcy de, *xiii*, 3

Pagu [*pseud.*]. *See* Galvão, Patrícia
parceiras, As (Lya Luft), 80
Parque industrial (Pagu), 5
Perto do coração selvagem. See under Lispector, Clarice
Piñon, Nélida, *xii, xiv,* 3
  A casa da paixão, 54
ponte das estrelas, A (Márcia Denser), 76
pornography
  defining elements of, 50–51
  versus eroticism, 50, 52–53, 119, 147, 151, 152
  and lesbian desire, 113
prazer é todo meu, O. See under Denser, Márcia

quarto fechado, O. See under Luft, Lya
queer, 143, 144, 162
  queer reading, 114, 117, 124, 141
Queiroz, Dinah Silveira de, *xii*
  Margarida La Roque: A ilha dos demônios, 76

Index

Queiroz, Rachel de, *xii*, 1, 5, 40, 53, 117, 159
   O quinze, xi
   As três Marias, 39
quinze, O (Rachel de Queiroz), *xi*
race, 13, 14, 17, 22, 23, 59, 62, 94, 124, 133, 149, 156
   and national identity, 11–12
   and sexual stereotypes, 24–25
Ramos, Graciliano, *Vidas secas,* 69
rape, 24
Reis, Maria Firmina dos, *Úrsula, x*
Ressurreição (Machado de Assis), 25
Ribeiro, João Ubaldo, *A casa dos Budas ditosos,* 53
Rich, Adrienne, 47, 122, 139, 153
Romanticism, Brazilian, 9, 16, 25, 35
Rota de colisão. See under Colasanti, Marina

Savary, Olga, 57, 183n3
   Carne viva, 57
seduction, 12, 18, 44, 72, 133, 144, 179Ch1n1
   and lesbian desire, 122
   in Lygia Fagundes Telles (*Ciranda de pedra*), 135
   in Sonia Coutinho ("Fátima e Jamila"), 131–32
seios de Pandora, Os (Sonia Coutinho), 96
sexual continuum, 139
Sontag, Susan, 98, 99, 101, 102, 111

Sortilegiu. See under Campello, Myriam

Telles, Lygia Fagundes, *xii*, 1, 3, 6, 40, 79, 85, 91, 112, 124, 141, 159, 161, 162, 180n11, 182n4
   "Uma branca sombra pálida" (*A noite escura e mais eu*), 182n4
   Ciranda de pedra, 53, 86, 135, 181Ch3n2
   "A escolha," 7, 123, 126–27, 135–38, 182n4
   As horas nuas, 76, 85–90, 91, 181Ch3n2
   As meninas, 135, 181Ch3n2
   Verão no aquário, 86, 181Ch3n2
"Tigresa." *See under* Denser, Márcia
três Marias, As (Rachel de Queiroz), 39
Trevisan, Dalton, 53, 146

último verão de Copacabana, O. See under Coutinho, Sonia
Úrsula (Maria Firmina dos Reis), *x*

"vampiro da alameda Casabranca, O" (Márcia Denser), 57
Van Steen, Edla, 3, 123, 124, 125, 130, 141, 182n5
"Intimidade," 7, 123, 127–29
Verão no aquário. See under Telles, Lygia Fagundes
Vidas secas (Graciliano Ramos), 69

About the Author of This Book

Gender, Discourse, and Desire in Twentieth-Century Brazilian Women's Literature

Cristina Ferreira-Pinto, Texas State University–San Marcos, was born and raised in Rio de Janeiro, Brazil. She holds a PhD in Brazilian and Spanish American literatures from Tulane University. Her major fields of research are Brazilian literature and feminist theory, and she has published numerous essays in academic journals in Brazil, the United States, and Spain.

Other PSRL Books of Interest

Machado de Assis, the Brazilian Pyrrhonian
   José Raimundo Maia Neto

Machado de Assis's subtle criticism of cherished institutions is evident to all readers, and critics have often mentioned his skepticism. Maia Neto traces Machado's particular brand of skepticism to that of the philosopher Pyrrho of Elis and reveals the modern sources through which he inherited that line of thought. He then shows how Machado's own philosophical development (as seen primarily through his fiction) follows the stages proposed by Pyrrho and his followers for the development of a skeptical worldview.
Vol. 5. 1994. xiv, 231 pp. Cloth

Other Books from PSRL

28 The Psyche of Feminism: Sand, Colette, Sarraute
Catherine M. Peebles
Peebles proposes that a feminist ethics, in order to be both feminist and ethical, needs to embrace psychoanalysis. She then applies this idea to works by the three authors named in the title and argues for a fundamental feminist rethinking of the ideal of equality.
2004. xiv, 232 pp. Paper

27 Orientalismo en el modernismo hispanoamericano
Araceli Tinajero
Drawing on ethnography, post-colonial studies, literary theory, art history, and travel theory, Tinjero analyzes a selection of modernist texts to show how writing at the "margin" of Western modernism-modernity is at once within and without the mainstream.
2003. x, 173 pp. Paper

26 The Great Chiasmus: Word and Flesh in the Novels of Unamuno
Paul R. Olson
This study views the whole of Unamuno's novelistic works as a great chiasmus in which the ending recalls—with variations—the beginning, and the whole of human life is likewise seen as a structure of chiastic repetitions.
2003. viii, 272 pp. Cloth and Paper

25 The Sunday of Fiction: The Modern French Eccentric
Peter Schulman
Schulman details the various means modern eccentrics employ to successfully transform the humdrum into the marvelous, work time into free time, or rather Mondays into Sundays.
2002. xii, 195 pp. Cloth

24 Narrative Transformations from *L'Astrée* to *Le berger extravagant*
Leonard Hinds
Hinds examines the historical transition from the idealist, pastoral romance to the more realist antiromance.
2002. x, 203 pp. Cloth

23 (A)wry Views: Anamorphosis, Cervantes, and the Early Picaresque
David R. Castillo
This study demonstrates that much of the literature of the Spanish Golden Age is susceptible to a mode of interpretation that permits, and indeed requires, "oblique readings."
2001. xiv, 182 pp. Cloth

Other Books from PSRL

22 Signs of Science:
Literature, Science, and
Spanish Modernity
since 1868
Dale J. Pratt
2001. x, 226 pp. Cloth

21 Constructing the
Criollo Archive:
Subjects of Knowledge in
the *Bibliotheca Mexicana*
and the *Rusticatio
Mexicana*
Antony Higgins
2000. xviii, 283 pp. Cloth

20 The Pleasure of Writing:
Critical Essays on
Dacia Maraini
Edited by Rodica Diaconescu-
Blumenfeld and
Ada Testaferri
2000. x, 277 pp. Cloth

19 Vidas im/propias:
transformaciones
del sujeto femenino en la
narrativa española
contemporánea
María Pilar Rodríguez
2000. xii, 222 pp. Cloth

18 Kingdom of Disorder:
The Theory of Tragedy
in Classical France
John D. Lyons
1999. xvi, 251 pp. Cloth

17 The Gendered Lyric:
Subjectivity
and Difference in
Nineteenth-Century
French Poetry
Gretchen Schultz
1999. xiv, 334 pp. Cloth

16 Fictions du scandale:
Corps féminin et
réalisme romanesque au
dix-neuvième siècle
Nathalie Buchet Rogers
1998. xii, 324 pp. Cloth

15 Reading Boileau:
An Integrative Study
of the Early *Satires*
Robert T. Corum, Jr.
1998. vi, 170 pp. Cloth

14 Conflicts and Conciliations:
The Evolution of Galdós's
Fortunata y Jacinta
Geoffrey Ribbans
1997. xvi, 352 pp. Cloth

13 Calderón y las quimeras
de la Culpa: alegoría,
seducción y resistencia
en cinco autos
sacramentales
Viviana Díaz Balsera
1997. viii, 237 pp. Cloth

12 Plotting the Past:
Metamorphoses of
Historical Narrative in
Modern Italian Fiction
Cristina Della Coletta
1996. x, 268 pp. Cloth

11 The Subject of Desire:
Petrarchan Poetics and
the Female Voice in
Louise Labé
Deborah Lesko Baker
1996. xvi, 249 pp. Cloth

Other Books from PSRL

10 Cervantes's *Novelas ejemplares:* Between History and Creativity
Joseph V. Ricapito
1996. x, 164 pp. PAPER

9 Cruzados, mártires y beatos: emplazamientos del cuerpo colonial
Mario Cesareo
1995. XII, 201 pp. CLOTH

8 André Gide dans le labyrinthe de la mythotextualité
Pamela Antonia Genova
1995. xiv, 212 pp. Cloth

7 Falsehood Disguised: Unmasking the Truth in La Rochefoucauld
Richard G. Hodgson
1995. XIV, 176 pp. 2 ILL. PAPER

6 Tournier élémentaire
Jonathan F. Krell
1994. XIV, 219 pp. 1 ILL. CLOTH

5 Machado de Assis, the Brazilian Pyrrhonian
José Raimundo Maia Neto
1994. XIV, 231 pp. CLOTH

4 Feminism and the Honor Plays of Lope de Vega
Yvonne Yarbro-Bejarano
1994. XIV, 324 pp. CLOTH

3 After Machiavelli: "Re-writing" and the "Hermeneutic Attitude"
Barbara J. Godorecci
1993. VIII, 212 pp. PAPER

2 Kinship and Polity in the *Poema de Mio Cid*
Michael Harney
1993. x, 285 pp. CLOTH

1 Writing and Inscription in Golden Age Drama
Charles Oriel
1992. x, 189 pp. PAPER